# WHITE HOUSE WEDDINGS

# White House Weddings

WILBUR CROSS

AND

ANN NOVOTNY

DAVID McKAY COMPANY, INC.

NEW YORK

WHITE HOUSE WEDDINGS

Library of Congress Catalog Card Number: 66-26034

MANUFACTURED IN THE UNITED STATES OF AMERICA

*Dedicated to three brides:*

Alice Roosevelt Longworth (February 17, 1906)

Alice Wilson McElroy (August 7, 1918)

Luci Baines Johnson Nugent (August 6, 1966)

*and to three bridegrooms:*

Francis Bowes Sayre (November 25, 1913)

Isaac Stuart McElroy, Jr. (August 7, 1918)

Patrick John Nugent (August 6, 1966)

# CONTENTS

*Illustrations follow pages 56 and 184*

CHAPTER I

# THE QUESTION

HEN the President and Mrs. Lyndon B. Johnson formally announced on September 10, 1967, that their elder daughter, Lynda Bird, would marry Captain Charles S. Robb of the Marine Corps in December, the nation was delighted to hear that the wedding would take place in the White House. Almost since the days of its first occupation, by President John Adams in November 1800, the White House has seemed to be the only appropriate place for marriage by members of the Presidential family. Millions of Americans were disappointed when Lynda's younger sister, Luci Baines, announced in 1966 that her wedding would *not* take place in the White House, as was evidenced by discussions and comments by members of the press and others who voiced their opinions in print or over the air.

The fact that Luci and her fiancé, Patrick John Nugent, were married elsewhere did not prevent the wedding from becoming the most publicized, the most thoroughly covered, in all Presidential history. As comedienne Edie Adams quipped at the time, "Nobody is invited except the immediate country." The President's daughter, despite her pre-nuptial expressions of wistful longing for a "private, family affair," could not have selected a less private place for the event: the National Shrine of the Immaculate Conception, the largest Roman Catholic Church in the United States, mosaic-domed and so vast that it has some 30 chapels within, in addition to the great central hall.

The wedding, which received major coverage by just about every publication in the country, including seven full-color pages in *Life* and four or five pages in newsmagazines, was in historical contrast to the first wedding of a U.S. President's daughter. When Maria Hester Monroe was married in 1820, her family managed to confine the guest list to fewer than 45 and keep the ceremony so private that the Washington newspaper reported the complete event in 34 words.

It was inevitable, though, that no wedding today in the Presidential family can ever be kept "private" in any sense of the word. In fact, from the very moment that Lynda and Luci Johnson moved into the White House, in January 1964, they came under the intensive eye of the press. There was already considerable speculation about a "White House Wedding," for at the time Lynda Bird was wearing the ring of Lieutenant (j.g.) Bernard Rosenbach, of the U.S. Navy. The engagement was never formally announced by President and Mrs. Johnson, although the romance had been going for several years, ever since Lynda had accepted Rosenbach's class pin at Christmastime, 1961. At the time, 16-year-old Luci had a regular boy friend, Jack Olson, whom she had been dating for about a year, but their ages and the fact that he was a college freshman precluded any serious speculation about marriage. Lynda Bird heightened the interest of reporters in the early spring of 1964 by discussing White House weddings of the past, mentioning that Grover Cleveland had been married in the Blue Room and Alice Roosevelt Longworth in the East Room. But on the last Saturday in April, the White House threw cold water on the whole idea by revealing that Lynda Bird had returned Lieutenant Rosenbach's ring the previous weekend.

New interest developed when, in the months that followed,

she began dating David Lefeve, a New York stockbroker who at the time was a Marine lieutenant, serving as a White House military aide. This was followed by a much-publicized romance with Brent Eastman, a medical student, during the summer of 1965. Lynda Bird dated him constantly, and visited him and his family at their Wyoming home while she was touring the West to help promote her mother's program for a more beautiful America. So much was the romance publicized, in fact, that Mrs. Johnson's press office protested that it was receiving more coverage than the subject of "beautification," which Lynda Bird had gone out to plug in the first place.

By the end of the summer, with Lynda's summertime romance somewhat fading, attention was focused on Luci. She was being seen more and more in the company of one Patrick John Nugent, whom she had first met at a party in the White House, celebrating her graduation from high school in June. Pat was a Roman Catholic, but, significantly, Luci was, too, having converted to Catholicism herself during the summer. It was not until late September that the press began predicting an engagement. When Pat and Luci flew to the L.B.J. Ranch in Texas to visit the President on October 29, 1965, when he was recuperating from a gall-bladder operation, it was widely rumored that the trip had really been made for the purpose of requesting parental permission to get married. This apparently was not true, and it was not until Christmas Eve—after much speculation in the newspapers that the President had turned down Luci and Pat's request—that a formal announcement of the engagement was released by the White House.

The big—and immediate—question was, "Will there be a wedding in the White House?" It was to remain for the time being an unanswered question. For one thing, no definite plans had been set. For another, a ceremony in the White House would require special permission from Roman Catholic

Archbishop Patrick A. O'Boyle, of Washington, D.C. "The prevailing rule," said a diocese spokesman, "is that the marriage ceremony is to take place in a church, but that exceptions can be made for special reasons."

Asked whether the Church often made exceptions, he replied, "This is an exceptional marriage."

The question had an old, familiar ring, for it has come up in the past whenever there has been an engagement within the Presidential family. Other aspects of the event and the plans for the wedding echoed events in American history from the beginning of the nineteenth century. There were frequent protestations from the White House that the wedding was to be "private," that the press should not intrude, that the ceremony would not be an "official" one, and other such statements that might have been copied from newspapers of bygone days. And when members of the House of Representatives let it be known that they were starting a collection to buy a wedding present, Luci did exactly what other brides-to-be had done before her: she protested.

Despite the protests, official and otherwise, gifts arrived from around the world. Luci almost received a wedding present that would have been unique indeed. It was described in the *New York Post* of August 2, 1966, as follows:

"Congressman Wayne Hays was not invited to the wedding. He barely knows Luci Baines Johnson. . . . But a couple of weeks ago, Rep. Hays produced a little present for the bride that could easily match anything she has yet received—from the $2,300 tea service Washington diplomats gave her last night, to a gold and diamond clip-on nose ring from Mrs. Orville Freeman, to the Texas-shaped cookie cutters from Mrs. Jake Pickle of Austin.

"The gift is House Resolution 16340, a bill to prohibit picketing within 500 feet of any church in the District of Columbia within a two-hour period of any religious service. 'I hope,'

Rep. Hays said fervently while introducing the bill, 'this will be passed before the sixth of August.'"

As it turned out on the day of the wedding, the bride and groom were greeted outside the church by pickets protesting U.S. participation in the war in Vietnam. But it was a fine Congressional gesture, anyway.

With the Johnson/Nugent wedding of August 6, 1966, a matter of history, the press could now focus fully on Lynda Bird and speculate once more on a White House wedding. The President's elder daughter was playing the game perfectly. She had been seen frequently in the company of handsome young actor George Hamilton, who was obviously enjoying her company immensely and who came from a background socially suitable for a good match. Speculation had reached a peak in March 1966 when Lynda Bird met George's mother, Mrs. Anne Potter Hamilton Hunt Spalding. On this occasion, her 22nd birthday, she had been the guest of honor at a party at Hamilton's $200,000 Beverly Hills mansion (once owned by Douglas Fairbanks and Mary Pickford), attended by such notables as Greer Garson, Eddie Fisher, Natalie Wood, Bobby Darin, and Elke Sommer.

Now, in the early fall of 1966, the romance was still going strong, although reporters were hard pressed to get any statements from either Lynda Bird or George as to their "future plans." By the spring of 1967, the odds were that, since nothing had happened thus far and since Hamilton was bouncing around the world as an actor while the President's daughter was pursuing her editorial career at *McCall's* Magazine, the possibilities of a wedding were remote.

It was therefore something of a shock to the press, and certainly to the public, when President and Mrs. Johnson announced, on September 10, 1967, that Lynda Bird would marry Captain Charles S. Robb. Even George Hamilton was caught off guard. "Well, it's certainly a surprise," he told a reporter. "I didn't know anything about it, and I don't know anybody who did."

While it had been common knowledge that Lynda Bird had been seeing the 28-year-old Milwaukeean, who was serving as a White House social aide, for several months, this was one romance that had received very little national attention.

The wedding would be on December ninth, in the White House. The place selected for the ceremony was the historic East Room, scene of half a dozen previous weddings.

Such unexpected happenings, along with unique events and colorful personalities, have made the stories of marriages within the Presidential family lively and fascinating. Yet few Americans could name even a handful of the Presidents or their sons and daughters who have been married during the term in office. One of the most unexpected conclusions reached after researching Presidential family weddings down through thirty-six administrations is their complete lack of pattern. Except for the fact that the Blue Room and the East Room were popular for marriages, or that the setting was a "bower of bloom," or that the bride looked "lovely," White House weddings might have taken place in a dozen different locations under the widest possible combination of circumstances.

A particularly surprising inconsistency is that the White House weddings have not all involved relatives of the President or First Lady: two couples married there were simply favored friends of the President, hospitably invited to become part of his household. Nor were all the brides and bridegrooms Americans: one Frenchman and an Englishman were married in the White House. Nine of the protagonists in this story had been married before. Three of the brides, surprisingly, were Quakers (or ex-Quakers) from Philadelphia, and one Roman Catholic marriage was celebrated in the mansion. There is one lucky constant, however, and that is marital happiness—only one White House marriage ended in divorce, and a second in separation. Twenty years after her White House wedding, and after her husband's death, one bride committed suicide.

Several weddings gained such notoriety that they were featured on the front page of newspapers around the world and were compared with the coronations of kings. Yet, surprisingly, some received so little publicity that they were overshadowed by such announcements as the price of livestock feed.

A few weddings turned out to be harmonious formal occasions that delighted Washington matriarchs and were recorded in gushing correspondence as the last word in fine taste and social accomplishment. Some, however, served to fracture Washington society, exclude long lists of the irate uninvited, and make the matter of protocol a prime issue of the moment.

Sweethearts were fickle, and unexpectedly deserted one lover for a new one. Others, less flirtatious, found themselves contending with everything from parental opposition to scandal and international crises. One romance actually blossomed because of a national disaster in which the girl's father, two Cabinet members, and two other prominent men were killed when the Navy's most publicized new cannon exploded. Another marriage might never have taken place had not a clever beau arranged to travel on a Congressional junket, where he successfully courted a President's beautiful daughter in the Orient, with all her other suitors left far behind.

Presidential family weddings, both inside and outside the White House, did not involve as much intrigue as, say, the maneuvering of European diplomats in bygone days to arrange royal marriages for political purposes. Yet they show a fair share of calculated, old-fashioned matchmaking. A woman like Dolley Madison might be expected to push and pull young lads and maidens toward the altar. But she ran a poor second to a man who was a most unlikely matchmaker: a President with a reputation for being a hard-nosed Army officer, often rude and uncontrollably irascible. Astonishingly enough, he had a record of having been a prime mover in helping almost a dozen love affairs end in marriage—as well as encouraging several that did not.

Down through the years, weddings in the Presidential family had their share, too, of colorful characters, ranging all the way from ambitious young diplomats, aging Civil War heroes, society queens, and missionaries to eccentric figures who gently wafted in and out of the White House like eddying breezes. Not the least of these was an "Auntie Mame" type, who wore so many bracelets, spangles, and other metallic ornaments that she could be heard from afar coming down the halls of the White House, jingling like an Oriental wind chime on a brisk spring day.

Because members of the President's family were so often in the public eye, minor matters sometimes became magnified out of all normal proportion. The question of drinking, for example, frequently became an issue. Presidents who liked a convivial glass on occasion—and there were more than a few—were taken to task for letting liquor flow at White House weddings. A number of wedding parties, no more spirited than those of any young people of the day, were reported smugly by the press as perhaps more boisterous than might have been expected in such quarters. Several reporters relished describing how the menfolk had retired to a back room after the wedding dinner for cigars, brandy, college songs, and an exchange of ribald jokes.

Somehow, too, it seemed difficult to imagine—in situations where the President himself was the bridegroom—that this august personage could enjoy kissing or courting like an ordinary human being. Such observations were rarely made in print, but they are evident between the lines of many an account of Presidential romances. A number of "January/June" marriages had the gossips quacking vigorously about the wide difference in ages, and what it really meant. One widowed President married a bride younger than three of his children. Another was particularly vulnerable because he was marrying his own ward, a luscious young thing less than half his age, so young that she drank nothing stronger than mineral water at their wedding reception.

A third President was roundly taken to task because he was romancing an attractive widow barely eight months after his first wife was in her grave.

"Outrageous!" sputtered the capital's conservative old matrons.

"Ill-advised," counseled the worried and nervous members of the President's own Cabinet.

"A national scandal!" whooped the delighted members of the opposite party.

"Love," murmured the President to his sympathetic family, "deep and all-consuming love."

One more Presidential wedding was ready for history.

The tale of these weddings has its own place in the social history of the United States. The personalities, the events, and the outcomes give fascinating insight into the manners and mores of their times.

CHAPTER II

# A LIE—AND THE WEDDING
# THAT HISTORY FORGOT

*he Washington Star* of February 11, 1923, carried a remarkable story, accompanied by two photographs and headlined:

## BRIDE IN 1862 GIVEN IN MARRIAGE BY LINCOLN TELLS OF ELOPEMENT AND WHITE HOUSE VISIT

The article was the result of an interview with an 80-year-old woman, Mrs. Elizabeth Chandler, of Anderson, Indiana. In 1862 Elizabeth A. Sheits and James Henry Chandler, after carrying on a courtship in secret for several months, eloped from their homes in Mount Sidney, Virginia, and ran off to Harpers Ferry to get married. Their plans were blocked, however, by local laws, and so they made their way to Washington, D.C. There, by chance, they ran afoul of a practical joker who told them that the only way they could get married in Washington was by going straight to the President. Being young and naive, they did so.

Abraham Lincoln, kindly man that he was, listened to their story, smiled understandingly, and sent for a nearby Baptist minister. The account of the White House marriage that followed is detailed and specific. A member of the Cabinet served as the best man. The preacher kissed the bride, although Lincoln, who gave away the bride, did not. And the wedding was followed by a small dance and midnight supper at which hot punch was served. Because it was a stormy night and they really had nowhere to go, the bride and groom were invited by the President to spend the night in the White House before proceeding on their honeymoon.

The story also appeared in the New York *Evening Sun*, and was later written into history in a book about Lincoln that was authored by a president of a historical society.

It is such an appealing tale and so colorful a morsel of Lincolniana that it is disappointing to find, upon researching history, that it is probably pure fiction. In a book privately published in 1926, *The Other White House*, Louis D. Carman states flatly that Mrs. Chandler "was not married in the Executive Mansion; she never was in Washington during the Civil War, having been within the Confederate lines during the entire war; and she never saw Abraham Lincoln."

According to records in the Clerk's Office of the Supreme Court, District of Columbia, Elizabeth A. Sheits and James H. Chandler were married on October 31, 1859—a year and a half before Lincoln came to office.

When "serious on the subject," Mrs. Chandler is said to have admitted that she was not married exactly in the White House, but in "what was called the 'White House Hotel.'" This was a popular designation for a three-story brick building, Rodier's Hotel, operated by Charles Anthony Rodier at the northwest corner of Wisconsin Avenue and Grace Street, and torn down around 1901. It was here, undistinguished by the presence of Mr. Lincoln or any other notable of the day, that Elizabeth and James Chandler apparently enjoyed their midnight supper and hot punch.

But the legend refuses to die, and at least two White House history books cite the incident as fact.

Many a White House wedding legend, equally fictitious, has somehow or other been written into history as "fact."

If one report is true, no one will ever know the exact number of marriages that have been performed in the White House. At the time of one White House wedding, in July 1942, *The Christian Science Monitor* reported: "In the past, when guards at the Executive Mansion were less eagle-eyed than they are today, sightseers sometimes arranged for a clergyman to meet them at a certain time in the East Room of the White House to perform a hasty ceremony so they could boast for the rest of their lives that they had been 'married in the White House.' "

There is no reason to believe that this kind of escapade did not happen from time to time, making it impossible to determine the true number of weddings. It would be a heroic task of research, too, to ferret out any marriages that have taken place in the servants' quarters of the Executive Mansion. Even as early as 1800, when it was called the "President's Palace," its first mistress, Abigail Adams, complained in a letter to her daughter that the chilly, unfinished mansion she had just moved into needed "about thirty servants to attend and keep the apartments in proper order, and perform the ordinary business of the house and stables." Out of the hundreds of people who served there, at least a few may have succumbed to the desire to be married within the historic walls.

Today's count of White House weddings ranges from fourteen to sixteen, in most cases. The confusion is nothing new: journalists and historians have always been muddled about the number. At the time of Nellie Grant's big wedding in 1874 (the *eighth* White House wedding in this book), *The New York Times* declared that "not more than one or two" weddings had previously been held in the mansion. *Harper's Bazar* (so spelled until 1929) said firmly that it was the *second*, while the *Daily Graphic* believed it was the *third*. Half a dozen intervening marriages were completely forgotten.

A great fuss was made by the press in 1913, when Woodrow Wilson's pretty daughter Jessie married Francis Sayre. The wedding was publicized as the *thirteenth*, and Jessie was constantly badgered by reporters who wanted to know whether she was superstitious about it. By way of answer, she deliberately included 13 in her wedding party to defy the pessimists. According to recently published lists, however, her wedding was only the eleventh, two earlier White House weddings having "disappeared."

One of the weddings that is missing from today's official list *may* have been the first of all. In 1801, John Adams left the White House to make way for Thomas Jefferson. James Madison and his wife, Dolley, had been living peacefully at "Montpelier," their Virginia estate, for four years since leaving the old capital of Philadelphia. They returned once more to official life when Madison was appointed Jefferson's Secretary of State, and Dolley was chosen to act as hostess for the widowed President. That year, a 24-year-old lawyer and engineer from Virginia, John George Jackson, was eagerly courting Dolley's youngest sister, Mary Payne, of Philadelphia.

Jackson had surveyed the lands west of the Ohio, and in 1801 was a member of the Virginia House of Burgesses. Two years later he was elected as a Democrat to the Eighth Congress. One of the "War Hawks" who stood for a strong foreign policy, a rugged, resolute man, quick to defend President Madison against the attacks of the Federalists, he later was lamed by a near-fatal bullet in the hip in a duel with North Carolina Congressman Joseph Pearson. During the War of 1812, he rose to the rank of General in the Virginia militia, and he ended his career as the first United States Judge for the Western District of Virginia.

But in 1801 he was simply a spirited young man very much in love.

His wedding is mentioned in a biography of a famous relative, General Thomas J. Jackson, written by "Stonewall's" nephew:

> He [J. G. Jackson] married Miss Mary Payne, sister of the famed Dolley Madison, and also a sister of Mrs. George Steptoe Washington, whose husband was a nephew of George Washington, and one of the administrators of his estate. This marriage of John G. Jackson and Mary Payne is said to have taken place in the White House, being the first ceremony of the kind solemnized therein.

When Mary (his loved "Polly") died seven years after the wedding, John George Jackson wrote a sorrowing note to Madison, which implies that Madison himself had given the bride away at the ceremony:

> My dear friend . . . I cannot write you without saying my miseries are past endurance; without speaking of my incalculable, and unparallelled misfortunes—you knew my Mary well, yes, you gave her to me at the Altar, you witnessed our union, and our happiness, you saw the little prattlers that she gave me—in the short period of seven fleeting years all those things took place, and above all but one,—and she too dearest of all has been torn from me in the same period—

Jackson family tradition continues to record this happy marriage as the *first* to be celebrated in the White House. Although most historians have either forgotten or disregarded the story, there seems to be no reason to doubt it. Henry B. Meigs, chronicler of Jackson's second wife's family, stated it as fact. And Mrs. John J. Allen, one of the children of John George Jackson and Mary, used to remark that she had often heard her parents tell the story of their White House wedding.

At the time of their wedding in 1801, the White House, named the "President's House" by Jefferson, lacked most of its present glamour. A recent writer described it as "a gaunt, naked-looking building standing aloof and yet all but surrounded with piles of debris, the oft-mentioned brickkilns, the mudholes and swamps spreading out in front. A sorry sight for the home of any President." The main stairway was unfinished. The gutters leaked. There was no running water, although other mansions had this luxury, and no sewer system. Water had to be carried from a spring six blocks away. The house required thirteen fireplaces, constantly in use, to provide heat that was far from sufficient in cold weather, and the occupants were constantly complaining about the difficulty of obtaining firewood. The lack of lamps kept the interior in semi-darkness. The surrounding roads were quagmires after a rainfall, and the view from most of the windows was one of garbage heaps and tree stumps.

Furthermore, there was hardly a room in this damp, chilly pile that was completed or adequately furnished. Referring to what is now the East Room, where half a dozen White House weddings have been held, Abigail Adams wrote in a letter to her daughter in 1800, "The great unfinished audience room I make a drying room of, to hang up the clothes in."

This was not the last time there were complaints that the White House was uncomfortable, drafty, half-furnished, and not fit to be married in. But the first marriage celebrated in the dark, damp, and half-empty building was a very happy one, as Jackson's grief at Mary's death testified.

After two years of mourning, he found a second mother for their "little prattlers." On August 10, 1810, he married the "amiable and accomplished" Mary Sophia Meigs, only daughter of Col. Return Jonathan Meigs, later the Governor of Ohio. This marriage took place in the Meigs home town, Marietta, Ohio.

There is a story that Jackson was married a third time, once again in the White House, and to another relative of Dolley Madison's. The bride this time has been described as a Miss Anna Todd, Dolley's niece or cousin, a "Quakeress from Philadelphia." Placed in 1811 or in 1812, this wedding is described as having been held in the East Room, "one of the brilliant functions of the year," with many "gay doings," and a "social sensation." The cold facts, however, do not support this tale. The story may be just a legend—a confused account of the first White House wedding (of 1801), or of the next, which is known to have taken place in 1812, when the bride was in fact another sister of the colorful Dolley.

CHAPTER III

# REJECTION AND ACCEPTANCE

*T*HINGS in Washington were never quite the same after Dorothea ("Dolley") Payne Madison came to town. Shortly after taking over as official hostess in the Jefferson Administration, she managed to stir up a storm in the British Embassy when the Ambassador's wife criticized her state dinners as "harvest-home suppers." With the Inauguration of her husband in 1809, she brought new color and radiance to Presidential functions. The White House, still rather barren and austere, began to undergo some startling changes. Liking mirrors, she had them installed by the dozen. She called in the noted architect, Latrobe, and with him planned a large-scale program of renovation. Fortunately, she had the winning personality to inveigle funds from Congress and other sources.

By the spring of 1812, the White House was, physically, ready for a wedding.

Fortunately, there were two candidates for just such an event: Lucy Payne Washington, Dolley's sister, and Judge Thomas Todd, both of whom had been widowed in 1811. Lucy was 35 at the time, and Todd 47.

Lucy and another of her sisters, Mrs. Anna Cutts, were "like the two Merry Wives of Windsor," according to Washington Irving. When she was only 15, Lucy eloped from Philadelphia with George Steptoe Washington, who was 17. Lucy's widowed mother, a staunch Quaker, was horrified that her daughter had married a "libertine person" outside their own sect. It did not matter that George was a nephew of the first President, or that his uncle had given him an outstanding education, or that he was heir to a large Virginia estate. At the time, her sister Dolley (then Mrs. Todd) and her husband John, both Quakers too, had also opposed the match that virtually "expelled" Lucy from the family. A document records the banishment in this manner:

> Minutes of Philadelphia Monthly Meeting. Adjourned meeting. 13th of 8 mo. 1793. Friends are appointed to assist women Friends in preparing a testimony against the misconduct of Lucy Washington, late Payne, who had by birth a right of membership among us, having disregarded the wholesome order of our discipline, in the accomplishment of her marriage with a person not in membership with us, before an hireling priest, and without the consent of her mother, after being precautioned against such outgoing. We therefore testify that the said Lucy Washington is no longer a member of our religious society, nevertheless desiring she may be favored with a due sense of her deviation and seek to be rightly restored.

Later, after about a year, the mother relented, gave up her residence in Philadelphia and moved into "Harewood," the Jefferson County, Virginia, home of her new son-in-law, who is said to have proved himself devoted to her.

After 18 happy years of marriage, George Steptoe died tragically from tuberculosis, collapsing by the wayside while traveling on horseback through North Carolina in search of a cure. Afterwards Lucy left "Harewood" to move to Washington to be near her sister, Dolley.

Lucy, described as the "least cultivated" of the lively Payne sisters, but by no means the least attractive, was a popular addition to Washington society, particularly from the masculine point of view. Within no time, she was fending off suitors, even though she had competition from a much younger lady, Phoebe Morris, the daughter of one of Dolley's oldest friends, who had been invited to the White House as a guest during the winter of 1811-12. It was during this winter period that Lucy met her husband-to-be.

Judge Thomas Todd had been born in Virginia and had earned his first income as a teen-age soldier for six months during the latter part of the Revolutionary War. In 1786 he had moved to Danville, Kentucky, to live with his mother's cousin, Judge Harry Innes, where he taught during the day and studied law in the evenings "by the light of a fire." He began practice "having as capital a horse, saddle, bridle and thirty-seven and a half cents." Eventually, he became a judge of the Court of Appeals of Kentucky and, in 1806, Chief Justice. In 1807, he was commissioned by Jefferson as an Associate Justice of the United States Supreme Court. It was in this capacity that he came frequently to Washington and met the attractive Widow Washington. He was described as a man of great patience, exceedingly benevolent and physically attractive. When he died in 1826, the editors of the *National Intelligencer* summed him up as "a gentleman as distinguished for his amiability and rectitude in private life as for his ability in the line of his public duty." According to the July 1836 issue of *Western Monthly Magazine*, "Judge Todd's person was finely proportioned, and his face a model of beauty and intelligence."

Dolley Madison referred to him in a letter to sister Anna as "a man of the most estimable character." Though described as "an aggressive suitor," he seemingly made little headway in winning the love of his intended, which is not surprising, since Lucy considered herself to be still deeply in mourning for her late husband. When he formally proposed to her, she rejected him just as he was to return to his home in Lexington, Kentucky. He is described as "riding mournfully" out of the capital in his carriage, having lost the battle. Lucy, however, had a sudden change of heart. As impulsively as she had abandoned her religion and her home to elope with her first husband at the age of 15, she now, 20 years later, decided to accept the proposal. A messenger on horseback was promptly dispatched to overtake the dejected Judge, which he did at Lancaster, Pennsylvania, and beg him to return. Needless to say, the Judge acquiesced, and returned with a great deal more haste than he had ever displayed in his years of riding circuit.

The suddenness of the decision, after a very short courtship, threw the White House family into confusion. Dolley, whose matchmaking efforts seemingly had been directed at marrying off the 20-year-old Phoebe Morris, was exceedingly fond of Lucy and had expected her sister to be a longtime resident of her household. "You may imagine," she wrote to Anna on March 20, 1812, announcing the wedding plans nine days hence, "my grief is not slight at the parting, and Lucy too is in deep distress."

Phoebe, who had looked upon the impetuous Lucy's "emotional adventures" during her brief stay in Washington with some amazement, wrote to her father on March 22nd:

My dear Papa

I write in the most delightful yet strange agitation possible—Mrs. Washington is to be married next Sunday to Judge Todd and Mifs Hamilton, Mifs Hay & myself are to be Bridesmaids & Mr Coles Mr Payne & Payne Todd Groomsmen—we have already shed so many tears on the occasion that we now begin to smile as we view the bright side of the Picture. The Judge is so estimable & amiable a man that every person respects & admires him; he is very rich, very handsome.

Poor Mrs. Washington had caused a great deal of distrefs to herself & all of us by this unexpected event they go off the next morning to Harewood & proceed from thence to the Judge's estate in Kentucky—Mrs W—will write you a postscript—Mrs Madison says she wishes most *earnestly* that you be here at the marriage. . . .

Lucy took the letter from her friend and dashed off a postscript:

Your flattering *Eulogium* very highly valued friend, I shall prize, and recollect when, *I am far away*—the prospect of separation now before me, from all my heart has been *accustomed* to love deprefses me beyond description, but, we must *yield* to fate—I hope your wishes in my favor may be availing—and be afsured they are sincerely reciprocated to you—for the last time perhaps I sign the initials of—

L.W.

It was not surprising that Madison should have invited Lucy and Judge Todd to be married in the White House. After all, he and Dolley had been married at Lucy's estate, "Harewood," in 1794. (It is interesting that Dolley married a Todd at her *first* wedding, and Lucy was to marry a Todd at her *second*.) The wedding was so quietly planned, for Sunday, March 29th, that it barely received mention in the press. For many years, in fact, it was completely overlooked by historians as a White House wedding. There were several reasons why the occasion was not the great social event it might have been under the hand of so masterful a planner as Dolley Madison. For one thing, the times were grave; the young nation was facing an imminent war with Great Britain, and official Washington was in no mood for a fling. For another, the President had politically affronted the Federalists so severely that, for a period, members of the party refused to dine with him or even to step inside the White House. Then, too, the romance had blossomed so quickly that few people were even to hear about it until after the wedding.

On Tuesday, March 31st, the *National Intelligencer* published a brief announcement:

On Sunday evening at the residence of the President of the United States by the Rev. Mr. McCormick, THOMAS TODD esq. one of the Judges of the Supreme Court of the United States, to Mrs. LUCY WASHINGTON, sister of Mrs. Madison.

The Reverend Andrew T. McCormick was referred to as being "of the proud faith, the Episcopalian," and was assisted by the Reverend Stephen Thomas Balch, "the disciple of predestination and the other essentials of Presbyterianism."

The wedding party was small, composed of three bridesmaids, Phoebe Morris, Miss Hamilton, and Miss Hay, and three "groomsmen": Edward Coles, Dolley's bachelor cousin, who was then serving as Madison's private secretary; John Payne, the bride's youngest brother; and John Payne Todd, Dolley's 20-year-old son by her first marriage, who turned out to be an idle young gallant and a spendthrift. It is likely that the wedding took place in the Blue Room on the main floor (then the sunflower-yellow "Oval Parlor" or "Elliptical Drawing Room"), since this is the room upon which Dolley had lavished most of her decorating attention.

To Lucy and her husband their departure for Lexington, Kentucky, and a new life together was a happy moment. Two sons and one daughter were to be born to them during their fourteen years of married life, before Todd died in 1826 (Lucy was to survive him by some thirty years). For Dolley Madison, however, it marked the beginning of a sad epoch in her life. She was losing a lively companion and beloved sister. And within less than three months she would be putting aside all thoughts of social life on the scale she had so artfully conceived, as the nation plunged into the War of 1812.

CHAPTER IV

## *WASHINGTON SOCIETY SNUBBED*

MRS. Elizabeth Kortright Monroe, wife of the fifth President, was not a popular woman in Washington. Although the Monroe Administration has been termed historically the Era of Good Feeling, notably for progress in developing good relationships throughout the Americas, this sentiment did not filter down to all the representatives of foreign countries in the U.S. capital. The President had adopted a policy of receiving foreign ministers only by appointment, and then in audiences which were brief and coldly formal. His wife, accustomed to the court circles of Paris, London, and Madrid, erased in one great swoop the warm and friendly image Dolley Madison had created as First Lady, by a public declaration that she would not follow the practice of making first calls at the homes of newly arrived diplomats. Nor would she return calls made to her by anyone.

Further arousing the fury of Washington's social élite, she proclaimed that whatever socializing was necessary for state reasons would be handled by her elder daughter, Eliza, the wife of George Hay, who lived in the White House. Then in her thirties, Eliza had attended school in Europe and had acquired manners considerably different from those of the affable, gregarious Dolley. Her best friend, Hortense de

Beauharnais, was Napoleon's stepdaughter and the future Queen of Holland. Eliza believed that the White House was on a footing with the royal houses of Europe and that the First Lady should no more accept the traditional calls than would a crown princess. She even felt that the President was not sufficiently regal in his manner and took him to task. In no time at all she had the Secretary of State, John Quincy Adams, up in arms at her snobbishness and vociferously complaining that he was spending much of his valuable time trying to calm down the foreign representatives, who were incensed by what he considered an "obstinate little firebrand." There is probably nothing that would have delighted Adams more than to have been able to turn Eliza on his knee and give her a sound spanking. Although his feelings were echoed by members of Congress, nothing could prevail on the Monroes to change their decision.

Matters reached such a state of tension that the Cabinet itself was called to a special meeting to determine matters of protocol and the right of precedence. Eventually, after great agitation, official Washington calmed down and was forced to accept the decisions of the Chief Executive. Not so, social Washington. The prominent women of the capital returned the snubs of Eliza Hay and Elizabeth Monroe by boycotting the White House. Dinners and receptions were largely attended by men, most of whom were put to the embarrassment of having to say that their wives were "indisposed" with one ailment or another. At some receptions, no women showed up at all, except for those in the immediate White House family.

Into the midst of all this controversy in 1820 stepped Maria Hester Monroe, a gracious young lady of but 17, some fifteen years younger than her sister. She had been born and brought up in France, but although little "Rias" was a precocious child, she affected none of the imperious qualities that were characteristic of the regal Eliza. Maria was only 12 when her father was elected President. When the Monroes had returned from Europe to Washington, in 1807, she was an attractive 4-year-old, described by one visitor, Judge St. George Tucker of Virginia, in a letter to his family:

> She was dress'd in a short frock, that reach'd about halfway between her knees and ancles [sic]—under which she display'd a pair of loose pantaloons, wide enough for the foot to pass through with ease, frill'd round with the same stuff as her frock and pantaloons. ... The little monkey did not fail to evince the advantage of her dress. She had a small Spaniel dog with whom she was continually engaged in a trial of skill—and the general opinion seemed to be that she turned and twisted about more than the Spaniel.

Maria had now fallen in love with 21-year-old Samuel Lawrence Gouverneur, her first cousin on her mother's side, then living at the White House and serving—as he had for the past two years—as private secretary to the President. Gouverneur was a sophisticated young man, who had become well accustomed to social functions, both in New York and in Washington. The Gouverneurs, like the Kortrights, were a fine old New York family, and Samuel was at the time considered one of the most eligible young men in the capital. One Washington newspaperman, Eliah Kingman, said, "He even possessed a seductive voice."

A White House wedding had been planned, but, much to the consternation of the young lovers, all of the planning had been snatched from their hands by the determined Eliza, who announced brusquely that the wedding was to be strictly a private affair. Not a diplomat was to be invited, nor were Congressional leaders, Cabinet members, military officers, and others who might logically have been expected to attend such an historic event—the first wedding of a President's daughter to take place in the White House. As for Washington society, even its most prominent members were deliberately excluded on the basis that the wedding was for close friends and relatives only. Gouverneur was furious at the treatment accorded his young fiancée, but he was hardly in a position to challenge the authority of the President's elder daughter, much less of her mother, who was then conveniently ailing and avoiding as much of the planning as possible.

The date was set for Thursday evening, March 9, 1820.

At this time, the new Executive Mansion, rebuilt after the British attack in 1814, had been well decorated. Monroe had developed a fine taste for furniture and furnishings when in France, and had ordered expensive items from abroad, often to the consternation of Congress, which had appropriated certain amounts for the White House, only to find that many of the estimated prices had been increased. The President had specified red damask, for example, for the Oval Drawing Room furniture, and it was found that "crimson silk trimmings, fringes, etc. are 50 percent dearer than other colors."

There were other unforeseen problems. Most of the French clocks had been designed, as was the custom, with pendulums shaped in the form of nude women. Nudes, said Mr. Madison, were certainly not appropriate for the American Executive Mansion. Hence an extra sum was required to substitute other forms. Then there was the matter of the French royal emblem. When the elegant and expensive furniture arrived at the White House direct from the master craftsmen of France, each article was glowingly decorated with the crown of Louis XVIII. Naturally, this embellishment had to be carefully removed and replaced with an American eagle, at considerable added expense.

Monroe had also ordered a magnificent Aubusson carpet in an oval shape, some 38 feet long by 25 feet wide, for what is now the Blue Room but has been variously called the Elliptical Drawing Room, the Oval Reception Room, the Circular Room, the Green Circular Parlor and the Blue Elliptical Salon. This was the room, then decorated in a rich rose, that was selected for the wedding. The carpet, which arrived in

Washington in February 1818, had a background of delicate green and was woven with the coat of arms of the United States, the traditional eagle with scroll in beak on which appeared *E Pluribus Unum*. The Stars and Stripes were there too, colorfully positioned above the eagle.

There is no doubt that the Blue Room provided an elegant setting for a wedding, but the reason for its selection over the larger East Room was chiefly one of size. Mrs. Monroe and Eliza had touched off a social explosion when they announced that the wedding was to be in "New York Style." What this meant, in effect, was that it was to be *exclusive*. The rumors had been true. Mrs. Seaton, the social commentator of her day, deplored the whole idea. And even John Quincy Adams was moved to enter in his diary that "there has been some further question of etiquette upon this occasion," pointing out that the foreign ministers, many of whom had made interested inquiries about what they should do in recognition of the important event, had been told that they "should not take notice of the marriage" and should treat it as though it had never occurred!

On Thursday evening, March 9th, Maria and Samuel stood in the Blue Room directly on the spot where the Grand Seal had been skillfully woven into the carpet and pledged themselves to each other. Maria was a petite little thing, with features like a head on a Grecian urn. She is said to have been one of the smallest, if not the smallest, of all the White House brides, her own daintiness accentuated by the strong figure of the handsome groom beside her. She was well proportioned, and, when younger, had been used by her mother to show off the children's fashions from Paris. She wore a rather simple wedding gown of blue silk, stiffened to give it body and a Continental style, intricately embroidered with red wheat stalks. Mrs. Monroe was dressed in black velvet. Both gowns had extremely long trains. In their hair they wore the latest word in headdresses—white ostrich plumes.

General Thomas Jessup, one of the heroes of the War of 1812, acted as the best man, and a small group of relatives and old friends witnessed the service.

Historical summaries of this wedding say that "The Reverend Mr. Hawley officiated," introducing a man who was to play a role in White House history for many years. Pastor of St. John's Episcopal Church in Washington, which had been founded in 1816, he had served first as associate rector, and was elected Rector in the spring of 1817, remaining there until he died in 1845. At the time of the Monroe/Gouverneur wedding, he was 35, but looking much older than his years, dressed in traditional British knee breeches, black silk hose, and the shoe buckles of a passing era. Although he came from Vermont, many people took him to be an Englishman because of his dress.

Dr. William Hawley was known as something of a character, a man who frequently spoke his mind bluntly. He was by no means bigoted, but he did criticize the election of a Unitarian as Chaplain of the House of Representatives in language so strong that it was later commented on by John Quincy Adams in his autobiography. Hawley, nevertheless, was quite tolerant, being friendly with the priest of St. Patrick's Roman Catholic Church, as well as with the pastor of the Presbyterian Church. He saw no harm in joining with other gentlemen in occasional card games. During his lifetime, he was friendly with many great figures of his day, including Presidents Monroe, John Quincy Adams, Andrew Jackson, Martin Van Buren, William Harrison, and John Tyler. In Washington, he was generally referred to as "Parson Hawley." Having served as an Army officer in the War of 1812, he was sometimes called "Captain" by old friends. Commodore Stephen Decatur refused to attend his church, however. It seems that Hawley, while in command of a company of divinity students enlisted to protect New York City, had refused to obey an order to march to the front to engage the enemy, in one incident during that war.

If the wedding in the Blue Room was smaller than the bride and groom might have wished, they at least had one consolation: after a brief, five-day honeymoon they returned on Tuesday for a White House wedding reception, at which Maria and her husband received the guests alone, while Mrs. Monroe and Eliza remained in the background. The reception on March 14th was to be followed by a round of balls, which it was hoped would assuage the hurt feelings being nursed by Washington socialites.

The reception was an immense success. The great East Room was in readiness, its chandeliers lit for the first time since its restoration. The first of the following balls, on March 20th, was a magnificent affair, given by Commodore and Mrs. Stephen Decatur, in their home on La Fayette Square. Decatur had been a national hero ever since his heroic conduct in the war with Tripoli. For the first time in many months there was social harmony throughout the capital, and Maria and Samuel were radiant.

Then a national tragedy occurred.

Two days after the Decaturs' ball, the Commodore went to Bladensburg, Maryland, just across the District line, on a disastrous mission—to fight a duel with Commodore James Barron. The latter had been suspended from naval service for five years by the sentence of a court martial in 1807, when his ship, the *Chesapeake*, had been boarded by the British and four of his seamen were forcibly removed. Decatur, as one of the Commissioners of the Navy, had resisted Barron's restoration to active duty. The hatred of the two men for each other never died. Decatur spoke of Barron in contemptuous terms, and Barron, returning from a long residence in Europe, accused Decatur of deliberately preventing him from obtaining deserved employment.

Matters came to a head after a series of harsh letters between the two and, according to the code of the day, a duel was unavoidable. Early on the morning of March 20th, the two faced each other with pistols. On the first exchange of shots, both naval officers fell. Barron was carried to Beale's Congress Hotel on Capitol Hill, seriously, but not mortally, wounded with a ball in his hip. Decatur was rushed to his own home and attended by Surgeon-General Lovell; he died shortly after nine that evening.

"Mourn, Columbia!" said the obituary in the *National Intelligencer* of March 23rd, "for one of thy brightest stars is set—a Son 'without fear and without reproach'—in the freshness of his fame—in the prime of his usefulness—has descended into the tomb."

The gay balls and dinners were promptly canceled, as Washington—and the entire nation—went into mourning.

In spite of this inauspicious start, Maria and Samuel Gouverneur enjoyed thirty happy years of married life together in New York before Maria died at 47. Samuel lived on another seventeen years. He was married again, to Mary Diggs Lee of Maryland, granddaughter of that state's second governor. Samuel and Maria had three children: James Monroe, who remained a bachelor; Elizabeth, who was baptized and later also married by Pastor Hawley, and had three husbands and four children; and Samuel, Jr., who served with the Fourth Artillery during the Mexican War, but later resigned his commission in a huff when the War Department refused to grant him a leave of absence to visit his mother when Maria was ill.

Samuel Gouverneur, Sr., matured into a man of the world, fond of race horses and owner of a much-celebrated horse, "Post Boy." He was deeply interested in the theater, and it was partly through his efforts that many brilliant stars were brought to the U.S. at the Bowery Theater, of which he was part owner. He and Maria gave brilliant parties and, according to one naval officer, "sixteen baskets of champagne were frequently consumed by the guests in a single evening." He entered the New York Legislature in 1825. President Monroe scrupulously avoided nepotism and did not favor his son-in-law with any government posts. Gouverneur had to wait for the next President, John Quincy Adams, to appoint him Postmaster of New York, a position he held from 1828 to 1836.

CHAPTER V

# THE TRAGIC MESSRS. ADAMS

EORGE WASHINGTON ADAMS had a distinguished name, a brilliant mind, and outstanding parents. The oldest son of President John Quincy Adams, he was a graduate of Harvard, had studied law in the Boston office of Daniel Webster, was admitted to the Massachusetts Bar in 1824, and two years later began what seemed to be a promising career by winning election to the State Legislature. During his earlier visits to Washington to see his father and mother, when Adams was still only Secretary of State, he had been seen more and more in the company of his orphaned cousin, Mary Catherine Hellen, a flirtatious little beauty who later lived in the White House and had her eyes open for a good catch.

George had fallen madly in love with this pretty young coquette and soon had convinced her that they should become engaged, although it looked as though the wedding would have to be postponed for several years until he became firmly established. Despite his good education and his keen mind, George was not a stable person. He wavered between the heights of ecstasy and the depths of despair, and was constantly seeking the love and understanding which his parents, he felt, had never given him. For a while it had seemed as though the engagement would prove to be the emotional anchor he needed. But George, passionate and poetic though he was in the presence of his sweetheart, somehow never got around to writing her very often during the long periods when he was away in Boston. Mary soon broke off the engagement, leaving the rejected suitor in one of his states of deep depression.

It is doubtful that Mary's change of heart had much to do with what followed, although it may have been a contributing factor. George had never had much of a head for business, and he spent a great deal of his time daydreaming about becoming a great poet and writer. He had talents in this direction—at Harvard he had once beaten Ralph Waldo Emerson in competition for a literary prize—but not the ambition and discipline necessary to accomplish any objective. His law business began to slip, as clients became discouraged with his inattentiveness to their problems and his delays in taking action. Romantic matters went downhill, too. Rejected by Mary, he turned to another cousin, Abigail Adams, who lived in nearby Quincy. While she and other young ladies in Boston found him attractive and entertaining when he was not in one of his dark moods, they all discouraged him from becoming serious.

George's decline was rapid. His practice fell off. He slipped heavily into debt. To top it all off, he "took up a relationship" with a young tart in town and got her pregnant. Overcome by despair and guilt, he had a complete breakdown, imagined that people were persecuting him, and finally left Providence on the steamboat *Benjamin Franklin* and jumped overboard early in the morning of April 30, 1829.

His former fiancée, Mary Catherine, was grief-stricken, as were all the members of the Adams household, but she must have long since realized that George's problems were not her fault. Fourteen months earlier, she had been married to one of his younger brothers, John Quincy Adams, II.

Mary Catherine Hellen has been mistakenly referred to in history books as Miss Helen, Miss Helen Jackson and Miss

Johnson—the last perhaps because of confusion with her dead mother's maiden name of Johnson, or with her older brother, Johnson Hellen, who also lived in the White House for three years. What with all the cousins and in-laws and the inter-family courting, there is some reason for editorial confusion. John Quincy Adams, Sr., had first courted Nancy Johnson, Mary's mother, before switching his affections and marrying her sister, Louisa Johnson. Nancy, described as a "plump, auburn-haired Hebe," then went on to marry Walter Hellen, by whom she had three children: Mary, Johnson, and Thomas Hellen. The three orphaned children moved into the White House with their aunt.

Young John Adams was a good student, but he had caused his father considerable grief by participating in a great student riot in his senior year at Harvard, in 1823, for which he was promptly expelled. Adams, Sr., in his position as Secretary of State, as well as one of the University's outstanding almuni, remonstrated with President Kirkland, but to no avail. To help the young man complete his education, he therefore brought him back to Washington to study law privately. In 1825, shortly after his Inauguration as President, he appointed him White House secretary.

Young Adams, businesslike and efficient though he may have been in comparison with his older brother, is not always treated very graciously by historians. While George is said to have had a "gentle disposition," John has been referred to as "little liked" and "arrogant." In 1886 Benjamin Perley Poore, recalling his sixty years in Washington, speaks of John as being "very obnoxious to the friends of General Jackson." He tended to be brusque and outspoken. On one occasion, a White House party was attended by one Russell Jarvis, an editor from the *Daily Telegraph*, which had recently printed anti-Adams sentiments. When he walked into the drawing room, John commented loudly that Jarvis would never have shown his face in the White House if he had been any kind of gentleman. "This led," wrote Samuel Bemis in his biography of Adams, Sr., "to an attempted nose-pulling in the Rotunda of the Capitol to provoke a duel. It took all the resourcefulness of the President's Cabinet, including Henry Clay, the Administration's most experienced duelist, to prevent a meeting of Jarvis and John."

Living in the same household and seeing each other day after day, Mary Catherine Hellen and John became fond of each other. After Mary had rejected George, their affection ripened into love. While John put up a cold and often antagonistic front to many an outsider, he had a tender heart and a great sense of loyalty to members of his immediate family circle. When, in late 1827, John announced that he wanted to marry Mary, the President was not pleased. A demanding father, he felt that his son was not in any position to support a wife.

When the President finally saw that he could not change the mind of either his son or his niece, he relented. The wedding was planned for Monday, February 25th, and was to be in the Elliptical Drawing Room (today's Blue Room) where Maria Monroe had been married eight years earlier.

The White House had been further decorated and improved. The Entrance Hall is said to have "boasted an oil-cloth carpet, two elegant brass fenders, two marble consoles, four mahogany settees, also a lamp with branching arms and a handsome barometer and thermometer." The East Room, then referred to as the "Large Levee Room," was still "woefully" bare. Although it had been the scene of the Gouverneur wedding reception, it now contained only eight pine tables, 24 armchairs, and four sofas. It was used in part as a store room, which one observer found "full of cobwebs, old chairs, benches and broken glass."

The Elliptical Drawing Room had the magnificent Aubusson carpet imported by President Monroe, over which hung an elegant chandelier, glistening with cut glass. The room was still not blue—not until Van Buren brought in blue upholstery in 1837. It contained the large pier table, looking glasses, upholstered chairs, and other Bellange furniture covered in the rose or pinkish-red silk that had been purchased during Monroe's Administration. The windows were draped in silk and surmounted by carved-eagle cornices.

President Adams conducted life by the book and by the clock. He was meticulous in adhering to a schedule, being proud of his punctuality. Writing in his diary, in December 1825, he declared:

> I usually rise between five and six—that is at this time of the year, from an hour and a half to two hours before the sun. I walk by the light of the moon or stars or none, about four miles, usually returning home in time to see the sun rise from the eastern chamber of the house. I then make my fire and read three chapters of the Bible with Scott's and Hewlett's commentaries. Read papers till nine. Breakfast, and from ten till five P.M. receive a succession of visitors sometimes without intermission—very seldom with an interval of half an hour—never such as to enable me to undertake any business requiring attention. From five to half past six we dine; after which I pass about four hours in my chamber alone, writing in this diary or reading papers upon some public business excepting when occasionally interrupted by a visitor. Between eleven and twelve I retire to bed, to rise again at five or six the next morning.

One of the few times that Adams departed from his custom and allowed himself to be seen publicly in gay spirits was at the time of his son's wedding. As old Perley reported, ". . . the President, usually so grave and unsocial, unbent for the nonce, and danced at the wedding ball in a Virginia reel with great spirit." It was a surprise to some that he could even dance!

The wedding was not large and was confined mainly to the family, immediate friends, and household servants. The lovely bride, attended by four bridesmaids, wore the traditional white satin, with orange blossoms and pearls. Once again, the Reverend Mr. Hawley officiated. The President not only went so far as to dance, but told a few jokes to the guests, and even sang parts of familiar love songs—as he could recall them. The festivities continued until midnight.

The bride and groom apparently spent the honeymoon at the White House, for there was a large formal reception in the Yellow Room on the next day, followed by a series of wedding dinners.

For a time, all went well. On December 2, 1828, Mary Louisa Adams, a White House baby, arrived, followed by a sister, Georgiana Frances, in Quincy, Massachusetts, a year and a half later. But by 1829, the end of the Adams Administration, the President's wife was suffering from fits of deep melancholy and the President was facing a serious financial crisis. Some six years earlier, he had bought grist mills along Rock Creek, intending to use them for retirement income, but they were operating at a loss, and he owed money on the loans he had obtained to purchase them. During the early 1830s, young John labored day and night to try to put the mills on a paying basis. He was partially successful, but by 1833, overworked and already ailing, he contracted a serious illness. Growing weaker and weaker, and often suffering from intense pain, he survived for almost two years, finally dying on October 23, 1834, just six and a half years after he had become the only President's son ever to be married in the White House.

In 1839, nine-year-old Georgiana Frances followed her father. The widowed Mary Catherine saw her elder daughter married and outlived that child, too, remaining in Washington until her death, as an old lady, in the early 1870s.

YORKE/JACKSON, JR.
November 24, 1831
EASTIN/POLK
April 10, 1832

LEWIS/PAGEOT
November 29, 1832
MARTIN/RANDOLPH
April 9, 1835

CHAPTER VI

# THOSE JACKSON AFFAIRS

ANDREW JACKSON was noted for a good many accomplishments, as well as for the toughness and ruggedness that earned him the nickname "Old Hickory." He is remembered as a rough-hewn Revolutionary War officer (slashed with a saber by an English officer whose boots he refused to clean), a merciless Indian fighter, expert marksman, deadly opponent in a duel, and the first of the "log cabin" school of American Presidents.

Readers not intimately acquainted with Jackson's life may therefore be considerably surprised to learn that our seventh President was also an emissary of Cupid and a more accomplished matchmaker than even the celebrated Dolley Madison.

Jackson's romantic avocation began in the Cumberland region of Tennessee one warm night in the year 1796, long before he reached the White House, and even before he became a congressman. On that notable occasion, he assisted his law partner, Sam Donelson, in an adventurous elopement. Sam had fallen in love with a pretty young maiden, Mary Ann ("Polly") Smith, daughter of General Daniel Smith, a courtly gentleman with an iron will. Smith had been violently protective of Polly who, although not quite 16, had already reached the maturity of a girl several years older. A vivacious, blue-eyed blonde, who had attracted would-be lovers from up and down the Cumberland, she had eyes for no one but Sam, revealing an attraction so evident that her father announced plans for sending her to school in Philadelphia to keep the two apart.

Andrew Jackson, braving the wrath of the General, not only urged Sam to elope, but materially assisted in the escape, the very night before she was to be bundled off to school. Stealing up to "Rock Castle," the Smith homestead, in the middle of the night, he and Sam approached a spot directly beneath Polly's bedroom window. Jackson then tossed up a ladder made of vines. It was caught by the agile Polly, who fastened it to the sill and scrambled down, partly with the help of a maple tree, skirts billowing, into the arms of her lover. The trio then sped to a parson, who had been alerted earlier, and Sam and Polly were married. Jackson "gave away" the bride and bestowed upon her a warm kiss.

The fact that he was never forgiven by the irate General (who boarded up the window and cut down the maple) did not in any way dampen Andrew Jackson's enthusiasm for encouraging love affairs among his relatives and friends.

Since he and his wife, Rachel, never had any children of their own, he was forever advising the sons and daughters of other people on matters of the heart. Their home was always full of other people's children; the rugged soldier could often be found bouncing some child on his knee and mouthing such seemingly out-of-character babblings as "This little pig went to market. . . ." One boy, the Donelsons' son, was particularly close to Jackson's heart. The happy union of Sam Donelson and Polly lasted barely eight years. In 1803, caught in a heavy snowstorm on his way to visit the Jacksons, Sam caught pneumonia from the exposure and died a few days later. By this time, however, he and Polly had a 4-year-old son, their second child, whom they had named Andrew Jackson Donelson. Jackson adored the boy and was instrumental in furthering the romance between him and another beauty of the region, a cousin, appropriately named Emily Tennessee Donelson. He merrily fostered the affair from the time the two were in their teens and delightedly saw them married in 1824, at which time Jackson was Senator from Tennessee.

The presence of numerous children in their household never quite balanced out the Jacksons' desire to have a child of their own. Just before Christmas, in 1809, an unexpected opportunity arose. On December 22nd, Rachel's brother, Severn Donelson, and his wife, Elizabeth, became parents of twin boys, whom they named Andrew Jackson and Thomas Jefferson. Since the mother was in poor health, and the Donelson finances were shaky, she permitted the Jacksons to take Andrew to their home, and shortly afterwards the boy was legally adopted by the General as Andrew Jackson, Jr.

Andrew, Jr., received more affection than if he had been the Jacksons' own son. In 1813, the General even brought him home a playmate, an Indian baby boy, named Lyncoya, who had been found abandoned after the battle of Talluschatches, and who then lived with the family for many years and was Andrew's constant companion. Andrew also played with Jefferson Davis, and with numerous cousins, including Andrew Jackson Hutchings and Andrew Jackson Donelson. With the proliferation of "Andrew Jacksons," it is no wonder that some of the family history is somewhat confusing. At one time, there were at least eight men and boys with the same name who were related to each other, and among their cousins there were five with the name "Mary," four of whom were married during Jackson's Administration.

Jackson was inaugurated as President in 1829, under tragic circumstances. His wife, Rachel, had died on Christmas Eve, shortly before they were to leave their home, "The Hermitage," for Washington to take up residence in the White House. The circumstances were ironic. During the bitter campaign, Jackson's enemies had tried to capitalize on a rumor that Rachel, who had been married first to one Lewis Robards, was not legally married to Jackson and that her presence in the White House would be scandalous. Now it no longer mattered.

With no First Lady to assist him, Andrew Jackson appointed the lovely and gracious Emily Tennessee Donelson to serve as official hostess, although she was only 21 at the time. Jackson was 62 at his Inauguration, described as "straight as a ramrod," over six feet tall, with a "shock of bristling white hair [that] gave him a certain air of distinction." He always wore black, with a ruffled shirt and high collar, and a band of black crepe on his arm in memory of his dead wife. Around his neck, he wore a miniature of Rachel, propping it at night on a table next to his bed. Although considered irascible and often implacable, he was always warm and deferential to women of all ages, and was ready at a moment's notice to push aside affairs of state in the interests of developing a romance between young lovers.

The White House during the Jackson Administration was an ideal trysting ground. Jackson had invited a whole flock of relatives and in-laws to come and visit at the White House. Among these were Emily's niece, Mary Eastin of Nashville (only three years Emily's junior); Mary Smith, of Abingdon, Virginia; Margaret and Rebecca Branch; Rebecca McLane; and Cora Livingstone. Watched over by a chaperone almost their own age and just as interested in merriment, the lovely young girls—and others who followed—turned the White House into a kind of young ladies' social club. "Uncle Andrew" not only encouraged them to be sociable in all ways, but saw to it that there was never a lack of handsome, eligible escorts for dances, dinner parties, soirées, and other activities. Jackson had just as many nephews, either blood relatives or adopted relatives, as nieces. Among them at one time or another were Andrew Jackson Hutchings, Daniel Donelson, Samuel Jackson Hays, Daniel Smith, and Edward and Anthony Butler. Jackson was so indulgent that he financed much of the socializing out of his own pocket. At one time he even paid a haberdasher's bill of $283, which young Hays had incurred buying clothes to keep himself presentable at all times to the young ladies, and he picked up not a few bills for the education of these fortunate Washington swains.

The President's chief interest was focused on Andrew Jackson, Jr., the boy whom he had adopted. Andrew, Jr., was an appealing young man, interested in making a way for himself, but never quite able to cope with financial matters or develop into a successful businessman. The General had spoiled him from the beginning. By the time he was 16, he was living "like a young lord," cared for by a personal manservant, and running up bills for such items as 76-dollar suits, 10-dollar hats and silk hose at a dollar fifty a pair. It was only natural that, with so many pretty young cousins and other Southern belles constantly in and out of "The Hermitage," he should have shown great interest in the opposite sex. At the age of 21, he was described as "one of the handsomest men in the country," proficient in all the social graces. By then, his father was President, and he was in a position to take full romantic advantage of the situation.

At about the time of the Inauguration, Andrew, Jr., was in love with a girl named Flora, of unknown parentage but under the guardianship of Colonel Edward Ward, a neighbor of the Jacksons in Tennessee. The President, so eager to promote romances among the young people around him, was now greatly concerned. In Flora he apparently saw evidences of a flirt, and he was concerned that the girl's fickleness might have a poor effect on his son. In July 1829, he wrote from the White House to Andrew, who was at "The Hermitage" for a while conducting family business:

> You can judge of the anxiety I have that you should marry
> a lady that will make you happy, which would add to mine,

seeing you so. You are very young, but having placed your affections upon Miss Flora, I have no desire to control your affections or interfere with your choice....

He expressed the feeling that "no good can flow from long courtship," advising Andrew, Jr., to get an answer from the girl at once, and if it should be "no," then to "give out all idea of Marriage for the present, until you see and advise with me."

Flora was not ready to settle down, and the rejected suitor was advised by his father that since the young lady "has given herself to coquetry ... you are now free from all engagements and I trust you will keep so until you advise with your father on this interesting subject."

In the fall of 1829, young Andrew returned to Washington, where Anne Royall, a newspaperwoman who might be described as the first White House social correspondent, wrote of him, "His countenance is sweetness and innocence itself, his eyes as soft as the dewdrops." There he met one of the White House belles, Mary Smith, the young lady from Abingdon, Virginia. She so charmed him that he followed her home, where he made the social mistake of professing his love to her and entreating her to marry him—all without having first expressed his honorable intentions to the girl's mother and father. The Smiths, fine Virginia folk that they were, could not conceal their indignation. The President himself, greatly disturbed by this breach of etiquette, wrote to Mary's father, sending the letter by his son's own hand, and pleading that his son, who had been "reared in the paths of virtue and morality by his pious and amiable mother," had erred only because he had been so smitten by the lovely Mary.

The lovesick young man did not go to Mary Smith's house alone. He was accompanied by a friend of his father's who had been asked to intercede for the young man and see what he could do to win Mary over. The mission, however, was in vain. Andrew, Jr., failed to win the heart of Mary Smith and returned to "The Hermitage" again to work on plantation affairs.

The President, ever the determined matchmaker, tried now to stimulate a romance between his son and Mary Ann Lewis, the daughter of Major William Berkeley Lewis, whom he had brought into the White House as part of his "Kitchen Cabinet."

"Have you seen Miss Mary Ann Lewis," he wrote to Andrew on September 16, 1831, "and presented my regards to her—you know she is a great favorite of mine, and that she also was of your dear departed mother—she is a sweet disposition, and I am sure will make a very fine and elegant woman, it is said here she is esteemed as one of the Belles of New York—I have no doubt but that she would make a sweet and affectionate companion."

Andrew, Jr., who was now nearly 22, needed no paternal assistance. Although Mary Ann Lewis was a pretty and charming girl, he had his eye on Philadelphia and a "demure little Quakeress" who lived there, Sarah Yorke. While walking along the street recently with a Captain McCaulley, he had met Sarah and an elderly lady, both of whom spoke to the Captain. "Andrew Junior turned to look at the young lady," reports an account in the *Tennessee Historical Quarterly*, "and at the same moment she, too, turned and flashed him a saucy smile. Both had fallen in love at first sight." The courtship that followed was described as "ardent."

Sarah Yorke had declared on one occasion that she would marry no one lower than a prince. She probably said this with tongue in cheek, although she did have every reason to hope for an excellent match. She came from an old, distinguished Pennsylvania family, which included Judge Thomas Yorke, her grandfather, and Captain Peter Yorke, her father, and she was related to some staunch old-line Philadelphia families—the Potts, Claypooles, and Lippincotts. Since her father's death in 1815, and her mother's in 1820, she had been brought up by an aunt. She was a petite, pretty girl with black hair and dark eyes and a dark complexion. By nature, she was amiable, though somewhat on the subdued side, with a gentle voice and delicate manners—qualities that perhaps set her apart in Andrew's mind from the gay, teasing coquettes who frequented the White House and delighted in playing the field.

Once Old Hickory got wind of the new affair, he became characteristically impatient. "My son," he wrote, "... the sooner this engagement is consummated the better," adding that "Sarah possesses every quality necessary to make you happy." The recommendation was not necessary. Andrew had made up his mind, and so had Sarah. On November 24, 1831, they were married. Fate was not kind to the President. On the day of the wedding, which took place in Philadelphia, urgent government business detained him in Washington, and the best he could do was to send the family friend and painter, Ralph E. W. Earl, in his place. With Earl, he sent as a gift an unusual ring of pearls, which contained a lock of the Presidential hair inside. The bride wore a low-necked gown, off the shoulder, with a narrow cape of the finest lace. The skirt was white mull, embroidered in panels with white silk floss in a satin-stitch floral design. The satin bodice was deeply pointed in a V, both in front and in back. She liked the dress so much that she later wore it several times in the White House. (It is now on display in the collection of dresses of the First Ladies at the Smithsonian Institution in Washington.) Sarah's hair was done in a style then popular and very becoming to her girlish simplicity: a Grecian knot worn high in the back, with the front parted and arranged in curls that trailed down each side almost to the shoulder.

The bride and groom journeyed directly to the White House after the wedding. As the carriage approached the door, Andrew turned to his bride and asked whether she could distinguish his father. She is said to have replied without hesitation, "Oh, there he is—like Saul among his brethren, head and shoulders above them all."

The President was in his glory. The romance had flowered, and even though he had not had anything to do with it other than to give his approval all along, he was almost as happy as though he himself had been the bridegroom.

Andrew and Sarah had five children: Rachel, who lived to be 96 and had nine children of her own; Andrew; Thomas Hugh, who lived only four years; Samuel, who served in the Confederate Army; and Robert Armstrong, who did not survive infancy. Andrew, Jr., died in April, 1865, at the age of 55. Sarah lived until 1888.

Family life among the members of the Jackson clan continued in a serene and rewarding fashion. Old Hickory was as fond of his new daughter as he had always been of his son. He was so attached to her that he even permitted her to hold one of his most sacred treasures, his dead Rachel's family Bible, and read to him aloud from it. And when in 1832 the Andrew Jacksons, Jr., presented him with a granddaughter, named Rachel after his wife, he was in a state of gushing bliss that was almost maudlin. She became his greatest pet, whom he played with endlessly whenever his son visited the White House from "The Hermitage" with his new family. In April 1834, another Andrew Jackson came into the world, and the old gentleman was ecstatic.

However, all was not as serene and happy on the romantic front as the President would have desired. He was still plagued —and was to be so during most of his Administration—by a scandal that was used often by his political enemies to place him in a difficult position. It had all happened at the very beginning of his Presidency, in early 1829.

The girl at the heart of the scandal was Margaret ("Peggy") O'Neale, a notorious beauty who had been brought up in a Washington lodging house and tavern run by her father. The inn, Franklin House, was patronized by many a Congressman who lived, ate, or drank there during the periods when Congress was in session. Andrew Jackson himself had lived at Franklin House when he had first come to Washington, and he had become acquainted with Peggy who, along with her more obvious attractions, had a gift for singing, dancing, and entertaining the male guests with her lively wit and conversation. At some point, Peggy had eloped with one Timberlake, described as "a rather dissolute Naval officer," who was a ship's purser and usually away at sea. One of Jackson's closest friends at the time, and fellow Senator from Tennessee, was John Henry Eaton, who became greatly attracted to Peggy, and she to him.

What followed is not altogether clear. The allegations are that Eaton rendered financial assistance to the tavern owner and that his daughter, either by choice or out of a desire to ensure the flow of money, saw to it that the young Senator from Tennessee enjoyed more than simply room, board, and drink. The dissolute Timberlake finally died at sea, supposedly of tuberculosis, but according to many by suicide because he had heard about his wife's amorous adventures. At any rate, Andrew Jackson, then President-elect, became greatly alarmed at the scandal that was about to erupt. Hearing rumors that the girl was pregnant, and knowing that at the very least her honor was at stake, he all but ordered the unfortunate Eaton to marry the girl. The ceremony that took place on January 1, 1829, shortly before Jackson's Inauguration, was about as close to a shotgun wedding as could be imagined.

The new Administration's political enemies had a field day. According to the whispering campaign, not only had Senator Eaton been intimate with Promiscuous Peg, but Jackson himself had shared her favors. Washington society began forming into two lines, a few people feeling that the scandal would blow over and it was better to stay on the side of the President, but a great many openly taking sides against him. Eaton's career appeared to be ruined. He had been talked about for a Cabinet position, but this was now impossible, since the wives of Washington officials were snubbing Peggy at every opportunity. It thus came as a shock to the capital when, barely five days after his Inauguration, Jackson appointed Eaton Secretary of War!

The scandal and the related problems invaded the White House to such a catastrophic degree that it almost broke up the harmonious family unit that the President had installed. Emily Donelson, as the official First Lady, refused to invite Peggy to social functions. At official events, when the Secretary and his wife had to be present, Emily, along with her niece and closest friend, Mary Eastin, and other young ladies, simply turned the other way when Peggy appeared. Mrs. Calhoun, wife of the Vice President, was so traumatically upset by it all that she had to pack up and return to her native South Carolina to avoid emotional crises.

In short, Old Hickory had cracked open a pretty bad nut.

Ever gallant, however, the President accepted Peggy warmly and did not attempt to hide the fact that he liked her, and always had. Martin Van Buren, a widower and at the time Secretary of State, also stood up for Peggy, thus securing the good graces of his Chief without seriously endangering his official position. Van Buren referred to the situation as "the Eaton Malaria," a term that was widely used. As the time for the winter "season" drew near, in November 1829, the Eaton Malaria grew worse. Van Buren tried to heal the breach in the White House by having a fatherly talk with the 22-year-old Emily, whom he admired. In his autobiography he described Emily and Mary Eastin as "unaffected and graceful in manners, amiable and purely feminine in disposition and character and bright and self possessed in conversation."

At this interview, Mary Eastin demonstrated her "purely feminine" disposition, and Emily nearly lost her self-possession. Van Buren argued and argued, while Emily grew more and more angry—until Mary, trying to control her agitation, withdrew into the "embrasure" of the window and sobbed aloud behind the damask draperies, luckily ending the interview.

The first real crack in family solidarity came in June of 1830 when Jackson insisted that Peggy Eaton should be invited to the White House and declared that if Emily Donelson continued ignoring the woman she would have to take herself back to Tennessee. Emily announced that she preferred Tennessee and promptly packed, leaving the White House within the week and taking Mary Eastin with her. She had carried the snubbing to such an extent that on one occasion, becoming ill during a boat trip on the Potomac, she had fainted rather than accept the fan and bottle of smelling salts offered to her by Peggy. During the 15-month period of "exile," while Emily and Mary were in Tennessee, Jackson flouted public opinion one time by inviting Peggy to sit at his right during a White House dinner. Washington society gasped, but Peggy seemingly enjoyed the public attention she received, even if at other people's expense, and was much taken to lampooning her critics. Since she was a superb mimic, and was not discouraged in this pastime, many an evening's entertainment was supplied through her caricatures of stuffy old Washington dowagers and others who were scandalized.

One of the most bizarre Cabinet meetings in the history of the White House took place when two ministers of the Church decided that the morals of the capital were in jeopardy. They took it upon themselves to make public charges that Peggy, while still the wife of Timberlake, had undergone a miscarriage, after the scurrilous Eaton had made her pregnant. Jackson and his Cabinet members gathered to face the aroused clergymen, having already compiled as many testimonies as they could get from people who were ready to defend Peggy's virtue. Jackson himself repudiated the assertions of the ministers and dismissed the charges, saying of Peggy, "She is as chaste as any virgin." That ended the meeting, but not the turmoil.

The family became reconciled after Emily and Mary had spent over a year in "exile" in Tennessee, Emily separated from her young husband (who, torn by his loyalties, continued to act as Jackson's secretary) and Mary from her many adoring beaux. In September 1831, Emily finally returned as First Lady to the White House with her two children and Mary Eastin and another young niece, Mary McLemore. But the Eaton Malaria was not fully cured until several years later, when John Eaton was appointed Ambassador to Spain and he and his wife departed for Europe, where no one was concerned over such trifling irregularities of amour, and where the voluptuous Peggy "enjoyed life to the fullest."

Among the many young men who frequented the White House at the beginning of the 1830s was Lucius Junius Polk, third son of Colonel William Polk and a cousin of the man who would become President some fifteen years later, James Knox Polk. He was an elegant Southern gentleman, from Columbia, Tennessee, a graduate of the University of North Carolina, and at the time about 30. In January 1832, Polk was deeply in love with the vivacious Mary Ann Eastin, Emily's 22-year-old niece and companion. He had met Mary ("The Cumberland Cinderella") at a party at "The Hermitage," and had intended to court her in Washington as soon as he could make plans. Mary had returned to the capital in time for the winter season of 1831. Then came a great blow. News reached him that his beloved Mary had met an older man of about 40, a naval officer named Bolton Finch who, according to the girl's uncle, Andrew Donelson, was "very clever and highly respectable." Polk might not have been so convinced about the second attribute, but there could be no doubt about the first. The fortunate suitor, described at a much later date by

*Harper's Weekly* as "quite a dandy" who had been engaged to several young ladies before he proposed to Miss Eastin, had engineered matters so favorably that the wedding date was already set.

Although Bolton Finch was a Lieutenant in the United States Navy, he was an Englishman by birth. A year after his courtship of Mary Eastin, he had his name changed by Congress to Bolton, and when he died in 1849 he was known as Commodore William Compton Bolton. The damnable man had selected as his wedding date Valentine's Day, February 14th, barely a month from the time Polk heard the unwelcome news. It was reported that Mary had already bought her trousseau, at a Miss Thompson's establishment in New York City. There could be little doubt about the report, since even the smallest details were described. Instead of the traditional bridal veil, Mary had selected a bonnet of white satin, at a cost of $11, and a wreath of orange blossoms at $2.

Gentleman though he was, Lucius J. Polk was not so sportsmanlike that he was going to bow out of the picture. He threw together some belongings and boarded the next stage to Washington. Within a matter of days, the surprised and chagrined Lieutenant Finch of the United States Navy found his romance scuttled and an Army officer in command of the situation. Old Andrew Jackson had observed some whirlwind affairs and abrupt about-faces, but never anything to match this. Characteristically, he had a hand in the affair, speaking on Polk's behalf and telling his niece, "Take care, my dear; with love, marriage is heaven, without it, hell." For a time, after Mary heeded his words, he thought that he would at least be spared the strain on his budget of an immediate wedding (he had promised to pay for hers, as he did for most of the others in the clan). The reprieve was short. The switch in bridegrooms merely changed the date from February 14th, 1832, to April 10th.

Uncle Andrew firmly suggested that the event take place in

the White House, a suggestion that could not be taken lightly, since he was footing the bill. Jackson did this out of affection for Mary, but he also may have been pleased to hold this wedding in the White House because of an old debt of gratitude to the Polk clan.

W. H. Polk, in his book, *Polk Family and Kinsmen* (1912), writes:

> The Jackson and Polk families had been intimate for years, in Mecklenburg County, N.C. During the Revolution, Andrew Jackson's father being dead, he and his two brothers joined the army. The eldest was killed at the battle of Stono, and the second died from a wound received, which was aggravated by British neglect in the hospital. During the absence of her sons in the army, Mrs. Jackson was often hard pressed for the necessaries of life, and was relieved in numerous instances by Col. Thomas Polk. . . . This kindness to his mother Andrew Jackson never forgot and hence he entertained an abiding friendship for the Polk family.

Glamorous though the idea of a White House wedding sounded, the mansion was at this time far from being the most elegant setting for a formal wedding. A Washington matron described it as "gloomy." And although the fact had little to do with the appearance, it also was infested with bedbugs. Even a year later, in 1833, the actress Fanny Kemble recorded in her *Journal* that the Executive Mansion was "comfortless" and that it had a "desolate reach of uncultivated ground down to the river behind." The East Room was the most presentable room in the house, with yellow wallpaper, bordered in cloth; four black Italian marble mantels, topped by magnificently framed mirrors; and three bronze chandeliers which, with the wall brackets, held a total of 180 individual candles. There were almost 500 square yards of Brussels carpeting on the floor, in blue, yellow, and fawn with a red border. During his two terms, Jackson was to spend about $50,000 furnishing and decorating the White House, but in 1832 he still had a considerable way to go. Much of the money went into the table settings, which were lavish by any standards, for Uncle Andrew was anything but frugal when it came to dining. He had a cellar of the finest wines and thought no dinner complete—even family affairs—without such fare as partridges, duck, wild turkey and an assortment of fish. Brandy and coffee followed every meal.

The announcement of Mary Eastin's engagement to Finch, and then to Polk, broke—or at least chipped—a good many male hearts in Washington. Mary had, or could have had, a different beau for every day in the week. As her contemporary, Cora Livingstone, expressed the situation in a letter, "Mary has half a dozen beaux who only wait for a smile to follow her to the ends of the earth." At one time she was seriously courted by Abraham Van Buren (son of the man who was to follow Jackson into the Presidency). This ex-beau was later to marry the beautiful Angelica Singleton, a relative of Dolley Madison.

On April 10th, Andrew Jackson was once again in his glory. Almost up to the last minute, Jackson had apparently had doubts about what Mary would finally do. On April 7th, he wrote to his nephew, John Coffee, "I believe I may say that Miss Mary Eastin will be married on Tuesday evening next to Mr. Lucius Polk. The gests [sic] are all invited and I trust that it will take place." All went well.

That evening, in full candlelight, Jackson had the honor of escorting Mary down the well-carpeted length of the flower-bedecked East Room to the altar where the now familiar Reverend Mr. Hawley beamingly concluded his third nuptial performance in the White House. The pastor had married Maria and Samuel Gouverneur, as well as Mary and John Adams, in the Blue Room. This is the first East Room wedding on record. Six-year-old Andrew Jackson Donelson, Emily and Andrew's son, may have been the ringbearer, and Mary Mc-

Lemore and Cora Livingstone the bridesmaids. History is murky about the details, and the daily press was little help. Three days after the wedding, the *Washington Globe* gave it a notice about the size of one of today's want ads:

> MARRIED, In this city at the President's on the evening of the 10th inst. by the Rev'd Mr. Hawley, Mr. Lucius J. Polk of Tennessee to Miss Mary A. Eastin.

It was considered indelicate to pry into the details of a matter so private in nature as a wedding and then to air them to the public at large.

After the marriage, Lucius Polk took his young bride back to live in Columbia, Tennessee, and the White House lost another popular belle. Within ten months, in February, 1833, they brought into the world their first child, a daughter whom they named Sarah Rachel, thus adding one more namesake to the rapidly increasing number in the Jackson clan. Before Mary left Lucius a widower, they were to have seven more children: Mary, Emily, William, Eliza, Frances, and finally twins, Susan and George Washington. Mary and Lucius are said to have lived "in elegant style" and to have entertained "most hospitably."

In his book of reminiscences about the White House, old Benjamin Perley Poore did not take too kindly to some of the young romantics who had invaded the capital from abroad during the past sixty years. "Washington society," he wrote in 1886, "was also kept in hot water by the young secretaries and attaches of foreign legations, who prided themselves on their success in breaking hearts. There were two classes of these foreign lady-killers. Those of the Castillian type had closely cropped, coal-black hair, smooth faces, with the exception of a mustache, and flashing eyes that betrayed an intriguing disposition." He went on to describe the other type, the fair-haired Saxons, and bemoaned the fact that "Every year or two

... some poor girl was captivated by the glitter of their small talk, and got more or less scorched before she could be extricated."

Among the Latin types in Washington, at about the time of the Eastin/Polk romance, who was to steal a fair prize and whisk her from the White House was one Alphonse Pageot. The jilted British-born Lieutenant Finch (alias Bolton) lost to him the distinction of being the first foreigner married in the White House. American writers and journalists seemed almost deliberately determined to put the man down a peg or two by referring to him as Paqueol, Paqeot, Depageot, Paquerel, and just about everything but his right name. Pageot was a young member of the French legation, about whom history records very little. Some sources say he came from Martinique. He was apparently quite a dandy, with the expected Continental manners, darkly handsome, and typically French in his dealings with the ladies. He was referred to later in a letter written by one of the White House frequenters, Mary Coffee, as "the upper cook," but the reason for this description is not clear. One surmise is that he was an amateur chef; another is that he resembled the White House chef. He was the brother-in-law of Serrurier, the French Minister, and he was a man of talent and experience in professional matters, for he served as Secretary of the French Legation when in his early twenties and later stepped into his brother-in-law's position as French Minister to the United States.

The young lady who was to succumb to his Gallic charm was Mary Ann Lewis, sometimes wrongly referred to as "Delia," the daughter of Major William Berkeley Lewis. Major Lewis, who enjoyed the distinction of being a member of Jackson's "Kitchen Cabinet," had come to the White House shortly after Jackson himself had moved in. Lewis was something of a controversial figure, coming under attack for a variety of things, ranging from rumblings that he was inept and inefficient to outright charges that he was involved in shady dealings. Andrew Donelson, Jackson's secretary, did not think that Lewis and his daughter should live permanently in the White House, and one of the President's closest friends, Alfred Balch, wrote to him on one occasion with great concern: "... those who are most attached to you, are the most distressed at the late events in Washington.... Great efforts have been made, to induce the people to believe that there exists at Washington 'a power behind the throne itself'.... It is my most decided opinion that Major Lewis should set up an establishment for himself ... disconnect himself from you and see you only in a ceremonious manner."

Lewis was also a brother-in-law of John Eaton, which placed him smack in the center of the "Eaton Malaria" scandal, on Peggy's side. But the President had utmost confidence in the man's ability and integrity and retained him for some time as his personal adviser. Lewis finally moved out of the White House in December 1831, but, to soften the blow, Mary Ann was invited to stay.

Lewis had been a neighbor of Jackson's in Tennessee, and had also served in the Army with him, particularly during the Natchez campaign, when he was the General's quartermaster and came out of the Battle of New Orleans with a brilliant record. He further earned a place in Jackson's affections by being one of the earliest of his associates to recognize Old Hickory's potential as Presidential timber. Although, officially, he was the second auditor of the Treasury, his real position was that of Presidential confidant.

Mary Ann Lewis did not enjoy quite the popularity of the other Mary Ann (Eastin) and was described in several contemporary letters in a rather unflattering way. One account, written by Rebecca Branch in late 1830, referred to her as a "strange girl," and said "... she acts in such a way as to have a good many malicious remarks made on her I pity her sometimes. She is very friendly with me, I believe has a good heart —Madame Rumour says she is terribly smitten with AVB

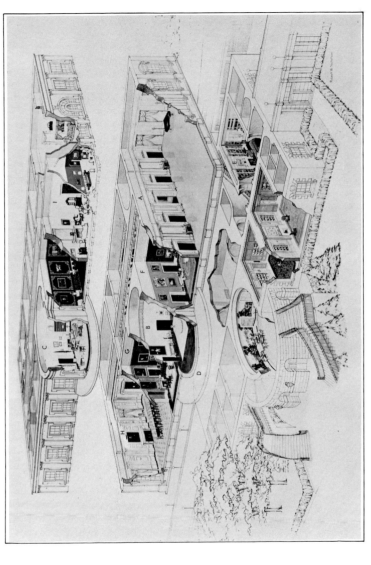

**A,** East Room. **B,** Blue Room. **C,** Yellow Oval Room. **D,** South Portico. **E,** Library. **F,** Green Room. **G,** Red Room. **H,** State Dining Room. **I,** Lincoln Bedroom.

View of Washington in 1800, year in which Abigail and John Adams became the first occupants of the White House, and the year before the first "forgotten" wedding in the mansion.

Lucy Payne Washington, Dolley Madison's widowed sister, in 1812 married the widower Judge Thomas Todd after a sudden change of heart. She was painted by Charles Peale Polk.

Todd's portrait, ordered by President Jefferson from the artist M. H. Jouett in 1807, vanished in 1964 at the death of the Judge's great-granddaughter. Albert Rosenthal, a Philadelphia engraver, etched this copy in 1889.

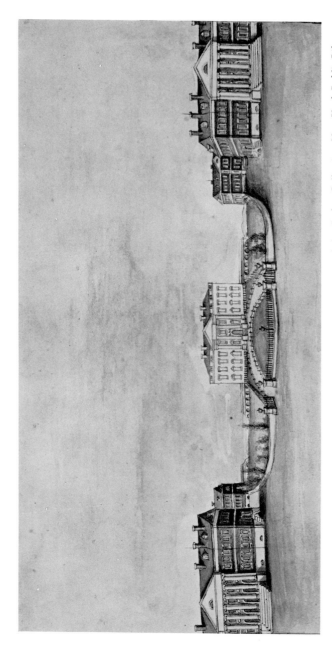

White House, rebuilt after the War of 1812, was sketched in 1820 by one of the foreign diplomats snubbed as a group and refused invitations to that year's White House wedding.

Maria Monroe at 17, portrayed in bas-relief by Cardelli,
in the year of her marriage to her handsome cousin.
He served in the White House as her father's private
secretary.

*James Monroe Law Office and Memorial Library,*
*Fredericksburg, Virginia*

White House as it looked in 1828 when John Adams, only President's son to have a White House ceremony, married his orphaned cousin.

St. John's Episcopal Church was sketched in 1816 (the year it was founded) by Benjamin Latrobe, who had helped Dolley Madison decorate the White House. Parson Hawley (opposite) was then the assistant rector. The White House, in background, shows scars of its burning by the British.

*From the portrait owned by St. John's Church, Washington, D.C.*

Parson Hawley, an eccentric Vermonter who wore British knee breeches and black silk hose, married Maria Monroe to her cousin in 1820, and John Adams to his cousin in 1828. Hawley ran St. John's Church for nearly thirty years and performed two more White House weddings in 1832 and 1842.

*Courtesy of Mrs. T. P. Yeatman, Mount Pleasant, Tennessee;
photo by Orman Photo Shop, Columbia, Tenn.*

Two of the four Marys who were married during Andrew
Jackson's Presidency. These two—Mary Eastin Polk and Mary
Ann Lewis Pageot—both had White House weddings in
1832. Their portrait by Ralph Earl has hung in the Polks'
home in Tennessee ever since 1833.

*Courtesy of Mrs. T. P. Yeatman, Mount Pleasant, Tennessee;*
*photo by Orman Photo Shop, Columbia, Tenn.*

Lucius Junius Polk in 1833, the year when he and Mary moved
into the house his father's slaves built for them in Tennessee.
The portrait and the home, "Hamilton Place," are still owned
by a direct descendant.

Andrew Jackson, Jr., the President's adopted son, painted by Earl. Andrew evaded the President's efforts to interest him in Mary Ann Lewis, and chose Sarah Yorke, an orphan in Philadelphia, instead.

*Ladies' Hermitage Association, Nashville, Tennessee*

Sarah Yorke Jackson was also painted by Ralph Earl, whom the President dispatched to the Philadelphia wedding with a pearl ring for the bride. Earl was a wandering portrait painter until the day he turned up at "The Hermitage" in 1821, becoming a member of Jackson's family until he died in 1838.

*Ladies' Hermitage Association, Nashville, Tennessee*

Angelica Singleton Van Buren was painted by Henry Inman four years after she married the President's son. To match her regal manner, she wears a court dress of white silk and plumes in her hair. Her portrait is in the White House collection.

Abraham Van Buren, Washington's most hard-
to-catch bachelor, was snared in a trap set by
Dolley Madison and her beautiful niece from
South Carolina.

About 15 years after her "scandalous" marriage to President Tyler, Julia Gardiner still looked young and regal as she posed for Francesco Anelli, an Italian painter. The portrait is in the White House collection.

President John Tyler, aged 51, sat for his portrait a year
before his daughter's White House wedding, and three years
before his own second marriage. The artist was Charles
Frederick, a German lithographer.

White House in early 1840s, during Administration that saw a White House wedding, a disastrous explosion, a Presidential marriage. Washington had 25,000 inhabitants, one paved street.

[Abraham Van Buren]—tho she told me she did not like him & from what I have seen, should think they dislike each other they met here a few evenings ago & her conduct on the occasion was truly ridiculous. . . ."

Such remarks could easily have stemmed from girlish jealousies. The President had quite another opinion of the young lady, describing her as "one of the belles of New York" when he tried to establish a match between her and Andrew, Jr. He had invited her to the White House to live in December 1831, and she had also stayed there earlier when her father lived there. During the 15-month absence of Emily Donelson and Mary Eastin, and when Mary Lewis herself was not away in New York, she was the only woman in Jackson's White House family.

In the spring of 1832, Mary Ann went to Philadelphia to visit friends. There she saw a great deal of Alphonse Pageot, who was on his way from Washington to New York to sail to France for several months. He managed to extend the stopover long enough to get from Mary Ann the promise that she would marry him shortly after his return in the fall. They were married on Thursday, November 29th of that year. Although the wedding took place in the White House—again at the request of the President—it was not a particularly lavish affair. Jackson's finances were strained, what with the White House wedding he had financed only seven months earlier, and he was still feeling the effects of the criticism that he had shown too much favoritism to his old friend Lewis. Consequently, guests were limited to Jackson's Cabinet, members of the diplomatic corps, Justices of the Supreme Court, and family friends and relatives (the latter alone being quite a sizable body). Jackson, rather than Lewis, gave the bride away. Probably the ceremony, like the previous one, took place in the East Room.

The ceremony was the only one of the Roman Catholic faith celebrated in the White House. The clergyman officiating was Father William Matthews, of the Catholic Church of Washington. The couple settled down in Washington in a large house provided by Lewis.

The marriage of Mary Ann Lewis and Alphonse Pageot brought one more element of controversy into the troubled Jackson Administration. Later, the French Minister, Serrurier, was recalled to France, and Pageot became the chargé d'affaires representing France. Rumor had it that King Louis Philippe had appointed Pageot so that he would be in a better position to "exercise supervision over his wife's valuable property in Tennessee," since the Lewises were believed to be rich landowners.

Pageot became even less popular when an international quarrel over 25 million francs strained relations between France and the United States. When diplomatic relations were broken off, Pageot was sent back to France with his wife and the son that had been born to them in the meantime—naturally named Andrew Jackson Pageot.

When relationships with France improved, the two countries came to an agreement to staff the embassies with entirely new personnel, in order to start afresh. To Jackson's astonishment, none other than Alphonse Pageot appeared back on the scene again, as the French Minister. Old Hickory, despite his delight at seeing Mary Ann and his little godson, thundered and roared at the French. He called the whole maneuver a despicable breach of faith. He softened his anger, however, when Major Lewis came to see him and admitted that he was behind it all. He had indicated to the French that nothing would please Jackson more than to have Pageot as Minister. It was the only way, pleaded Lewis, that he could get back the daughter he loved and his little grandson.

Jackson let his heart make the decision, and the Pageots remained. They became well known during their years in the diplomatic circles of Washington before they finally returned to France, where Mary Ann died in 1865.

Although there were no more White House weddings during the Jackson Administration, there were numerous other marriages within the sprawling family network. On November 14, 1833, another one of Jackson's grandnieces and a frequent White House occupant, Mary Coffee, married his ward, Andrew Jackson Hutchings, from Alabama. Mary Coffee and Mary Eastin were cousins, and their parents had been married in a double ceremony at the Donelson mansion near Nashville in 1809. Only a few months before Mary Coffee's own wedding, when her fiancé had come of age, Jackson had turned the Hutchings estate over to him and had written, on his favorite subject:

> One word as to matrimony—seek a wife who will aid you in your exertions in making a competency and will take care of it when made, for you will find it easier to spend two thousand dollars, than to make five hundred . . . think before you attempt to select a wife when you find one such, and I think you can, then would I say to you that you cannot too soon settle yourself.

The formula worked to perfection. In Mary Coffee, the President saw a girl who had an "amiable temper, good sense and economy" and who would be for Hutchings "a treasure to your good welfare and happiness in this world."

In February 1835, another family romance ended in the marriage of the fourth Mary in the White House—Mary McLemore, who was a cousin of both Mary Eastin and Mary Coffee. In her parents' home, in Nashville, she married a young physician, Dr. James Monroe Walker, who came from a distinguished Virginia family and had only quite recently come to the Cumberland.

And that same year, two months later, Elizabeth Martin—a cousin of these three Marys—married Merriwether Lewis Randolph, a grandson of Thomas Jefferson and the youngest child of the Governor of Virginia. Elizabeth was another of the White House belles. She had gone to live there early in 1834 at the age of 18, fresh from the Nashville Female Academy. Although gentle and shy, she attracted suitors rapidly. Emily Donelson wrote that she was "more admired than any of my western charges," and she was described by a dinner guest as "a very pretty little girl from Tennessee." She had the best singing voice of any of the beauties in the White House. She must have overcome her shyness quickly, for as early as March of that year she received a letter from an aunt cautioning her not to forget "the one thing needful" (presumably meaning her virtue) since it was indeed "a pearl of great price." Her uncle, though, was not quite so concerned about her falling victim to the temptations of the big city. His message to "Pretty Betty Martin" was that "if there is any danger of your falling in love while you are in Washington to be sure he is a clever fellow beforehand."

Lewis Randolph probably was "a clever fellow" for he was highly esteemed by Jackson, who had for some time used his services and wanted to advance his career. Together with secretary Andrew Donelson, Lewis had been one of the floor managers for the ball at Carusi's, held for Jackson's second Inauguration in March 1833. After the summer holiday in 1834, during which Betty and Lewis managed to see a lot of one another, Andrew and Emily persuaded Betty not to return to Washington with her fiancé and the White House family. They felt the President would be freer to forward Lewis's interests if he were not already "one of the connections."

Two months before their wedding, Jackson appointed Randolph Secretary of the Territory of Arkansas, replacing William Fulton, who was made the territory's Governor in February 1835. On April 9, 1835, Betty and Lewis were married by the Reverend R. A. Lapsby, M.G. (Minister of the Gospel), at "Clifton," the Tennessee home of the Martins, not far from "The Hermitage." After the wedding, Lewis went out first to Arkansas and Betty joined him later, happily looking forward to a lifetime of love and accomplishment. Within a year, tragedy struck; Randolph suddenly became ill and died. Betty returned to her home in the Cumberland, to try to get over her loss. Within less than five years, her adored little son, Lewis Randolph, also died.

Fortunately, the Jackson clan with all "the connections" was well adapted to such tragedies. In 1836, Emily Donelson died, almost in Betty's arms, leaving her husband Andrew a widower. In 1841, Betty Martin started a new life by marrying her widowed friend and cousin.

Whatever else the Jackson Administration accomplished, or failed to accomplish, there can be little doubt that the White House saw more romances, engagements, marriages, births, baptisms, and other matters of the heart than in any comparable period before or since. Jackson's record as a matchmaker stands unique.

CHAPTER VII

# ONE PRESIDENT'S SON

SATURDAY, March 4, 1837, was an auspicious date for the ladies of Washington, D.C. It was the day that Martin Van Buren took office as the eighth President of the United States. He was a 54-year-old eligible bachelor, a widower for some eighteen years, and he brought into the White House with him four bachelor sons between 18 and 29 years old.

To the delight of Washington society, the new President had courtly manners and cultivated tastes, so much so that the White House was once again referred to by its old name, the "President's Palace." He had imported a noted chef from abroad and not only had the talent and the wherewithal to arrange magnificent banquets, but he did so at every opportunity. The White House wine cellar was filled with fine sherries, brandies, ports, and other liquors. Even the smallest affairs were usually accompanied by orchestral music and refreshments of one kind or another. He delighted society, but shocked Congress, by ordering from Europe a set of gold dessert dishes, with gold spoons to match, which actually incited the legislature to recommend that "all articles purchased for the President's House shall be of American manufacture, so far as that may be practicable and expedient." He launched what was eventually to be a $60,000 program to have the rooms and furnishings cleaned, the furniture fixed and refinished, and the ceilings repaired and painted. The Elliptical Salon, which was the parlor he favored for his select, elegant parties, became blue for the first time. By the end of his term, he was to have spent so much time, effort, and money on the Executive Mansion that one Congressman indignantly referred to him as "Martin the First" and railed against the "extravagance" of his August Majesty in buying such luxuries as a "private bath" (which had actually been installed by the Monroes) and some "foot tubs." Most outrageous of all, said the Congressional critic, was a bill for $100 for artificial flowers.

With the White House inhabited by this kind of man, whose sociability and tastes were becoming ever more apparent to the capital during 1837, there was certainly an excellent chance that the widowed Van Buren or one of his four sons might provide the occasion for a lavish White House wedding. During the years following the death of his wife, Hannah, in 1819, Van Buren had shown interest in a number of lady friends. On one occasion, some fifteen years before he became President, he had courted Ellen Randolph, granddaughter of Thomas Jefferson and the elder sister of Lewis Randolph, and visited her at the Jefferson home, "Monticello." She was in her early thirties, fourteen years younger than Van Buren. But Ellen had been dismayed by the prospect of trying to take on four sons as well as their father, and in 1825 she had married Joseph Coolidge, of Boston, instead.

It was a big disappointment, therefore, when Van Buren went through all four years in office without once displaying enough romantic interest in anyone even to start a rumor.

It remained for the famous Dolley Madison, who was living in Washington again after a 20-year absence, to set things right. Seven years earlier, during the Jackson Administration, she had tried to stimulate a romance between her niece, Dolley, and Abraham Van Buren, the President's oldest son, a handsome West Pointer, who was then 23 years old. Abraham Van Buren was one of Washington's most hard-to-catch bachelors. In the winter of 1829-1830, he had been Mary Eastin's beau, and by the end of 1830 rumor reported that Mary Lewis was "terribly smitten" with him. By July 1832, when Mary Lewis was engaged to Monsieur Pageot, Emily Donelson wrote to Mary Eastin (now Mrs. Polk of Columbia, Tennessee) that "the little Major" was devoted to another White House belle, Rebecca McLane.

Dolley deliberately arranged a social occasion to introduce her niece to Abraham. But in March 1830 she had to write a disappointed letter to her niece from her home at "Montpelier":

> In my quiet retreat I like to hear what is going on, and therefore hope, my dear, you will not be timid in telling me, though your statements shall be seen by no one else. I wish that circumstances would have permitted you to have accepted Mr. Van Buren's invitation, but I cannot doubt you had a good reason for declining.

That matchmaking effort had failed, but Dolley returned to live in Washington in October 1837 and at once enlisted another likely candidate, her cousin Angelica Singleton, the daughter of a rich planter, Colonel Richard Singleton of Sumter County, South Carolina. One look at Angelica should have convinced any skeptics that this time Mrs. Madison could not fail, and Abraham would ultimately be caught. Angelica was a striking beauty of the Old South, with aristocratic yet pleasingly sensuous features, and wide dark eyes. Later, she was to favor dresses that were daringly décolleté, with tight bodices that did justice to her full, fashionable figure.

Abraham was introduced to Miss Singleton during the early winter of 1837-38, at a time when he had resigned, at least temporarily, his Army commission as a Colonel to serve as his father's personal secretary. When he met Angelica, she had just graduated from a fashionable school, Madame Grelaud's Seminary at Philadelphia, and seemed very much the innocent little girl, with ringlets of "corkscrew curls" around her cheeks. To make certain that the two would have every opportunity to see each other, Dolley had arranged for the girl to pay an extended visit to kinfolk, Senator and Mrs. William C. Preston of South Carolina, and live in their Washington home. She remained there until Congress adjourned, before returning South to her own home. It was long enough for her to become a great favorite at the White House—with all five men in the family. Not only was she visually attractive, but she was an excellent conversationalist and possessed poise, graciousness, and real Southern charm.

Dolley Madison's romantic coup did full justice to the clever old matchmaker. Although gossips said Van Buren's eldest son would marry the daughter of Van Rensselaer, the Albany "patroon," Abraham and Angelica fell in love and were married within a year of their meeting, on November 27, 1838. Dolley failed in only one respect: she was never able to engineer things so that the wedding took place in the White House. It was held, instead, at the Singletons' Home Plantation in South Carolina. After the honeymoon, the couple took up residence in the Executive Mansion, where Angelica became the official First Lady for the widower President. In that position she was extremely successful and played her role with queen-like grace.

In the following spring (1839), the young Van Burens went on a holiday to Europe. Their success there equaled that of Abraham's younger brother, John, who had been nicknamed "Prince John" after the warm reception given him in the summer of 1838 by Queen Victoria. Angelica's uncle, Andrew Stevenson, was the American Minister to Great Britain, where he entertained them. Angelica was much admired when she was presented at the English court and, later, at the French court. No American couple received such attentions. Queen Victoria was gracious; and, after dinner at St. Cloud, Louis Philippe himself took them on a tour of his palace.

Washington society, too, adored Angelica, who had made her first appearance as acting First Lady on New Year's Day, 1839. At White House levees, Angelica presided on a dais, dressed regally in a long-trained gown of purple velvet.

Typically, it was in a court dress that Angelica posed for her portrait by Henry Inman, four years after her marriage to Abraham. Now hanging in the White House, the painting shows her in a dress of white silk, with plumes in her hair, a pearl necklace, and a pendant on her forehead suspended from her jeweled headband.

Abraham and Angelica Van Buren had three sons, Singleton, Travis, and Martin, III, all of whom continued the "hard-to-catch" tradition of the Van Burens and never married. In 1841, Abraham and Angelica accompanied Van Buren into retirement at Kinderhook, New York, after he had been defeated by Harrison. Abraham died in March 1873, at the age of 65, but the records are not clear about Angelica's fate or how long she lived.

CHAPTER VIII

# ANOTHER PRESIDENT'S DAUGHTER

*T*HE next wedding within the Presidential Family—this time in the White House—took place only a little more than three years after the Singleton/Van Buren marriage. When John Tyler took the oath of office as tenth President of the United States in April 1841, he entered the White House with two formidable disadvantages. The first, of course, was that he was a "substitute" Chief Executive, filling the shoes of William Henry Harrison, who had caught pneumonia at his Inauguration and died after only a month in office. Some say that if the slogan "Tyler, too" had not rhymed so neatly with "Tippecanoe," he would have been quite forgotten during Harrison's campaign and brief Presidency. The second drawback was that his wife, Letitia, who might otherwise have stood at his side during national crises, was a helpless invalid, having two years earlier suffered a paralyzing stroke.

The Tylers' four eldest children were all grown up and married—Mary (Mrs. Henry Jones), Robert, John, and Letitia (Mrs. James Semple). Still at home and single were Elizabeth ("Lizzie," aged 18), Alice (14), and the youngest son, Tazewell (11). Robert and his wife, Priscilla, lived in the White House, and Priscilla assumed the role of official hostess with a remarkable degree of success, since she made it a point to consult frequently with Dolley Madison, then in her seventies and considered the Grande Dame of all Washington society.

Priscilla and the Tyler daughters spent a great deal of time with Mrs. Tyler in her upstairs bedroom. Priscilla wrote to her sister soon after she had moved into the White House: "Mother with a smile of welcome in her sweet calm face, is always found seated in her large arm chair, with a small stand by her side which holds her Bible and prayer book, with her knitting usually in her hands, always ready to sympathize with me in any little homesickness which may disturb me." But Priscilla found her mother-in-law unable to give much useful advice on White House entertaining, despite the experience she had acquired when her husband was Governor of Virginia and later a U.S. Senator. She was a patient, cheerful woman and passed along to the girls a sense of responsibility and decorum for which her husband was especially grateful.

In the tradition of the times, the Vice President was expected to do little except to preside over the Senate, and Tyler found himself to be something of an outsider in Washington, a man who was expected to be President in name only. Tyler has been placed rather low on the Presidential ladder by history. He was more beloved, said one writer, for his mint juleps, eggnogs, and Southern hospitality than for his politics. Many politicians, including John Quincy Adams, thought that Tyler should be addressed as "Mr. Acting-President" or "Mr. Vice-President." But Tyler refused to be made into a nonentity, and he firmly stood up to his duties as Chief Executive. He made the White House into a home of considerable warmth and unostentatious charm. He continued to live exactly as he had done in Virginia, riding in an old carriage discarded by the Secretary of the Navy, and outfitting his waiters in second-hand livery bought at a foreign minister's auction. In the evenings, the family sang ballads around the piano while Tyler (who had once wanted to be a concert performer) played his violin. Open-air concerts were started on the White House grounds on Saturday afternoons, so that all Washingtonians might enjoy the music of the Marine Band.

It is a shame that Mrs. Tyler, a woman with a fine background as the daughter of a Virginia planter, could not have participated in the social life of Washington. On only one occasion during her year and a half in the White House did she appear downstairs in public at a large gathering. That was when the Tylers' third daughter, 19-year-old Elizabeth, was married on January 31, 1842. "Our dear mother was downstairs on this occasion for the first time . . . since she has been in Washington . . ." wrote Elizabeth later, "her face shaded by the soft fine lace of her cap;" and she praised "her sweet gentle self-possessed manner. . . ."

The bridegroom was William Nevison Waller, of Williamsburg, Virginia, the home town of the Tyler family. His parents were Colonel William Waller, a member of the House of Delegates, and Mary Stuart Griffin, daughter of Major Thomas Griffin of New York. The Waller family could trace their ancestry back all the way to Alured de Waller, a Norman, who settled in the English county of Kent and died in 1183. From him descended a long line of distinguished gentry, including Richard Waller of Groombridge, Kent, who captured the French prince (Duke of Orleans) at the Battle of Agincourt in 1415, and to whom Henry V in gratitude gave a crest showing the arms of France suspended on an English oak.

The bridegroom did not get to know his prospective father-in-law very well before the wedding, yet he did have parental approval, because he had been described as an "artless, unsophisticated, generous, honorable man of pure and sound principles—ardent and affectionate in his attachment to all his relatives."

Pastor Hawley officiated for his fourth time at a White House wedding, held in the large East Room. The Washington *National Intelligencer* gave the occasion its usual brief treatment: "Marriage; on the 31st ult., by the Rev. W. Hawley, William Waller, Esq., of Williamsburg, Virginia to Elizabeth Tyler, third daughter of the President of the United States."

Although one account has the wedding attended by "all Washington society," it was anything but a pretentious affair. While consideration for Mrs. Tyler's illness certainly ruled out a wedding in the grand manner, another factor also limited the size of the function. Tyler had many enemies within his own Whig party because of his reputation as an independent. Consequently, whenever appropriations were requested for redecorating or even adequately maintaining the public rooms of the White House, they usually were turned down. The situation reached such a state that the Executive Mansion was designated the "Public Shabby House." The President even had to pay for his own light and fuel.

It is easy to see why the wedding, which took place in the East Room, was not one of the outstanding events of that generation. The guests included Cabinet members and their wives and daughters, foreign ministers, some personal friends, and the incomparable Dolley Madison. Another distinguished guest was Daniel Webster, then Secretary of State. Priscilla wrote: "I heard one of her bridesmaids express to Mr. Webster her surprise at Lizzie consenting to give up her belleship, with all the delights of Washington society and the advantage of her position, and retire to a quiet Virginia home. 'Ah!' said he, 'Love rules the court, the camp, and the grove; and love is heaven and heaven is love.'" Priscilla Tyler, who was responsible for most of the arranging, considered the event a large success and later described it as a "grand wedding" for her sister-in-law, Lizzie. She added that Elizabeth looked "surprisingly lovely in her wedding dress and long lace veil, her face literally covered with blushes and dimples" and that "she behaved remarkably well, too."

At least one interesting literary effort marked the occasion. Maria Monroe Gouverneur, described as "somewhat literary in her tastes," wrote a poem in tribute to the White House bride whose wedding followed twenty-two years after her own, giving her encouraging advice:

## TO MISS TYLER ON HER WEDDING DAY

The day, the happy day, has come
   That gives you to your lover's arms;
Check not the tear of rising bloom
   That springs from all those strange alarms.

To be a blest and happy wife
   Is what all women wish to prove;
And may you know through all your life
   The dear delights of wedded love.

'Tis not strange that you should feel
   Confused in every thought and feeling;
Your bosom heave, the tear should steal
   At thoughts of all the friends you're leaving.

Happy girl may your life prove,
   All sunshine, joy and purest pleasure;
One long, long day of happy love,
   Your husband's joy, his greatest treasure.

Be to him all that woman ought,
   In joy and health and every sorrow;
Let his true pleasures be only sought
   With you today, with you tomorrow.

Believe not that in palace walls
   'Tis only there that joy you'll find;
At home with friends in your own halls
   There's more content and peace of mind.

More splendor you may find 'tis true,
   And glitter, show, and elevation,
But if the world of you speak true,
   You prize not wealth or this high station.

Your heart's too pure, your mind too high,
  To prize such empty pomp and state;
You leave such scenes without a sigh
  To court the joys that on you wait.

Some seven months after the wedding, the First Lady, aged 52, died on September 10, 1842. Priscilla had left Washington for a brief visit with her sister in New York. Mrs. Tyler, sensing that she was dying, sent her son, Robert, on an emergency mission to bring Priscilla home. But they were too late. Robert never saw his mother alive again. Priscilla spoke of the agony he had gone through. "My poor husband suffered dreadfully when he was told that Mother's eyes were constantly turned to the door watching for him. Nothing can exceed the loneliness of this large and gloomy mansion, hung with black, its walls echoing with sighs."

The President was almost overcome by grief, even though he had known for many months that Letitia could not survive her illness for long. Priscilla served as the official First Lady for the next two years, and then her sister-in-law, Letitia Semple, briefly took over the role.

In 1844, William Waller was appointed Justice of York, and he and his wife moved to Lynchburg. Five children came along, before Lizzie died in 1850: William, John (who died in the Civil War), Letitia (who did not live longer than infancy), Mary Stuart (married 1867), and Robert.

CHAPTER IX

## THE "PRESIDENTRESS"

O N Wednesday, February 28, 1844, the new vessel *Princeton*, the first screw-propelled battleship in the fleet, steamed down the Potomac in a short trial run. On board were many notables, including the widowed President of the United States, John Tyler, his Cabinet, legislators, high-ranking naval officers, foreign diplomats, and numerous wives, relatives, and other civilian guests. One of the reasons for the excursion was to demonstrate a gigantic new piece of ordnance at the bow, a 10-ton, wrought-iron gun that the Navy had proudly named "The Peacemaker."

The *Princeton*, which had been designed by John Ericsson, later to gain fame for his Civil War *Monitor*, was under the command of Captain R. F. Stockton. Under sunny skies and with her rigging bedecked with flags, the new steam-powered man-of-war sailed smoothly along, while her officers thrilled and delighted the spectators by occasionally firing "The Peacemaker" and other guns aboard. The sound, echoing up and down the Potomac, brought crowds to the riverbanks, while others, prepared for the much-publicized occasion, floated out into the river in barges and other small craft for a closer look. On the return trip, the guns were silenced until onlookers pleaded for just one more salute from the big one. Several Cabinet members were standing by, as was David Gardiner, former State Senator from New York, who had been invited aboard with his two daughters. President Tyler, who had witnessed several firings, was not present at the moment—and with good reason.

Although a few ladies remained on deck, many of them had complied with the polite request to go below so as "not to be annoyed with the smell of powder, or the noise of the report." There they had been served a "collation." Tyler had gone below to join several of the ladies, and one in particular, Gardiner's elder daughter, Julia, a gray-eyed beauty with black hair, "the clearest olive complexion," and a "playful disposition," who had enlivened Washington's social season during the past three winters. She attracted the most eminent men of her time, and was courted by judges, senators, and governors, among others.

Many years later, Julia (then 68 years old) recalled the occasion in an interview with the famous Nellie Bly, published in the New York *World*, October 28, 1888. Julia had been invited to join the President, this account related, and as she started down the stairs a gust of wind caught her veil and blew it upward. "Take care of your streamer," said her father, who was accompanying her down, as he caught it deftly with his cane.

"When we got down," said Julia, "the President seated me at the head of the table with him and handed me a glass of champagne. Father was standing just back of my chair, so I handed the glass over my shoulder, saying, 'Here, Pa.' He did not take it, but he said, 'My time will soon come.' He meant his time to be served, but the words have always seemed prophetic to me. That moment some one called down for the President to come and see the last shot fired, but he said he would not go as he was better engaged. My father started with some other gentlemen."

When the President replied that he was "better engaged," he was referring directly to his desire to take the opportunity of enjoying Julia's company. Tyler, whose wife, Letitia, had died in the White House in 1842, had for some time been attracted to the girl, whom he described as "the most lovely of her sex . . . the most beautiful woman of the age." The musically inclined President wrote her a love song entitled, "Sweet Lady, Awake." She had to some extent reciprocated, even though he was then in his middle fifties and she was only 23, but when the affair became serious rather than flirtatious, she had backed away from the thought of marriage. Tyler had not pressed the matter, although he continued to favor the girl with his attentions, and she continued to think of him as a person of great charm and urbanity, with a "silvery sweet" voice, graceful in bearing and easy in conversation.

In the cabin, the Presidential party could hear the sound of "The Peacemaker" speaking out for the last time. As expected, the deck shuddered and the timbers shivered. Suddenly, smoke began coming down the companionway. "Something must be wrong," said Julia to a young man sitting on one side of her.

He started up to see, reached the door, and turned around with a look of horror. The great gun had exploded, mowing down onlookers with jagged fragments of hot metal. The dying and wounded were strewn about the deck, while those who had escaped stood frozen in shock or began crying out in panic. The President rushed out immediately and, at about the same moment, some one screamed, "The Secretary of State is dead!"

"I was frightened," Julia supposedly told Nellie Bly, "and I tried to get up the stairs. 'Something has happened. Let me go to my father!' I cried, but they kept me back. Some one told me that there had been an accident, the gun had exploded, but that there was such a crowd that it would do no good for me to try to get there. I cried that my father was there and I must learn his fate. I was told then that he was wounded. That drove me frantic. I begged them to let me go and help him, that he loved me and would want me near him. One lady, seeing my agony, said, 'My dear child, you can do no good. Your father is in heaven!' "

Later purists have accused the resourceful Nellie Bly of getting most of this dramatic "interview" from earlier written accounts rather than from Julia herself. It is undoubtedly true that Nellie became carried away by the story and exaggerated when she wrote that Julia fainted and did not regain consciousness until she was later being carried down the gangplank—in the President's arms.

In all, some thirty persons were wounded, and seven were killed. The other dead, besides David Gardiner, were a sailor and a young Negro servant of Tyler's; two members of the Cabinet, Secretary of State Upshur and Secretary of the Navy Gilmer; naval Commander Kennon; and Virgil Maxcy, ex-Minister to The Hague. Gardiner's body was carried with the other government officials' to the White House, to lie in state for a day in the East Room. All of Washington went into mourning, and the victims were given a State funeral on March 2nd. Before the mile-long procession left for the Congressional cemetery's vaults, a religious service was held by three ministers. One of them was the aging Reverend Mr. Hawley, who had seen so much happiness and festivity at the White House, but whose last previous function there had also been a sad one, preaching Letitia Tyler's funeral sermon 15 months earlier.

On June 26, 1844, John Tyler and Julia Gardiner were married.

In the intervening three months between the funeral and the wedding, Julia had become closer and closer to the President because of his sympathy and understanding. He had admired her courage at the time of the disaster. She in turn could feel the extent to which he had suffered, emotionally and politically, from the tragedy. It is interesting to speculate whether Julia would ever have married Tyler if her father had not been killed. Julia's mother willingly gave her approval when Tyler wrote to her in April asking for her consent. But the courtship touched off a great deal of criticism—against Tyler for carrying on an outlandish affair at the age of 54, and against the girl for being an opportunist. Tyler's seven children by his first marriage did not take at all kindly to the idea. They resented the intrusion into the family of a Northerner, who took over Letitia Semple's role as White House mistress. Three of them were older than 24-year Julia, and they had already presented Tyler with at least four grandchildren.

Former President John Quincy Adams, then in his late seventies, recorded bluntly in his diary:

> ... Tyler and his bride are the laughing-stock of this city. It seems as if he was racing for a prize banner to the nuptials of the mock heroic—the sublime and the ridiculous. He has assumed the war power as a prerogative, the veto power as a caprice, the appointing and dismissing power as a fund for bribery; and now under circumstances of revolting indecency, is performing with a young girl from New York, the old fable of January and May.

As the tone indicates, old Adams was not exactly pleased with Tyler to begin with, and had the President married someone his own age, he would probably have been roundly lambasted for some other reason.

Tyler's January-May romance, as well as his Southern fondness for juleps and eggnog, may have added venom to the bitter and fantastic attack published in the following year by one H. Cumming, entitled *Secret History of the Perfidies, Intrigues, and Corruptions of the Tyler Dynasty:*

> Though I intended not to meddle with your private character, and the example you have set for your sons, and their vile associates; yet, as connected with your term, it might not be improper, as public men are public property. How often have you, in their presence, become so inebriated that your servants had to assist you to your bed, and of the sons, I will now only ask, whether they did not follow your example, and tread in the

footsteps of their illustrious sire? Will you deny that you frequently with them, were engaged in bacchanalian reveries [sic] in the Presidential mansion, which were succeeded by scenes at which the heart recoils, and humanity shudders? Will you deny that, after scenes of blasphemy and revelry, that in connection with them, and with their full knowledge, you have prostituted your accidental residence for purposes too base here to be related? Why many would ask were you at one time rather pleasant, and at another, so neglectful, and abusive of your best friends, as well as of strangers? Because you were constantly engaged in all kinds of dissipation and licentiousness in private life, as well as public, which made your naturally bad temper sour and uneven.

... Think of the influence your example must have exerted upon private, as well as public morals; not only on those around you, but throughout the land; Heaven only knows when its direful effects will no longer be felt. Thousands of pure young men, since you came into power, have visited this den of iniquity, and contracted habits that will prove their ruin.

The wedding did not take place in the White House. The ceremony was performed in New York City on June 26— four months almost to the day from the time of the explosion. The wedding was privately held in the Church of the Ascension on lower Fifth Avenue, an event so well concealed that the marriage was not publicly known until the couple returned to Washington. It marked the first time in history that a President of the United States was married while in office, and, in fact, it was probably the most secretive of all the weddings that have concerned Presidential families. Tyler left Washington by ship with his son John (the only member of his family who knew of the wedding date), saying he was going on holiday to Point Comfort, Virginia. But the vessel turned *north*, instead. Tyler arrived in New York late on the evening of June 25th, unheralded. The immediate Gardiner family, Bishop Benjamin T. Onderdonk, and the livery keeper who was to provide the carriage were the only New Yorkers who were prepared for the first Presidential wedding in the country's history.

The Gardiners' neighbors in Colonnade Row on Lafayette Street were given the first clue as to what was happening the next morning, a Wednesday, when a carriage drawn by four white horses drew up outside the town house, and a little later John Tyler led out Miss Julia Gardiner, dressed in a wedding gown. As the family drove to the Church of the Ascension on lower Fifth Avenue, the news spread like wildfire. By the time the ceremony and the wedding collation were over, and the newly married couple had driven in the afternoon to the harbor to board the *Essex*, flags were flying from every vessel in the bay. A later issue of *Harper's Bazar* tells a romantic tale: "As the boat on which were the President and his bride pushed away from the dock, the two stood together on the deck, and just then a frigate fired a salute, and the smoke formed into two rings, intertwined, floated upward. Thus there was another happy augury of the happy life that followed."

From Perth Amboy, they took the train to Philadelphia, accompanied by John, Jr., the younger Miss Gardiner, and three servants, and at Hartwell's Hotel they were joined by Robert and Priscilla Tyler. The New York *Herald* tells us that the party sat down to a most elegantly prepared supper consisting of cold woodcock, pigeons, chicken salad, oysters, but, surprisingly, "no wines, not a drop of liquor of any kind, this being strictly forbidden by the bridegroom and assented to by the bride." The next morning they were up for a six o'clock breakfast of omelets, spring chicken, pigeons and woodcock, ham and eggs, salmon, beefsteaks, kidneys, boiled eggs and young duck, served in Black Dan's Parlor. "The President was in high glee, laughing heartily all breakfast time, and cracked jokes incontinently, diving all the time into the best part of a young duck." In spite of the enormous menu, they ate all this in record time, catching the 7:30 train; that evening they stayed in Baltimore, and they reached the White House on Friday evening.

On Saturday, June 29th, the President and Mrs. Tyler held a reception—it was really more of an unofficial Open House—in the White House. Despite the fact that there had been no formal announcement in the papers, the Executive Mansion was mobbed. Cabinet members, foreign ministers in court dress (no doubt including M. and Mme. Pageot of the French legation), and military officers in uniform arrived with their wives or other ladies. Dolley Madison, now 76, was naturally among the guests. If the critics were absent, they certainly were not missed, and their number did not seem in any way to diminish the crowd.

Julia was led into the dining room on the arm of John Calhoun, the Secretary of State, who helped her cut a magnificent bride's cake while the champagne was poured. Outside, the grounds were thronged with people who listened to the regular Saturday afternoon concert by the Marine Band and watched Tyler and Julia on the portico of the White House receiving the congratulations of more well-wishers. Julia wrote her own account of the day (published years later in *Harper's Weekly*):

> The company who waited upon me with their most respective compliments comprised the talent and the highest station in the land. For two hours I remained on my feet, receiving quite in queenlike state, I assure you.
>
> At six o'clock, I had to appear on the balcony, it being music afternoon, and go through introductions. Throughout, everything has been very brilliant—brilliant to my heart's content, as much so as if I were actually to be the Presidentress for four more years to come.
>
> Crowds followed me whither I went. My high estate has been thus far altogether pleasant to me.

During the mere eight months left to her as "Presidentress," Julia managed to achieve a remarkable, if not always favorable, reputation. She had been born into an old, aristocratic family, on Gardiner's Island itself. She had been given what was, for her day, a good education, in East Hampton and at boarding school in New York City. At Saratoga Springs, the most fashionable resort in the country, she had met society. Before her formal debut, she had spent two years abroad with her parents and young sister, Margaret, acquiring European tastes and learning other languages. It was natural that she should envision the duties of the mistress of the White House in rather Continental terms. She was described by her admirers as regal, fashionable and exciting, and by her detractors as having a "queen complex." She dressed in majestic fashion. Many of her costumes were purple and fashioned with a train. Frequently, she wore a headdress that resembled a coronet. She even outdid the regal Angelica Singleton Van Buren. She set up her own "court," receiving visitors while seated on a low dais in the Blue Room, with as many as twelve "maids of honor," dressed all alike, surrounding her. When a large group was expected, the First Lady would deliberately wait until they all arrived, before sweeping into the salon to make a queenly appearance.

What a contrast it was to the first two years of the Tyler Administration, when affairs had been for the most part colorless and the Executive Mansion was referred to as the "Public Shabby House"!

John Tyler approved when Julia enlarged the White House ball programs of quadrilles and polkas by adding the new dance, the waltz—which he had once forbidden his daughter Mary to dance because he thought it "rather vulgar"! Washington had a social whirl like nothing since the days of Dolley Madison.

For the most part, the social élite of Washington—particularly the older women—resented this ostentatious display, feeling that it was done deliberately to put them on a lower plane. They did not approve of her dashing through the streets in her coach and four, in a style that put most others—including the Imperial Russian Ambassador—to shame. But the men all found her exceedingly attractive and appealing. They could understand why Tyler had fallen for her. Daniel Webster used to raise toasts in her honor; John Calhoun whispered endearments at the dinner table; the British Minister avowed his devotion to her; and in one instance fifty members of Congress paid their respects to her in a body, "all at one time." As her letters to her mother reveal, Julia loved every moment of it.

It is unfortunate that circumstances prevented a wedding in the White House, for it might have been one of the events of the century—at least judging by some of the formalities she introduced during her eight-month "reign." She instituted the custom of playing "Hail to the Chief" upon the appearance of the President at state functions. She revived the custom of having a footman formally announce her guests in European fashion. There can be no doubt that whenever there was a social function in the White House, she was the center of attention. She was able, too, to take criticism with all the calm self-assurance of someone royally born. Newspapers occasionally tried to ridicule her by referring to her as the "Lady Presidentress" or "Her Serene Loveliness," but she simply took these titles seriously and was not offended.

If Julia Gardiner Tyler was not a White House bride, then at least she was very much a White House wife. Regardless of the difference in ages, the Tylers had a great deal of real love for each other. Julia's sister even had to chide her for a breach of decorum, when she kissed her husband in front of other people. They retired to "Sherwood Forest," on the banks of the James River in Virginia, where Julia became mistress of a typical Southern plantation, adopting the way of life and politics of her husband's family, and even learning how to speak and write in the Southern idiom. Although she always referred to him as "the President," they were romantically happy for their remaining seventeen years together. Tyler, the most prolific of all the Presidents, fathered another seven children by her. The first, David, was born in July 1846; and the last, Pearl, was still a babe in arms when Tyler died at the age of 72.

There is a strange and haunting story about Tyler's death. He had gone to Richmond in mid-January 1862, to attend the state secession convention, leaving his wife at home. That night Julia had a nightmare. In her dream, she saw her husband suddenly before her, deathly pale and holding his tie and collar in hand. The vision was so vivid that as soon as dawn broke she awoke the nurse and with her and her baby, Pearl, she drove to the riverboat and headed for Richmond. When she arrived, though, she found the former President apparently in good health and sheepishly had to make some excuse for the sudden appearance. There was only one vacant room left in the hotel, and it was too late to return home. The next morning, Tyler went downstairs for breakfast, while Julia and the nurse and baby remained in their room.

A few minutes later, there was a fumbling at the door. Tyler stumbled in, *deathly pale and with his tie and collar in hand —exactly as in the dream.* He had suffered a heart attack and was dying.

By strange coincidence, the same hotel saw the end of Julia's own life, twenty-seven years later. She died there on July 10, 1889, after seeing her son Lyon installed as President of The College of William and Mary.

Tyler's will left control of all his property to Julia, for her use and that of their children, earnestly desiring his first seven children to do nothing to interfere with this arrangement. But much of the money was lost during the Civil War. Julia never married again, nor did she return permanently to the North. She settled into the Southern way of life in Richmond, and there, in the 1870s, she became a Roman Catholic, In 1873 she traveled north to place her youngest daughter in a convent school near Washington, and at the same time asked Congress for a pension to help her through financial difficulties. And that is how she came to be living quietly in Georgetown at the time of the next White House wedding.

CHAPTER X

## THE WHITE HOUSE BELLE

N Saturday, May 23, 1874, a New York newspaper carried a public lament, which began:

It's of no use. We are utterly unable to meet the demand for today's issue of THE DAILY GRAPHIC, notwithstanding that our presses have been running without cessation since Friday night. Before nine o'clock this morning orders had been received for more copies than we can possibly fill today. With nine steam presses constantly in motion, we cannot approach such a demand, and we are therefore obliged to say to such as are unable to buy occasional copies of THE GRAPHIC, that the only way to be sure of getting a good thing is to subscribe for the paper and receive it by mail....

The editors were capitalizing on the most romantic event within public memory. The occasion was the wedding of Ellen Wrenshall ("Nellie") Grant, daughter of President Ulysses S. Grant, and Algernon Charles Frederick Sartoris, of the British legation. It was the first White House wedding in 32 years, and for long afterwards it was referred to as "the greatest social event" of the eight-year Grant Administration and "the most brilliant wedding in the history of the White House."

The *Graphic* also took pains to announce that it was publishing, on Sunday, a special 12-page pictorial "Wedding Number," which would be available at newsstands across the country for the modest sum of 10 cents. The issue was quickly bought out by eager crowds, all fans of the President's only daughter.

When Grant took office in 1869, Nellie was only 12 years old, a plumpish little girl with silken brown hair and tip-tilted nose and soft brown eyes. She had three brothers, Fred, who was 19, Ulysses, Jr., who was 17, and Jesse, a year younger than she was. Despite her role from the beginning as "Belle of the White House," she matured into her teens in a quiet, demure way, without ever becoming the slightest bit spoiled. Her father, like many a President before and since, was persistent in his efforts to protect his children from publicity. Her mother was equally severe and strict in demanding discipline from daughter and sons alike. The four children were educated as nearly as possible like other children and taught to have respect for their elders, no matter what their political or social rank.

As Nellie grew older, her plumpness developed into an attractive figure that made her highly popular with the young men of her age. She had a round, pretty face, with a full, sensuous mouth and a perfect peaches-and-cream complexion. She was an excellent dancer, a good conversationalist, and a great asset to any dance or party she attended. At least one historian (Grant's biographer, W. H. Woodward) believed that Nellie was "probably the most attractive of all the young women who have ever lived in the White House."

In the summer of 1872, when she was just 17 (in July) and had finished school, the Grants sent her abroad with family friends, Mr. and Mrs. Borie, for an extended tour of Europe. To her astonishment, Mrs. Borie found herself playing more the role of a lady-in-waiting to a half-fledged princess than the part of a schoolgirl's chaperone. Wherever she went, she was greeted with delight and was treated as the "American Princess." She was described as a "sensation," and was the guest of honor at many dinners and balls. She wore long gowns for the first time in her life. She danced her way across England and the Continent, winning friends for Grant and the United States as a kind of unofficial ambassador. At Buckingham Palace, she had an audience with Queen Victoria, then in her middle fifties, and won the lady's heart. Although she might have had her choice of any number of young British dukes and Continental noblemen, she had no serious romances until she stepped aboard the steamer *Russia* for the return trip home late in the fall.

On board the ship was a British junior diplomat, Algernon Sartoris, four years older than Nellie and said to be heir to some $60,000, a considerable fortune at the time. His father, Edward Sartoris, had been a minor British diplomat at capitals in southern Europe, as well as a Member of Parliament and a prosperous merchant in the "East India trade." Young Sartoris, educated in the best tradition at Eton, was heir to the family fortune and estate—Warsash House near Titchfield, Hampshire, between Southampton and Portsmouth, on the south coast of England ("opposite the Queen's summer palace on the Isle of Wight," commented one delighted newspaper writer—but the royal residence at Osborne would have been barely visible across the 10 miles of Southampton Water that separate Warsash from the Isle of Wight). The young man was a grandson of Charles Kemble, the actor, and a nephew of the famous stage star, Fanny Kemble. Perhaps he was endowed with a little of their emotional and dramatic flair. At any rate, the magnetism of both Sartoris and Nellie was such that they took one look at each other and that was enough. Sartoris had the appealingly British rumpled look (an appearance not unlike that of Nellie's father) and he wore his rather straight and shaggy hair parted in the middle. He had a sporty mustache and later a full beard. A reporter from the *Daily Graphic* described him as "a handsome blonde, manly and firm in his bearing, . . . [who] does not resemble the constitutional

English traveller." He was at the time newly assigned to the British Legation in Washington. His eyes were deep and serious, almost hypnotic, and it is not surprising that Nellie was immediately drawn to him.

The voyage was all too short for the young lovers. They dined and danced and stole away to the darkened decks for kisses whenever Nellie could shake off her chaperones, which was quite frequently, since they were usually confined to their stateroom with seasickness. By the time the *Russia* reached American shores, they were as engaged as they could be without the official consent of the President and Mrs. Grant. Over cigars in the President's study, after dinner at the White House, Sartoris formally asked for Nellie's hand. "I knew my time had come," said Sartoris, recalling the awful moment. "I waited and hoped the President would help me, but not a word did he say. He sat silent, looking at me. I hesitated and fidgeted, and coughed, and thought I should sink through the floor. Finally, I exclaimed in desperation—'Mr. President, I want to marry your daughter.'"

It is easy to imagine the look of shock that came over the faces of the President and his wife when they learned the news. They had sent away a pretty little schoolgirl, and they were welcoming home a would-be bride, who now wanted to leave home for good. Nellie had grown up remarkably in the few months that she had been away, but even so, the President insisted that she was too young for marriage. It was not that he had anything against the Englishman—although, out of patriotism to his country, he would have preferred an American suitor—but Nellie had known Sartoris for too short a time to be certain that she was really in love. The fact of the matter is that Grant spoke more from an emotional viewpoint than he did from a patriotic or rational one. He loved Nellie dearly, and he did not want her to be whisked away to another country.

Finally, when Grant and his wife, Julia, realized how much

the two were in love, they gave their consent—on condition that they would wait for a year and a half. They reasoned that if the love continued as strong as it was for that length of time, then there was little that they, or anyone else, could do about it. There were a good many young men around Washington during those months who wished heartily that Sartoris had never left his native England. Still, the engagement did not entirely dampen young social life at the White House. Nellie was given a debut, which had been promised to her before the European trip (although it was said to have been changed from a ball to a "formal reception"), and there were numerous dances and dinners of one kind or another. She was the "White House Belle" at her father's second Inauguration. As her father began to realize that the engagement was for keeps, and as he saw the time nearing when he would lose his pet forever, he went out of his way to plan special occasions for her—not only parties, but family excursions, picnics, and horseback rides in the park.

By the end of 1873, a wedding date had been set: Thursday, May 21, 1874. The President and his wife decided that the ceremony would be a small one and accordingly planned for fewer than 200 guests, including Cabinet members and their wives, and top-ranking military officers. The only member of the diplomatic corps to be invited was Sir Edward Thornton, then British Minister, with his wife, to represent the bridegroom's native land and family. The other diplomats, along with an additional list of guests—numbering some 500 in all— were to be invited to the reception afterwards.

May of the President's fifth year in office was a propitious time for a wedding, in an era that could truly be called "brilliant." It was a period when there was tremendous public interest in social affairs of all kinds, when Americans were becoming acutely conscious of fashions from Paris, when magazines were beginning to multiply, to tell in pictures and words all about life in the elegant homes of Washington and other cities. The female society writer made her first appearance.

Mrs. Julia Grant was constantly followed by reporters and fashion and society writers who were eager to describe the First Lady's activities and her costumes.

Some three years before the wedding, Orville Babcock, Grant's Commissioner of Public Buildings and Grounds, had examined the White House carefully and written a damning report. He described the Executive Mansion as being in an alarming state of disrepair, with decaying beams, a damp basement, and a leaky roof. "There is hardly a ceiling which has not cracked," he reported, adding that "One large ceiling fell last year, but fortunately when the room was unoccupied." He noted the lack of closet space and other necessary facilities. The White House had received little structural attention since the time of President Monroe, after the fire of 1814.

As a result of Babcock's revelation, repairs and redecorating were planned. The East Room was greatly affected, done over in what one account describes as "Pure Greek," but what was actually an overwrought "steamboat-palace" style. The classic simplicity vanished under the heavy hand of the decorator. The ceiling was divided into three panels, all lavishly painted in oils. From each panel hung an elephantine German chandelier, said to contain 5,060 pieces of cut glass. The floor was ornate with a massive figured carpet, the gift of the Sultan of Turkey, the windows clothed with weighty drapes and the walls hidden by dark maroon hangings and by huge mirrors that reflected and multiplied the ornate splendor. Where the wallpaper still showed, it featured raised figures gilded to make them stand out even more against the pearl-gray background. Brass spittoons were obligingly placed along the perimeter for the menfolk.

It was in this unbecoming setting—rather than in the old East Room of classic grace, where Lizzie Tyler had married William Waller thirty-two years before—that the lovely, girlish Nellie, with the pert look and the upturned nose, was to be married.

As the wedding day approached, orange blossoms were transported all the way from Florida to decorate the East Room, in addition to the lilies, roses, spirea, and other flowers. The setting for the wedding became "a perfect bower of bloom," wrote *Harper's Bazar*. "The whole house, indeed, overflowed with flowers, massed and matted here and bunched there, here in trailing and netted vines, there in whole branches, heaped profusely on console and bracket, and waving in feathery sprays from the tops of the tall and slender gilt tripods."

Under the great east window, a low platform was built and banked in the back with green ferns and vines and more roses and lilies. Over this, on a rope of flowers, was suspended a huge wedding bell, made of white flowers and tea rosebuds, a gift from New York. On each side of the bell hung wreaths of green with the initials of the bride and groom, N.W.G. in one and A.C.F.S. in the other. The four great columns were patriotically draped with flowers of red, white, and blue.

The perfume from all these flowers was "almost oppressive in its sweetness," said one reporter. Even the chandeliers were festooned with flowers, but not so heavily as to interfere with the hundred gas jets in each, which were to be lit before the ceremony (no more candle wax dripping on the guests, as in Tyler's day).

By eleven in the morning of May 21st, a great crowd had gathered outside the White House to catch a glimpse of the arriving guests, driving up in seventy fine carriages. In the East Room, the bridegroom waited with his best man, Lieutenant Colonel Fred Grant (although some reporters put these two into the wedding procession). The 40-man Marine Band began the traditional march, and in came the wedding party —including Nellie's two younger brothers, her mother, and the eight bridesmaids: Miss Edith Fish and Miss Sallie Frelinghuysen, daughters of Cabinet officers; Miss Lizzie Porter, daughter of the Admiral; Miss Minnie Sherman, daughter of the Commanding General of the Army; Miss Bessie Conkling, daughter of the New York Senator; Miss Maggie Dent, a cousin of the bride, and Miss Fannie Drexel of Philadelphia; Miss Anna Barnes, the maid of honor, was the daughter of the Surgeon General of the Army. They wore dresses of white corded silk, with over-dresses of a transparent material, and sashes of white silk arranged in a succession of loops from the waist downward.

Finally, from the Blue Room where she had been waiting, came the figure that all of Washington—and indeed the country—wanted to see, the lovely bride herself, on her father's arm. She wore a white satin gown, elaborately trimmed with rare Brussels point lace, described in three separate accounts as being worth $1,500, $2,000, and $4,000. She had a white tulle veil that completely enveloped her, adorned with the traditional orange blossoms interspersed with green leaves and white flowers. The bridal bouquet was a cluster of tuberoses and orange blossoms around a center of pink rosebuds. From this delicate center jutted a tiny flagstaff with a little banner on which was written the word LOVE.

Nellie was radiant, but the General is said to have looked a little bit dour, undoubtedly because he was now about to turn his daughter over to another man. Years later, Jesse Grant wrote in his memoirs that, young as he was, he remembered "father, silent, tense, with tears upon his cheeks that he made no movement to brush away." Mrs. Grant looked a bit wan and tired; although most of the female guests were in bright and lavish costumes (low-cut dresses in the French manner were then in style) hers was rather simple, since she was in mourning for her father. She wore a mauve-colored silk dress, trimmed with a deeper shade of mauve, puffs and ruffles of black net lace, and bunches of dark-colored pansies, tied with lavender ribbons.

Standing under the white bell, the bride and groom were married by the Reverend Otis H. Tiffany, pastor of the Metropolitan Church (Methodist Episcopal), where the President and his family attended services.

"After the ceremony was all over," wrote Thomas F. Pendel, who served as White House Doorkeeper for nearly forty years and was at the wedding, "the invited guests repaired to the Red Parlor; that is, the ladies did, and I had the pleasure of presenting to them the wedding cake—put up in little white boxes about six inches long and three inches wide—for them to dream on, that those who were single might dream of their future husbands." Each little box was inscribed with the initials "G.S." and tied in white satin.

All of the guests, including members of the diplomatic corps and others who had not actually witnessed the ceremony, then went to the State Dining Room for a wedding breakfast, described by one White House chronicler, Kate Dickinson Sweetser, as being "as elaborate as money and thought could make it," from which "every guest carried away a menu printed in gold on white satin to keep as a souvenir."

President Grant sat proudly erect at the head of the large state table, with Nellie and Sir Edward Thornton on his left, Mrs. Grant and Algernon at his right. From the center of the table rose the flags of the two nations and the wedding cake, decorated with wedding bells, roses, and white doves. Gold knives, forks, and spoons were used. He presided over a feast that included chicken croquettes with peas, lamb cutlets, woodcock and snipe on toast, aspic of beef tongue, broiled chicken, and soft crabs from the Maryland coast. Dessert was strawberries and cream, as well as ices, confectionery, chocolate, coffee, and punch.

In the upstairs library, the wedding gifts were displayed, along with the names of the donors, while the Marine Band played in the background. "The wedding presents were costly and superb," said a contemporary account, "these comprised a superb set of laces, solid silver service, complete dinner service of silver, jewelry of every description, silver pieces of all kinds, laces, fans, handkerchiefs, etc." A silver fruit dish from Tiffany's had been given to Nellie by the White House staff, because of "the sweetness and amiability of her disposition."

One of Nellie's most unusual gifts was a poem composed especially for the occasion by Walt Whitman:

## A KISS TO THE BRIDE

Sacred, blithesome, undenied
With benisons from East and West
And salutations North and South.
Through me indeed today a million hearts and hands,
Wafting a million loves, a million soul-felt prayers:
—Tender and true remain the arm that shields thee!
Fair winds always fill the sails that sail thee!
Clear sun by day, and bright star at night beam on thee!
Dear girl—through me the ancient privilege too
For the New World, through me, the old, old wedding greeting:
O youth and health! O sweet Missouri rose! O bonny bride!
Yield thy red cheeks, thy lips, today
Unto a Nation's loving kiss.

The bride and groom made no attempt to slip quietly away. At 1:30 the President himself and Mrs. Grant escorted the young couple to Union Station in their state carriage, drawn by four matched horses. Nellie wore a traveling dress of rich brown silk. "A pleasant incident occurred as the carriage was leaving the door of the White House," reported *The New York Times* the following day: "Two little girls, daughters of Marshal Sharpe and Collector Casey, came out upon the porch and each threw a slipper after the departing couple, and the omen of good luck was made complete by the directness with which they were aimed, one striking the bride and the other her husband." As the carriage drove through Washington to the railroad station, the bells of the Metropolitan Church pealed Mendelssohn's "Wedding March," "Hail Columbia," and "God Save the Queen."

At 1:40 the newlyweds started on their way to New York in one of two Pullman "palace cars" built for the Vienna Exposition at a cost of $16,000 each. The woodwork was black walnut, inlaid with gold and beryl. Crimson velvet covered the furnishings, and Wilton carpets and costly chandeliers put the finishing touches to this epitome of 19th-century luxury. For the occasion it was, of course, decorated from end to end with American and English flags, flowers, and evergreens.

Some eight hours later at 10 P.M., the Pullman palace rumbled into Jersey City, where friends met Mr. and Mrs. Sartoris and helped them transfer by carriage to the ferryboat for the final leg of the long journey. Nellie had a trousseau of a hundred dresses, packed with other belongings, in thirty trunks and cases. It was late at night when they finally drove up Broadway and Fifth Avenue to the Fifth Avenue Hotel at 23rd Street.

By 8:30 the following morning, even though it was a business day (Friday), a great crowd had already gathered in front of the hotel, trying to catch a glimpse of the bride in the windows of their suite. The *Daily Graphic* reporter noted the crowd showed "no special interest" in the groom. They were rewarded before 10 o'clock by the arrival of President and Mrs. Grant, their three sons, and a group of friends, all of whom had followed the honeymooners to New York to give them a second send-off. The line of carriages rolled down to the pier at the foot of West 24th Street. There the party embarked on the *Grant*, a Coast Guard cutter appropriately named after the President and flying the U.S. Revenue flag, the Stars and Stripes, *and* the British Red Ensign.

(The *Grant* was, in fact, probably chosen for her name rather than for more practical reasons. Because she was bark-rigged, her yardarms did not allow her to lie alongside either the pier or the larger steamer, and the whole party had to be transferred onto and off the *Grant* via a tug and another cutter, the *William E. Chandler* and the *Jessamine*.)

A collation and the final farewells took place on the *Grant*, on the way to her rendezvous with the *Baltic*, a trans-Atlantic steamer waiting out in the Narrows. The Grants had taken two days to see their beloved Nellie off, and judging from the emotional scene that took place, it is a wonder that Algernon and Nellie managed to cross the last gangplank to the *Baltic* and get off to England alone!

Doorkeeper Pendel, in his book, *Thirty-Six Years in the White House*, recalled vividly the feelings of the Grants:

After Miss Nellie had sailed for Europe, one night after dinner, the President took a walk down town, and everybody had left the house with the exception of Mrs. Grant, Jerry Smith, the old colored duster and myself. When the President had been out probably fifteen minutes, Mrs. Grant, who was sitting in the Blue Parlor, seemed very lonesome. She called me away from the front door to come in near the Blue Parlor door and be seated, as the house was perfectly deserted, except for us three. While I was there, the conversation turned to Miss Nellie. I said to her, "I am very sorry, Mrs. Grant, that Miss Nellie has gone away. We all miss her very much." Mrs. Grant spoke up and said, "Yes, but we will have her back home again." I chatted with her until the President returned and then took my post again at the front door.

Taking their cue from Walt Whitman, lesser poets (and non-poets) tried their hands at paying tribute to the newly-weds. Those unfortunate non-subscribers who were unable to buy copies of the *Daily Graphic* missed two such verses penned specially for the occasion, as the bride and groom sailed away across the sea:

### BON VOYAGE!

Lo! upon the far horizon
  Looms the good ship on her way,
O'er the ocean path she hies on,
  Under the soft skies of May.

Lightly launch the fairy slipper,
Halcyon emblem of good speed,
Steered by Cupid, elfish skipper,
Neptune's nereids it will heed.

Smoothly they will lull the ocean,
Softly lap its curling crests,
For a nation's fond emotion
On the good ship Baltic rests.

Beareth she to Albion's beaches
Floweret of Columbia's pride;
May the luck that heavenward reaches
Follow Sartoris and his bride!

## BON VOYAGE

Ship, bear them merrily,
Safely and cheerily.
Swiftly and airily—
Not dull and drearily,
Slowly and wearily!
May no storms lower;
No clouds pour
Turbulent shower;
No tempest roar.

And, as of old,
In the age all golden,
Even though thunders rolled,
Love's bark was holden
By the stout sea-gods
(Big gods and wee gods)
Safe from the tempest shock,
Safe from the hidden rock,
So may the ship be guarded,
And from danger warded,
Till, every peril past,
Harbored it be at last.

In spite of all the poetry and good wishes, this is one White House wedding story which does not have a happy ending. The young couple lived in England at first, with Sartoris' parents, who adored Nellie and initiated her into British customs such as afternoon tea. Two sons (Grant Greville and Algernon Edward) followed by two daughters (Vivien and Rosemary) were born between 1875 and 1880. But, after a few years, Nellie found it impossible to continue living with Algernon Sartoris. One of the problems (ironically, shared by Nellie's father) was Algernon's drinking. Even his family sided with Nellie; after she left him, they provided her with a large income and continued to be her close friends. Sartoris died of pneumonia, in the Hotel Schweizerhof on Capri, in 1893, at the age of 42.

Nellie had already returned to the United States, where her American citizenship was reinstated by a special Act of Congress. No sooner had Sartoris died than there were rumors that she was to be married again. Her supposed fiancé was a bachelor from Baltimore, General Henry Kyd Douglas, Adjutant General of the State of Maryland. But Nellie did not marry again until she was 57 years old, and then it was not to Douglas. On July 4, 1912, at her summer home in Cobourg, Ontario, on the Canadian shore of Lake Ontario, Nellie was married to a childhood sweetheart, Franklin Hatch Jones of Chicago. The ceremony was performed by the Rev. Carron Spraggs, of "The English Church" (who had earlier married her daughter, Vivien, to Frederick R. Scove). But sadness was to strike this second marriage, too. Just three months after the wedding, Nellie became ill and, eventually, paralyzed. She remained an invalid until she died in her Chicago home at the age of 67, in August 1922.

CHAPTER XI

## A PRESIDENT'S SON IS MARRIED

ℐN early May of 1863, General Ulysses S. Grant was leading his troops up the Mississippi River toward Vicksburg in an attack on Confederate strongholds. On leaving Bruinsburg for the front at Port Gibson, he had left behind another Grant, whose Civil War exploits have been little chronicled. "I left my son Frederick," he says in his autobiography, "who had joined me a few weeks before, on board one of the gunboats asleep, and hoped to get away without him until after Grand Gulf should fall into our hands; but on waking up he learned that I had gone, and being guided by the sound of the battle raging at Thompson's Hill—called the Battle of Port Gibson—found his way to where I was."

Fred had no horse, and when he arrived at the front he discovered that there were no rations and thus had to forage as best he could for food. The supply train was slowly crossing the Mississippi some seventy miles downriver. He accompanied his famous father throughout the Vicksburg campaign and siege, at one time receiving a slight bullet wound and on one occasion becoming very seriously ill. Despite all of this, according to the General, his son "caused no anxiety to me or to his mother, who was at home. He looked out for himself and was in every battle of the campaign." The most remarkable fact of the story is that, as it turned out, young Frederick was at this time not quite 13 years old, and he was only 14 by the time he had completed two years of service on the battlefield and the Civil War ended! He had run away from school three times, and been packed home again twice by his father before the General finally relented, deciding that soldier blood must run in the family and there was nothing he could do about it.

When Frederick served as best man at Nellie's wedding in 1874, he had just turned 24 and was a lieutenant colonel, a graduate of West Point, stationed in Chicago under Lieutenant General Sheridan. He had been in the field the previous year on the Yellowstone expedition and was about to set out on the Black Hills expedition that summer.

The year 1874 was an important one for Fred for another reason. In Chicago, he had just met Ida Marie Honoré, a 20-year-old beauty. She had lovely brown hair, worn in a classic Greek coil and fastened with a golden arrow. Her nose turned up slightly. But no young man could escape from her large and expressive gray eyes, which shone with intelligence and feeling. Fred had fallen completely in love with the girl. Freshly graduated from the Convent of the Visitation in Georgetown, she was said to be a fine singer and an excellent player on the harp and piano. "According to public and private reports," the press noted, she was "as good as she is lovely, and gifted not only with grace, refinement, and beauty, but high intelligence fostered by careful cultivation." Another report noted that Fred was lucky to obtain "this prize in life's lottery." Ida was a good catch for any young man.

The Honoré family, too, must have been pleased at Ida's impending marriage with Fred, the fourth young man in history to be married while his father was President of the United States. Henry Hamilton Honoré, originally from Paris, had married a wife of English family and had lived in Chicago for 20 years. He now owned some of the best real estate in the city (the post office building alone brought him yearly rents of

$20,000), and the Honorés were counted among the social and financial leaders of the region.

The family began making wedding plans as soon as the engagement, which was allowed to last only three months, was announced. It is possible that the wedding might have taken place in the White House, following close on the heels of Nellie's, but the matter was taken out of the Grants' hands by Ida's elder married sister, Bertha, Mrs. Potter Palmer. A well-known society leader in Chicago, she had seen the previous White House wedding at first hand and was among the guests who followed Nellie and Algernon to New York for the final farewell on the *Grant*. Perhaps one White House wedding was enough for her. At any rate, the Honorés saw Ida's wedding as an excellent opportunity for arranging *the* social affair of the Chicago season. A White House ceremony would have been memorable for the bride and groom. But how much more distinguished from the Honoré point of view it was to be able to have the wedding in Chicago, where Mrs. Potter Palmer would introduce the President's son to her own social peers!

Mrs. Palmer and the Honorés may have planned the social affair of the season, but in popular appeal they were upstaged by an unusual wedding that took place a day earlier, in (or rather, over) Cincinnati. Nearly 50,000 spectators watched as one of P. T. Barnum's balloons, under the guiding hand of the popular balloonist Donaldson, rose majestically from the Hippodrome, carrying a wedding party of seven. In the skies over the city, Charles Bolton, a circus ticket-taker, was married to Mary Walsh, an equestrienne, by a Swedenborgian minister from Pittsburgh. When they landed in half an hour, however, they drove to the cathedral and were remarried by Father Quin, "to satisfy the bride," who apparently did not have absolute confidence in "the first bona-fide marriage in mid-air on record."

The following day, on Tuesday, October 20, 1874, Fred Grant and Ida Honoré were married. The *Daily Graphic*'s editor was very happy (quite apart from his soaring sales) about his readers' sentimental interest in the wedding: "It shows that with us marriage has not yet been pushed from its pedestal by the evasive theories of free love." But reporter Jenkins of the Chicago *Times*, hunting for a story to match the aerial wedding, was coldly rebuffed by Fred, who "declined to assuage the thirst for information," and the reporter accordingly described the bridegroom as "a stolid-looking, sullen-faced young man."

The marriage took place in the Honoré summer residence, on the corner of Vincennes Avenue and Forty-Seventh Street in Chicago, and it was indeed the social affair of the season, although it was said to be "informal." The house, surrounded by croquet lawns and shaded walks, was furnished with a Swiss-chalet style of willow furniture, interspersed with marble statuary. In accordance with current fashion, it was turned into a floral bower by Mr. Reissig, the "celebrated German florist." In contrast to the brass instruments of the Marine Band at the White House weddings, the soft low notes of Johnny Hand's orchestra entertained the guests. The famous caterer, Kinsley, with his uniformed servants, provided the collation, which included a pyramid of ice creams of every variety then known— white, orange, pink, buff, lemon, and green. The jellies, in particular, caught the eye of Miss Jemima Jenkins, the *Daily Graphic*'s lady reporter: "pure amber masses of quivering translucence catching the wine-colored prisms of perfumed light, and holding them in tremulous mirrors of rosy beauty." The bride's cake was "a magnificent structure of solidified sweetness."

Fred's younger brother Ulysses acted as best man. General Sheridan was there with his entire staff, in full dress uniform. The President and his family and numerous notables came from Washington and, all in all, the wedding was a great success for everyone concerned. "Honore to the Chicago bride!"

punned the *Daily Graphic* happily; "Grant Honore and peace to the new household!"

President Grant was delighted with his new daughter-in-law. Back in Washington five days after the wedding, he wrote to a friend in England: "Fred's wife is beautiful and is spoken of by all her acquaintances, male and female, young and old, as being quite as charming for her manners, amiability, good sense, and education, as she is for her beauty. Mrs. Grant and I were charmed with the young lady and her family. . . . We expect them to spend the winter with us."

Fred received six months' leave from the War Department. After the honeymoon, the newlyweds moved into the White House, where Ida gained a reputation as a lovely and gracious "assistant First Lady," helping Mrs. Julia Grant during the lengthy periods when Fred was away on military expeditions to fight Indians in the West or assist the government's surveys of Montana and the Arizona deserts.

In June of 1876, a 13-pound daughter, Julia Dent Grant, named after the First Lady, was born in the White House and later christened in the East Room, with the President (a proud godfather) and his Cabinet in attendance. A baby brother, Ulysses S. Grant, III, followed patriotically on the Fourth of July five years later. He grew up to serve as one of Theodore Roosevelt's military aides and was an usher at the wedding of the girl who in 1906 followed his Aunt Nellie as the bride in the next really large White House wedding.

Julia also followed the path of her Aunt Nellie, in that she married a foreigner and led a colorful life abroad. Her father had seen Europe before his marriage, as a young second lieutenant, General Sherman's aide-de-camp. He had been in France then, just after the Franco-Prussian War, and had traveled to Tiflis and across the great steppes of Russia, bearing a report to the Czar in St. Petersburg. In 1889, Frederick Grant, now a businessman of nearly 40, was appointed by President Harrison to be Envoy Extraordinary and Minister Plenipotentiary to Austria-Hungary, and he and Ida moved their family to Vienna.

Thirteen-year-old Julia received her first taste of Europe and, four years later, made her debut at the Viennese court. During later travels abroad, she met Prince Michael Cantacuzene, Count Speransky, then a Russian diplomat in Rome. They were married in a large wedding in Newport, where the prince's splendid Russian uniform caused quite a stir, and then they traveled to St. Petersburg to live in the declining courtly world of Czar Nicholas II, the last of the Russian emperors. They were caught up in the revolution of 1905, beginning with "Bloody Sunday." When the court finally fled into exile and Princess Julia Grant Cantacuzene-Speransky returned safely to the United States, she was welcomed with great relief by her mother, who had been looking after her three children during the European turmoil.

Fred Grant and Ida had not spent the intervening years just worrying about their daughter, however. After Fred's years as a diplomat, he had been Police Commissioner of New York City, an officer in the Spanish-American War, then commander of troops in Puerto Rico and the Philippines, ending his career as a major general. He lived to be 62, when he died in New York in 1912, just three months too soon to see his sister Nellie married in Canada to Frank Jones. He was buried with honors at West Point. Ida lived on to enjoy her children and grandchildren for many years, until she died in 1931, an elderly lady of 77.

CHAPTER XII

# A DRY OCCASION

*Y*ou will not find it in the history books, but President Rutherford Birchard Hayes and Lucy Webb Hayes were "married" in the White House on December 30, 1877. On that Sunday afternoon, the wedding took place in the Blue Room, where John Adams had married Mary Hellen nearly fifty years before. Lucy was radiantly happy, wearing an old-fashioned wedding dress of white flowered satin. A circle of White House servants and twenty old friends and classmates surrounded the couple and brushed away sentimental tears. "Our friends from Ohio filled the house," wrote Hayes contentedly in his diary.

The Reverend Dr. L. D. McCabe of Delaware, Ohio (the home state of both the Hayes and Webb families), conducted the service. Later, President and Mrs. Hayes and their guests moved into the private dining room for refreshments. General Manning F. Force read letters and poems sent by absent friends. They all had "a fine dinner," recorded Hayes, and there was singing in the evening.

It should be explained here that this "wedding," carried out in detail, even to the participation of the guests and minister, was the Silver Anniversary of a marriage that had taken place on December 30, 1852, when 30-year-old Hayes had married

19-year-old Lucy Ware Webb in her Cincinnati home. It was the first time that such an event had been celebrated in the White House.

Hayes had finally proposed in June 1851, to the sweet, intelligent, proper Lucy Webb, a graduate of the Wesleyan Female College in Cincinnati, after dithering for two years and trying to choose between her and another girl who was just her opposite—an exciting, sophisticated coquette named Helen Kelley. Even after his proposal was accepted by Lucy, Hayes took a long time to bring himself to the point of marriage. When they had been engaged for more than a year, with no final date in sight, a friend blurted out in his hearing, "Why doesn't the young fool marry her? I don't believe she'll have him." This gave the reluctant bachelor the needed push; he became a bridegroom four months later.

Mrs. Hayes, slightly plumper now at 44, and the mother of eight children, squeezed into her flowered satin wedding dress, after letting the seams out. Laura Mitchell, her husband's favorite niece, stood by her side holding her hand as she had done as a little girl at the wedding. Tears were shed at what one of Hayes's biographers has called a "sentimental orgy."

Immediately afterwards, three christenings took place. Mrs. John W. Herron, one of the original wedding guests, who attended the anniversary celebration with her husband and 16-year-old daughter Helen (later to become Mrs. Taft), had her 7-week-old baby christened Lucy Hayes Herron, in tribute to the bride. Two of the Hayes children, 10-year-old Fanny and 6-year-old Scott, were also baptized.

The guest list at this celebration reveals something telling about the character of this quiet and little-noted President. One of his old schoolmates, a Mr. Deshla of Columbus, is reported to have put it this way: "I knew him when we called him 'Rud'; when he was called 'Mr. Hayes,' then 'Colonel Hayes,' and 'General Hayes'; then 'Governor Hayes' and now that he is President, we are equally good friends." The President himself noted in his diary some two weeks later: "At the time of our silver wedding it was mentioned as remarkable that the friends with whom I was most intimate when I married in 1852 were all still my most intimate friends. . . ."

A second—public—celebration, one of the most important social functions of the Hayes Administration, took place the day after the anniversary. At 9 P.M. the Marine Band played Mendelssohn's "Wedding March" as the President and First Lady came down the staircase and stationed themselves in the East Room, amid masses of flowers and vines, with their backs to two immense flags that hung from ceiling to floor and completely covered the large east window. Lucy wore a gown of striped white brocade that evening, with the fashionable wide straight skirt of the time, decorated with ruffles and rows of tasseled fringes. The heart-shaped neck was decorously filled in with tulle. Below her half-length sleeves she had on long white gloves, and her dark hair was fastened back with a silver comb. The President wore evening dress.

One hundred guests filed by to offer their congratulations, including Cabinet members and a delegation from the Twenty-third Ohio Volunteer Infantry, which Hayes had commanded during the Civil War. The Regiment had sent the only anniversary present the President was willing to accept, which was proudly displayed in the Blue Room. It was an ebony-framed silver plate, engraved with a sketch of the log hut that had been his quarters at Camp Reynolds, Kanawha Falls, West Virginia, early in 1863.

As might be expected, chroniclers have been somewhat confused by this double event. Some accounts combine both celebrations into one. But of one fact, history can be absolutely sure: the occasions were completely dry, for both the President and the First Lady (nicknamed "Lemonade Lucy") were teetotalers.

Mrs. Hayes had decreed that no liquor would ever be served in the White House during their Administration. They relented only once, when the anguished Secretary of State convinced them that the Russian grand dukes Alexis and Constantine would be highly insulted if no wines were served at a state dinner in their honor—but the wine was served to no Americans at the table, only to the foreigners!

A legend, probably based only on wishful thinking, persists that some ingenious citizens found a way to get around Mrs. Hayes's decree without her knowledge. By giving the waiter a certain signal at dessert time, the story goes, they would be served oranges filled with *rum* instead of the normal flavoring. (Another version has it that the President had directed that the fruit be flavored with "a liquid similar to rum but containing no spirits.") But the strongest drink served at these two celebrations probably was coffee. After the second reception, supper was served in the State Dining Room, and the party continued until midnight, disbanding when the bells of the city rang and the guns of the military posts were fired, announcing the arrival of the New Year.

Less than six months later, there was a real White House wedding. It was a small affair, referred to by Hayes in his diary as "the family event of the month" and a "quiet, beautiful wedding."

It is easy to see why the actual number of White House weddings is a subject of some contradiction. A newspaper of the day referred to it as the *ninth; Harper's Weekly* of February 17, 1906, called it the *eighth* (so did the bridegroom); Edna Colman's *White House Gossip* of 1927 listed it as the *eleventh;* and the 1907 White House memoirs of Esther Singleton assure the reader that it was the *seventh. The New York Times,* which used barely 130 words to cover the entire affair the following day, did not hazard a guess. In fact, the editors were rather timid about the whole event, making such unenlightening statements as "Mr. Platt, the father of Miss Platt, gave the bride away."

The bride was Emily Platt, the fifth child of Rutherford Hayes's idolized sister, Fanny. Fanny had died 22 years before, and Emily, who was now 28 years old, had spent most of her youth with her aunt and uncle. When the Hayes family moved to the White House, she became the First Lady's assistant in social affairs.

The bridegroom was General Russell Hastings, formerly Lieutenant Colonel of the Twenty-third Regiment of the Ohio Volunteer Infantry, who had met his sweetheart through his association with his old Army friend and commander, Colonel Hayes. She had been scraping lint and rolling bandages for the Civil War when he caught his first glimpse of her in Columbus, Ohio, in 1861. Visiting the White House in October 1877, he saw her for the second time. In his own words:

> It being Cabinet day, I was, after the first meeting, taken to the library, just off the Cabinet room, and requested to amuse myself for a time. This library, during the Hayes administration, was used quite as a family room. I had not been there very long when a young lady entered escorting several of her young lady acquaintances who seemingly were making a morning call. At the time they entered I was sitting in the deep recess of a window opening to the South and was partially screened by the curtain. I made noise to let them know I was there and kept my position, while the coterie took seats at the farther end of the room some forty feet away. I wished I had eyes in the back of my head so that I might see the quality of the people I could not help overhearing in their young lady chit-chat. I did catch a glimpse of the young lady without a hat.... I felt relieved when the young ladies went away.

At lunch that day, Hastings saw again the young lady who was called Emily by the President, and "Minnie" and "Miley" by the Hayes children and young relatives living in the White House.

Russell Hastings did not travel on to Florida for the winter, as he had planned. He was a guest at the Silver Wedding Anniversary at the year's end, and a frequent guest at the White House during the next few months. The announcement of their engagement was apparently a surprise to many of Emily's friends. Hastings was a widower, 15 years older than Emily, but he himself did not regard the marriage as inappropriate. Although he admitted he was 42, he included himself among the "young folks" who would stay behind, after the Hayes evening assemblies broke up at 10 P.M., for snacks and idle chatter in the second-floor library. In his manuscript autobiography, he was very scathing about John Tyler's marriage to Julia Gardiner: "Certainly a union of December and June. I hope she was happy."

Hastings's maturity, as well as his military reputation and bearing, may have made him all the more attractive to Emily. He was a fine-looking man, with a full beard. An air of heroism clung to him, as he limped noticeably from the knee wound suffered at the Battle of Opequon, in Virginia, in 1864. After the Civil War, he had been a member of the Ohio Legislature and Marshal of Ohio's northern district, before moving to Rockford, Illinois, to become a banker.

On June 19th, at seven in the evening, the guests assembled in the Blue Parlor for the first "real" wedding to be held there since 1828, when the room was still rose-colored. There were no bridesmaids or ushers, but just a simple procession of six people: President Hayes with his favorite niece, Mrs. Laura Mitchell; Mrs. Hayes with the bridegroom; and Emily, in a dress of ivory brocade, cut in the princess style, on her father's arm. Although most accounts indicate that the President gave the bride away, that role was actually performed by Emily's father, William Augustus Platt, who came to the wedding with his second wife. The couple were married by Dr. Thomas A. Jagger. Speaking of Jagger, one Washington columnist must have broken some kind of record for those days, when she publicly admitted having made an error in reporting. Said "Miss Grundy" (Augustine Snead) in the New York *Daily Graphic*, two days before the wedding:

> ... Bishop Jagger will perform the ceremony, but I made a terrible blunder when I said he was a Methodist. I came to the conclusion because I supposed all the President's relatives were Methodists. Miss Platt is, however, an Episcopalian, and Bishop Jagger is of the Southern Diocese (P.E.) of Ohio of the Protestant Episcopal Church.

The bride and groom stood under an enormous bell of 15,000 buds and blossoms, suspended over the center of the room, where the circular divan usually stood. There were "floral medallions of the initials of the bride and groom" and many imported plants.

The Marine Band was again on hand, to play the "Wedding March" and, later, several "airs," including a selection from *Norma*, Schubert's "Ave Maria," the fantasia from *Il Trovatore*, and the "Pizzicato Polka."

An elaborate supper, complete with gold cutlery and two cakes initialed in blue, was served in the family dining room to about sixty guests, including Cabinet members and their families, Emily's many Washington friends, and about fifteen of her young nephews, nieces, and cousins. It may have been one of the merriest of all White House weddings. Tea, coffee, and lemonade were served—but no wine.

At 9:30 that evening Russell and Emily, the latter wearing a handsome dark green traveling suit, left by train for a long honeymoon in the North. Mrs. Hayes had told the press that she wanted no allusions made to the bride's trousseau or to her wedding presents. She said that many brides, feeling that their clothing would be publicized in the papers, were thus lured into being extravagant in purchasing their trousseau in order to receive public approval.

Their story has a surprising ending: When ex-President Hayes visited them twelve years later, they were happily running a flower-bulb plantation in Bermuda, raising Easter lilies on Saltine Bay (where they had built a home, "Soncy") for sale in the United States. In addition to the son of Hastings's first marriage, 16-year-old Clive, they had three children of their own: 10-year-old Lucy (who today lives in London); 8-year-old Fanny (who died in New York City in 1950); and 5-year-old Russell, Jr. (who lives in California).

Russell himself died in September 1904 in Massachusetts, at the age of 69. Emily survived him by eighteen years, dying at the age of 72 in 1922.

CHAPTER XIII

# A PRESIDENTIAL "FIRST"

DEER PARK, Maryland, in the Allegheny mountains at the extreme northwest corner of the state, lay deep in the heart of the forest. Yet in early June of 1886 it was the scene of a most curious spectacle. Although it was a full three weeks before the opening of the vacation season, the tiny summer colony was as lively as though it were the Fourth of July. The railroad station bustled with activity. A new telegraph office had just opened. Carriages came and went, often bearing rumpled-looking men with writing cases or bulky cameras. The activity was particularly noticeable in the neighborhood of what looked like an ordinary summer cottage, a wooden frame building two and a half stories high, in the "Queen Anne" style, painted gray, with dark-red shutters. Men, singly or in groups, stood at the edge of the unfenced grounds looking toward the building, which had the simple designation, "Cottage No. 2." Local hill folk and their families stood there, too, as though waiting for the house to burst into flames.

As new arrivals appeared, they conversed with others already on hand. "Have you seen them yet?" was a standard question.

The objects of all this concentrated attention were the President of the United States and his young bride, who had wishfully imagined that they could escape for a "simple" and "quiet" honeymoon, some two hundred miles away from the hectic whirl of Washington, D.C.

Stories of the press intrusion were considerably exaggerated later. One report went so far as to claim that a group of reporters had erected a pavilion on a high rise of ground, from which they peered with spyglasses, took notes, and tried to take long-distance photographs. While it is doubtful that any such pavilion existed, there can be no doubt that the invasion was far beyond anything President Cleveland had anticipated.

There were many reasons why the nation and the press were fascinated by the wedding, which took place on June 2, 1886. For one thing, it marked the first time in history that a President had been married in the White House. For another, there was an intensely romantic interest in the idea of this portly 49-year-old bachelor marrying a slim, dark-haired 22-year-old girl who was without any doubt one of the most beautiful and attractive ever to serve as First Lady.

Grover Cleveland had known Frances Folsom all her life. "Frank" was the daughter of Oscar Folsom, his law partner in Buffalo, New York. It is said that Cleveland had either given the baby her first carriage or had been present when it was bought in the mid-1860s. At that time, he was a bachelor in his early twenties and probably not greatly interested in infants of either sex. Later, when he held the office of Sheriff and she attended the very proper French kindergarten run by Madame Boucher in Buffalo, he began to take a fatherly interest in her. He gave her a frisky bull-terrier puppy. She called the Sheriff "Uncle Cleve" and loved to climb upon his broad knee when he came to visit her father and mother.

In 1875, a tragic accident occurred. Her father was killed in a carriage accident. Later it was learned that Folsom had legally appointed Cleveland as guardian of his child. At that time, "Frank" was only eleven.

For several years, Cleveland saw little of the girl. The

mother, heartbroken by the tragedy, moved back to her own home town, Medina, New York, to live with her widowed mother. When "Frank" reached her mid-teens, she returned to Buffalo to attend the Central School, and Uncle Cleve saw her occasionally.

It is curious that hardly any of the writers who tell this story manage to get the young girl's name right. The rumor got around that she had actually been christened "Frank" (although official records disprove this). The author of *Bride of the White House* gave an ingenious account of how this name was changed to "Frances": because she often was included on the boys' list at school, she invented "Clara" as a middle name, he asserted, and then slowly changed it from "Frank C." to "Frances"! Newspaper reporters persisted in nicknaming her "Frankie." This must have made poor Frances shudder. "I am never called Frankie, and dislike the name very much," she wrote later to a Kentucky mother who wanted to name her baby after her. "Will you do me the favor not to call her Frankie, but Frances or Frank?"

By the time Frances entered Wells College, at Aurora, New York, on the shores of Lake Cayuga, Cleveland was Governor of the state and well on his way toward nomination for the Presidency. His letters to his ward, now 18, already indicated more than avuncular interest. While she was at college, he sent her flowers nearly every week from the Governor's Mansion in Albany (and later from the White House conservatories).

During one college vacation, he attended the Music Festival in Buffalo and came to call on her. She had just come home through a drenching rain, and had gone to bed; she kept the Governor waiting while she struggled into a dress. "Five minutes more that time," historian Allan Nevins reports he used to say, "and we should never have been married!"

In March of 1885, Frances and her mother spent her last spring vacation from college as Miss Cleveland's guests at the

White House, where they helped the newly inaugurated President and his sister Rose to receive visitors. Cleveland wanted to wait until "Frank" graduated before he formally proposed to her, as she later told historian Nevins. Whether an actual proposal still had to be made or not, there was certainly a very close attachment and understanding between them at this time. Rose Cleveland said later that she had known for two years that a marriage was probable, and that it had definitely been agreed upon for one year before June 1886. It sounds as if it was during this springtime White House visit that Cleveland, too impatient to wait until Frank's graduation, proposed. He told a friend: "I often say to my wife, 'Poor girl, you never had any courting like other girls,'" and he added, "It is true I did say some things to her one night, when we were walking together in the East Room, when she was here visiting my sister."

After graduation that summer, Frances left with her mother and cousin for an extended trip to Europe, as was the custom in families of education and means. During another White House visit before they sailed, the wedding may have been tentatively set for the following June. Publicly, rumors began to spread. When Frances and her mother went abroad there was talk that the President had underwritten the trip. But her uncle, X. F. Harmon, of Boston, strongly denied this when interviewed shortly before their return. "Among the many rumors that have appeared," he said, "is one to the effect that the expenses of her European trip were paid by Mr. Cleveland. There is not a particle of truth in it, and I do not see how it originated."

Letters to friends in Buffalo and Troy (perhaps read aloud at the breakfast table before the reader saw the closing injunction to secrecy) started rumors—later denied, of course—that Miss Folsom was indeed engaged to the President. Another interesting rumor was that the President was secretly engaged, not to his ward, but to the good-looking widow, *Mrs.* Folsom.

There is no evidence of any romantic interest on either side.

By April of 1886, with the return of the Folsoms imminent, speculation grew, and the ladies at tea and the gossips on Washington street corners could hardly contain themselves. On the one hand, there was a group that backed a prominent Democratic Congressman who offered great odds that there would be a wedding before fall. On the other hand, there were many of the President's old-line associates who maintained that he was a bachelor for life and that he was all business and had time for nothing but his job. In spite of his paunch, his rotund features, and his heaviness, Cleveland was, and always had been, a beaver for work.

Sometime during the second week in April, the newspapers printed a third-hand report from ailing Colonel John B. Folsom—Frank's grandfather, who was affectionately known as "Papa John"—that the engagement was a fact, that the marriage would take place in June, and that the bride-to-be was already purchasing clothing in Europe for her trousseau. How did he know? He had given the young lady $1,600 when she went abroad, and he had to forward her $600 more for that very purpose!

Frank's uncle, Mr. X. F. Harmon, made another statement to a reporter from the Boston *Globe*, a week after the rumors began about the trousseau. "I suppose the main question of interest is, 'Is there any doubt that President Cleveland is going to marry Miss Folsom?' Frankly speaking, there is none. It was not her intention to announce the engagement until some little time before the wedding, but unfortunately it was made public by a breach of confidence on the part of friends in Buffalo."

Whenever the press approached the White House for information, they left as uninformed as when they had entered. It was considered a breach of journalistic etiquette to ask a direct question, and the reporters had to content themselves with indirect approaches, usually to Colonel D. S. Lamont,

Cleveland's private secretary, whom the President had appointed for his well-known ability to keep his mouth shut. When one young woman, a society columnist, bluntly asked the President whether he was engaged or not, she came away "uninformed" after she had received what one of her delighted male colleagues referred to as "a severe wigging for her impertinence."

As the first and second weeks of May came and went, it was evident that there was some change in the White House attitude. No one there would take it upon himself to *deny* reports of the engagement, it was just that the matter was too delicate for public discussion. In an editorial datelined May 25th, *The New York Times* finally stuck its neck out and said, "The President is to be married to Miss Folsom on June 10." Although the paper referred to its source of information as "trustworthy," there was an air of indecision in the text, with much use of phrases such as "it was understood . . ." and "it is expected . . ." and "they say. . . ." The editors ended up rather apologetically, and not a little grumpily: "The curiosity about the wedding is altogether the expression of friendly concern, not vulgar impertinence or a desire to meddle in anybody's private affairs."

Despite this piqued disclaimer, *The Times* would have sacrificed its City Editor to achieve a journalistic scoop.

Although Frances Folsom was 27 years younger than the President, she had many attractive attributes that promised to make her socially and intellectually equal to the task of being First Lady. She had a facility for learning things rapidly and, as one of her secondary-school teachers expressed it, she "always put a little of herself into her recitations." She was clever enough to skip freshman class at college and to enter in the middle of the year, at that, without taking any special examinations. She had a reputation for common sense, self-motivation, and independence, and she was ingenuous and unspoiled, though she came from a well-to-do family. Acquaintances described her as intensely loyal to her mother and other relatives, mature beyond her years, with excellent taste in clothing and decoration, and with a rare gift for letter writing.

Physically, she had the appeal and the presence that would have endeared her to television audiences had she been born years later. She had a tall, well-proportioned figure, enhanced by a regal bearing, which earned for her one writer's unofficial title at Wells, "Queen of the College." She had the stamina, combined with graciousness, that on a future occasion was to see her through a New Year's Day reception that required more than 3,000 handshakes without once looking tired or uninterested. Her hair was dark brown, soft and wavy, and usually worn combed back from her forehead, but loose enough so that impish ringlets occasionally curled down by her cheek. She had eyes of a deep blue, so deep they were sometimes described as "violet," or "black," set off by heavy, expressive eyebrows. Her lips and chin were particularly pleasing and one artist, Farnham, is said to have remarked that "Miss Folsom has the most beautiful mouth I have ever seen."

It is no wonder that, after the wedding, many contemporaries were to describe her as the loveliest and most exciting First Lady since Dolley Madison.

When Frances Folsom and her mother returned from Europe on the steamship late in May, with the rumored trousseau carefully packed in their trunks, several events confirmed suspicions about an impending marriage. Reporters believed the two were on the *City of Chicago*, landing in New York on Friday, May 28th, but the passengers were really on the *Noordland*, which arrived the previous evening. They were met by Colonel Lamont, Cleveland's private secretary, on the revenue cutter *Chandler* and spirited away to the Gilsey House in Manhattan before anyone knew what was happening. It was learned that the President intended to visit New York, ostensibly to officiate at Decoration Day functions.

Then, late on May 29th, handwritten notes to fewer than

thirty people went out on the stationery of the Executive Mansion. They were short and to the point:

My dear Mr. ———

I am to be married on Wednesday evening at seven o'clock at the White House to Miss Folsom. It will be a very quiet affair and I will be extremely gratified at your attendance on the occasion.

Yours Sincerely,
Grover Cleveland.

The speculation was over—with only four days to go!

The wedding almost did not take place in the White House at all. Frances had intended that the ceremony would be at the home of her grandfather, "Papa John" Folsom, near Buffalo. But his recent death ruled that out when she and Cleveland were making plans. The President did not belong to a church, and he did not feel that a public hall was appropriate. So the White House was selected, not so much by choice as because it was the only appropriate alternative.

White House social life had become somewhat dreary during the past few years. Although Rose Cleveland was a capable hostess, a scholar, and an author of a book on poetry, she was not a particularly artistic or imaginative woman, and state affairs tended to be dull and infrequent. Current wits alleged she greeted guests at receptions with one hand, while holding a book in front of her eyes with the other. The President himself, usually immersed in his work, did not encourage social affairs. Now, suddenly, the White House became a romantic attraction. On May 30th, there was an influx of Sunday strollers who entered the gates and craned their necks to see signs of wedding preparations. It was reported that even a *Congressman* brought his family to look the place over.

That Sunday, the morning after the invitations were sent

out, the President did indeed travel to New York, riding with three friends in a special railroad car and being met at the Pennsylvania Railroad Station in Jersey City at about 10:30 P.M. by Secretary of the Navy Whitney (in whose Fifth Avenue mansion he spent the night) and by Benjamin Folsom, Frances's cousin, who had also been along on the European tour. The President smiled broadly as he alighted, waved at the crowd that had gathered, and walked briskly along the platform through the station to a waiting carriage. He was in such a jovial mood that when the carriage had boarded the ferry to New York and an audacious youth thrust his arm through the window, the President shook his hand warmly and said "Good evening." The crowd waved their hats and showed great respect—all except for "one unmannerly boor" who "held a lighted match up to the carriage window in order to get a look at the President."

Sunday, May 30th, was a day of quiet for Frances Folsom. There was speculation in New York as to which church she would attend on her last Sunday before heading for Washington and the White House. Some said it would be the Church of the Transfiguration. Others, knowing she was a Presbyterian, supposed that she might go to the Reverend Dr. Hall's Church on Fifth Avenue. As a result, both houses of worship were jammed, to the delight of the officiating clergymen. Miss Folsom, however, slept late, not breakfasting until 10 A.M., and consequently decided not to go to church at all.

She stayed in the suite the entire day, receiving several letters and a magnificent bouquet of flowers from the President, lunching with her mother at one o'clock, receiving lady friends during the afternoon, and then dining in the parlor with her mother and cousin from 6:30 until 9 P.M. She saw her fiancé, for the first time since she had returned from Europe, between 11 and midnight when he reached New York and he and Benjamin Folsom spent an hour in the home (adjoining the hotel) of the proprietor of the Gilsey House. Then she went to bed, to rest for the Decoration Day celebration, which would start the following morning.

Her last full day in New York began at 8:30 on Monday morning, when she rose and had breakfast. At 11:30 A.M. she and her mother went by carriage to the Fifth Avenue Hotel, to the second-floor apartment of Postmaster and Mrs. Vilas. There the ladies could conveniently look down on the parade and, more importantly, see the stand occupied by President Cleveland.

Among the marchers were one Gilmore and his band of 65 musicians and a drum corps of 20 men. The imaginative Mr. Gilmore had, as the papers reported, "conceived a most brilliant idea on Saturday night." He had "labored unceasingly" with his men, and all was prepared. When the band reached the grandstand directly opposite the President, it would, at a signal, instantly stop the music it was playing and swing into Mendelssohn's "Wedding March." "It is expected," said one paper, "that the consequent cheers will be deafening."

It was a touching moment. The bride-to-be, dressed in a tight-fitting gray suit, tailor-made to fit her full figure, was all but overcome by the procession. She applauded heartily; "her little gloved hands were continually smiting each other." At the end, as the President was being escorted to his carriage, he looked up. "There was a little flirt of her dainty handkerchief," and then she was gone. That night, they dined together with friends at the Gilsey House and heard a Memorial Day concert at the Academy of Music before Cleveland returned to Washington on the overnight train.

When Cleveland had left for New York, many of his friends in Washington—knowing his strict attention to duty—were afraid that he might become so involved in the official affairs of the day that he would have no time for his fiancée. It was a great relief, therefore, when word came that the President actually did get around to seeing Frances and that in fact they had attended to a number of details, including the arrangements for the wedding cake. The cake was to be prepared on 48 hours' notice by a noted *New York* caterer (Washington society was horrified!), J. B. Pinard's Sons, of 6 East 15th Street. It was to weigh 25 pounds, to be modestly decorated, and to have the initials "C-F" in the center, surrounded by orange blossoms. The frosting was to be plain, except for delicate scrollwork around the border. In addition, there were to be 150 smaller cakes, about five inches by two inches, nestled in oblong white satin boxes, each bound with a white ribbon and bearing in hand lettering the "C-F" monogram and the date, June 2, 1886. Space was left to attach a card on which the bride and groom would inscribe their names. (One of the little cakes was thoughtfully sent to Julia, the 66-year-old widow of President Tyler, living in Richmond.)

The designs for the cards and boxes, as well as for the cake's frosting, were not left up to the caterer, but carefully worked out by the creative hand of one Mr. Whithouse, engraver for Tiffany & Co.

Among the few people in New York who did not get Decoration Day off and who had to miss the parade were the young ladies who worked for the Spooner Manufacturing Company on West 27th Street. Late Sunday, Mr. Spooner received the startling news that he was to manufacture immediately the 150 special containers for the wedding cakes. He hastily rounded up his employees and promised them double pay for missing the parade and various outings that they had planned. Complete with contents, cards, tinfoil and real point lace wrapping, the satin boxes are said to have cost up to $20 apiece.

After the President had returned to Washington, Frances Folsom and her mother and cousin made preparations to follow a day later. On the evening of Tuesday, June 1st, they left the hotel in a two-horse carriage for the Desbrosses Street wharf, where they were just in time to catch the 8:30 ferry. Although a crowd had waved them off, they were now anonymous. The carriage edged into position behind a butcher's wagon, which had some difficulty maneuvering off the ferry on the other side, causing a slight delay in their arrival at the railroad station. There was some confusion, and the private car of Mr. Roberts, president of the Pennsylvania Railroad, in which they were to ride, was late. During the delay, word spread and a small crowd gathered. One of the railroad officials had the presence of mind to usher the party into a parlor car standing nearby, where they remained for some five minutes until their own car arrived.

At 5:30 in the morning of June 2nd, the long train, which had eleven coaches and several baggage cars, steamed into the Washington station. The private car, at the end, with red curtains tightly drawn, was switched to a track adjoining Sixth Street. A carriage hastily drew alongside, and out stepped Rose Cleveland, in a bright-red shawl. She entered the car and within a few minutes reappeared, followed by Frances, who was dressed in a silk dress, dark-gray jacket, and "peaked ship hat" with black and white trimmings.

A number of spectators, mostly men, had quickly gathered. Because the lower step from the car to the walk was longer than expected, Rose navigated the distance awkwardly with skirt slightly askew, and the onlookers were treated to "rather more of the anatomy of the President's sister than is usually to be seen in public."

Frances saw the amused smiles, and, not to be caught in such a predicament herself, "with a dainty kick, she gathered her skirts about her and jumped to the walk with only her boot tips protruding."

"It was a lover's June morning," wrote one reporter, happily ignoring the rain, "the air laden with sweetness and the twitter of birds, and with no other sound save the soft crunching of the carriage wheels over the gravel roadway." It might have been even more romantic had Grover Cleveland himself been on hand to embrace his bride-to-be. But, even at that hour, he had some state business to attend to.

The carriage entered the East Gate of the White House, on Pennsylvania Avenue, and by the time Frances had stepped out and been escorted by attendants under the portico and in the door, it was exactly 6 A.M. There, at the entrance to the corridor, the President stepped forward to greet her. True to tradition, his pretty fiancée "blushed clear to the forehead" as he held out both hands to her, and she in turn "let her hands fall trustingly in his."

The attendants, who expected to witness at least a decorous embrace, were disappointed. The President displayed great restraint. He gave her a squeeze of her hands and then turned to greet his future mother-in-law and her nephew. Frances was shown to the South Room, on the second floor, which had previously been occupied by President and Mrs. Grant, and which was now transformed into a "bower of flowers." Breakfast was served by eight o'clock for a family group that included the bride's aunt and uncle, Mr. and Mrs. Harmon of Boston; the President's brother, the Reverend W. N. Cleveland; his second sister, Mrs. Hoyt; and his former law partner, Wilson S. Bissell of Buffalo.

Immediately after breakfast, the President excused himself and went off to his office. Wedding day or not, there was work to do. He did return, however, for lunch, and afterwards paused long enough to sit down for a chat, partially to discuss plans and partially to calm Frances's apparent nervousness. A little later, they met for a brief rehearsal with the Reverend Dr. Byron Sunderland, who was to marry them. Toward the end of the rehearsal, Frank became a little bit tearful, and the President gently escorted her back to the South Room so that she could rest, undisturbed, until it was time to begin dressing for the ceremony. As might have been expected, he then calmly returned to the Presidential office to dispense with a pile of official papers and to meet with various members of his

Cabinet. At one point in the afternoon he relaxed by going for a short drive, alone, in his coupé.

Right up until the eleventh hour, the White House was besieged with requests from journalists and artists to attend the wedding so that it could be accurately reported in the newspapers. All appeals were politely, but positively, turned down. It was unfortunate, intoned numerous editors, that the press —interested solely in historical documentation—was to be totally excluded. But that was the President's desire, and who were editors, however distinguished and responsible, to argue with the Chief Executive?

There were the usual number of ambitious, unprincipled would-be gate-crashers. One ingenious young man is said to have gone to the office of Professor John Philip Sousa, "The March King," who was to conduct the Marine Band, and asked him whether he would like to earn $50. Sousa replied that he had no aversion to money, if honestly come by.

"Well," said the young man, "I want you to lend me a red coat and triangle and let me go with you to the White House as a member of the band. It will be fifty dollars in your pocket if you will do this."

The offer was quickly, and not very politely, turned down.

While the President and Colonel Lamont worked in the office, all around them was a tremendous bustle and commotion. There was some concern about the weather and the necessary arrangements in case of storm. Although the Weather Bureau officials had been whimsically reported as "exerting themselves all day to get up appropriate conditions of sky and air for the wedding ceremony," rain continued and there were rumbles of thunder in the distance.

The Reverend Dr. Byron Sunderland, a small, stout man, was one of the most energetic bustlers. Not only did he have to attend to the wedding rehearsal and other ministerial matters, but he was constantly being cornered and given unsolicited advice. Some of the President's friends were anxious that the bride and groom should not be forced to kneel to receive the blessing. Another group maintained that kneeling was absolutely necessary, regardless of the portliness of the bridegroom. There was also some debate about the length of the prayers. Dr. Sunderland, however, had his own ideas. He had been Pastor of the First Presbyterian Church in Washington since 1853, except for several years' absence when he was at the American Chapel in Paris, and he had served four years as Chaplain of the United States Senate.

Another man described as being considerably "unsettled" that day was Professor Sousa. As leader of the Marine Band, he had heard that he was to play before, during, and after the ceremony, probably in the vestibule, and he had assumed that dress would not be formal. Suddenly, however, he had received orders that it was to be an "official" performance and that the members of the band would appear in full dress uniforms.

The kitchen was in a state of confusion because so many of the instructions had been withheld until the last minute. In one corner, a chef was wrestling with one of the largest salmon ever taken from the Connecticut River, weighing more than twenty pounds. It had just been received as a gift for the bridal table from Fish and Game Commissioner Blackford, as evidence that the fish-stocking program of the Commission was proceeding nicely. In another corner, Mr. John A. Pinard of New York was nervously supervising the unpacking of the wedding cake, four sections high. He had personally escorted it on the overnight train to Washington, all but carrying it on his lap en route, to make certain that it arrived in the same condition as when it had started.

"I would not trust it to anybody!" he asserted to all who cared to listen. "Suppose anything should go wrong!" Once unpacked, the cake was to be moved gently to its place of honor in the dining room, on a bed of green vines and white Cornelia Cook roses.

Also in progress were the enormous flower arrangements.

The Blue Room, where the wedding was to take place, was encased in "a wall of green," so dense that it cut out the light from some of the windows. At the entrance were two tall candelabra with gold branches (a gift to Andrew Jackson), and extending from them down the length of the room were potted plants, some of them shoulder high. The mantel was blooming with flowers, and beneath it on the inside of the hearth lay a mass of bright red begonias, designed to represent a glowing fire. Across the mantel the inscription "June 2, 1886" was spelled out in light-colored blossoms against a panel of dark pansies. All the mirrors were festooned with roses. The famous circular divan had once more been pushed out of the way from the center of the floor. Over the entrance to the corridor, where the band was to play, hung an ingenious scroll of flowers in red, white and blue, with others arranged to spell "E PLURIBUS UNUM."

The wedding was scheduled for seven in the evening. Before six o'clock, people had begun to gather outside the White House grounds. Then, finding no guards on duty, they entered and moved as far as the steps leading to the building before they were finally stopped. Although one account speaks of a "great crowd," there were probably not more than several hundred orderly onlookers. By this time, the rain had generally let up.

Among the first to enter the White House were the members of Professor Sousa's Marine Band. As directed, they wore full dress uniform with scarlet jackets, blue trousers, blue caps, and swords with red and white cords and tassels.

The first guests to arrive were Colonel Lamont and his wife. They was followed by Secretary Lamar, the Reverend Dr. Sunderland and his wife, the Postmaster General and Mrs. Vilas, and Cleveland's law partner, W. S. Bissell, "whose round face looked as merry as Pickwick's," according to the Washington *Evening Star*'s reporter on the spot. They were followed by Secretary of War Endicott and his wife, Secretary of State

Bayard, and Secretary of the Navy and Mrs. Whitney. The last to arrive was Secretary of the Treasury Manning, paying his first visit to the White House since partially recovering from a stroke; his wife helped him to limp up the steps. When the door closed behind them, it was exactly five minutes before seven. With the friends and relatives already in the White House, there were no more than 28 guests in all.

One guest remained conspicuously absent: Attorney-General Garland. The reason? He had long let it be known that he would never appear in public in a swallow-tailed coat!

Inside the White House, as the clocks chimed the hour, the Marine Band struck up Mendelssohn's "Wedding March" and the crowd outside hushed expectantly, straining to catch every note. (Sousa, in arranging the musical program, was said to have taken care "to leave out all airs from comic operas as being inappropriate to the occasion.") Across town at the arsenal, cannon began booming in an official salute, and all over Washington—and in many other cities near and far—church bells rang out. The President and Frances stood waiting in the private dining room at the west end of the corridor until the appropriate moment, then advanced into the Blue Room and stood beneath the chandelier. The small group of guests formed a loose semicircle. After Dr. Sunderland (who received a brand-new $100 bill, which he gave to his wife to keep as a memento) had joined them in marriage, the Reverend William Cleveland stepped forward to conclude the ceremony with a blessing. According to *Harper's Weekly*, the President did not kiss his bride.

The wedding was about as simple as Cleveland had wished. He had purposely avoided a fancy floral wedding-bell arrangement or horseshoe to stand under. The weekly periodical *Puck*, however, could not stand this restraint. Indulging in the usual sentimentality of the day, it ran an illustration depicting the couple (rather gloomy of countenance) standing, not under one, but under *both* of these objects. Carrying this maudlin display to the extreme, it also printed a poem entitled "Puck's Congratulations," of which the first of four stanzas went:

> God rest you, Mr. Cleveland,
> May nothing you dismay—
> Mugwump and Spoilsman, Rep. and Dem.
> Hail you this happy day.
> The sweet alliance which you make
> No party disapproves—
> E'en politicians will admit
> You've made the best of moves.

The wedding gown was amply described, by the *Paris Morning News*:

The wedding gown is a poem in its pure simplicity, of thick ivory satin of the kind that stands alone. The round, plain jupe is draped from side to side with a very soft silk Indian muslin, attached on the left side, and nearly joining the traine de cour. The muslin is ourle, or bordered, with a very narrow band of orange flowers and leaves that outline the draping. The traine de cour is attached on to the plain bodice, just below the waist behind, and measures four meters in length. It is slightly rounded and falls in full organ plaits on the ground, no trimming upon it whatsoever. The bodice is extremely neat. Two scarves of the soft, filmy muslin start from the shoulder seams, cross the bosom, and are bordered with a narrow band of orange flower, to correspond with the skirt. The scarves at length hide away beneath a broad ceinture, or lappet of satin that crosses the bodice from left to right, and fastens on the hip. The effect is simple and exquisite. The sleeves are made to reach just below the elbow, and have three crossway bands of Indian muslin, forming plisse. Attached at the elbow point, on the inner side of the arm, are tiny blossoms, buds, and two or three leaves of "oranges." The veil is of plain white silk tulle of enormous length, to be dressed high on the head with an upstanding piquet of myrtle and orange blossoms; the six meters of tulle lightly covering the entire train.

Immediately after the ceremony, the bride and groom and the guests moved into the dining room for the wedding dinner —timed to coincide with the President's regular meal hour. There the guests were greeted with another profusion of flowers. But the main focus was the table where "a revelation in floral art confronted the assembly." There, floating on a huge mirror said to have been purchased by Dolley Madison, was the good ship *Hymen*, bearing white flags of love and the familiar monogram, "C-F." Besides the ship itself, there were "shoals" and "rocks" and "banks," all made of appropriately colored flowers.

Except for the diamond necklace presented by Cleveland to Frances, there were no wedding gifts on display.

As a contemporary account has it, the bridal party was served "terrapin and a lot of dainty French dishes, of which no one knew the name." The bride duly cut the cake. Then everyone rose to pledge her health. According to one report, the Secretary of the Navy proposed a toast to the bridegroom, which he drank in sparkling champagne. But Frances drank hers in mineral water!

Queen Victoria sent a telegram of congratulations from London, and other good wishes arrived from Fred Grant and Ida in New York.

It was dark by now, and as the gas lights flickered cheerily (this was the last wedding before electricity came to the White House), Grover Cleveland and his bride prepared to leave. At about 9 P.M., the President came downstairs and received a premature shower of rice. He was not quite ready to go. Shortly afterwards, Frances appeared in a dark-gray traveling dress and waistcoat, with fifty or sixty narrow white stripes that formed a hem about twenty inches deep. She wore a large gray hat, lined with velvet and crowned with ostrich feathers and a bow of picot ribbon.

As Cleveland escorted his bride down the steps of the South Portico to the waiting carriage, guests threw rice and several old shoes, while the band played selections from *Lohengrin*, "Bright Star of Hope," Mendelssohn's "Spring Song," and other appropriate numbers. By 9:30 the bride and groom had reached the station without incident and were happily seated in the private car Frances had taken from New York. They had not been long under way, however, when John W. David, the railroad representative in charge of the special three-car Presidential train, received word that "at least two and he didn't know how many more" newspapermen were hot in pursuit, having left Washington around 11 P.M. on the Chicago express.

During the honeymoon at Deer Park, President and Mrs. Cleveland received more newspaper coverage than they had before or during the wedding. Although he did manage to get in some fishing, Cleveland was not happy about the publicity. He was outraged at the Peeping Tom tactics of the press. Some reporters lifted the covers from dishes sent from the hotel kitchen to the cottage, to see what the bridal couple would have for dinner. Some actually used spyglasses. And others managed to get their hands on the Presidential mail, to see who was writing letters of congratulations. Cleveland, who had long harbored a resentment against the sensational journalism of the day, spoke of the "newspaper nuisances" and the "animals" who sat on a nearby bridge that marked one of the boundaries of the restricted area and watched, "waiting for some movement to be made which will furnish an incident."

Finally, he wrote an angry letter to the New York *Evening Post*, damning the correspondents:

They have used the enormous power of the modern newspaper to perpetuate and disseminate a colossal impertinence, and have done it, not as professional gossips and tattlers, but as the guides and instructors of the public in conduct and morals. And they have done it, not to a private citizen, but the President of the United States, thereby lifting their offence into the gaze of the whole world, and doing their utmost to make

American journalism contemptible in the estimation of people of good breeding everywhere.

Cleveland's decision to return to Washington after only a week was motivated less by spying correspondents than by his desire to get back to the work he knew was piling up in the White House. Far more distressing to him than the ever-present reporters was the unauthorized commercial advantage that was later taken of the First Lady's beauty and popularity. Her pictures came to be seen everywhere—on patent medicines, perfumes, candy, and packages containing ladies' underwear. The President's protests finally culminated in the introduction of a bill in the House of Representatives in March of 1888. It read in part:

> Be it enacted, etc. That any person or persons for themselves or others or for corporations who shall publicly exhibit, use or employ the likeness or representation of any female living or dead, who is or was the wife, mother, daughter or sister of any citizen of the United States without the consent in writing of the person whose likeness is to be used shall be guilty of high misdemeanor and shall upon indictment be fined not less than $500, nor more than $5,000, and stand imprisoned until fine and costs are paid.

Mrs. Cleveland was as popular with Washington society as she was with the advertisers. At the first of her Saturday afternoon receptions, a group of delighted ladies, gazing back at her over their shoulders as they walked away, bumped right into the palms screening the ever-present Marine Band; panic and confusion followed, and "order had to be restored by force" by the White House guards. Enthusiasts at other receptions got into line twice, just to see the lovely Mrs. Cleveland smile again and to shake her hand a second time. Her friendliness and charm attracted people to a continuous round of public receptions and the other social events that had been neglected before she became First Lady. No one, it was said, had been so popular since Dolley Madison.

The White House began to look more homelike, as Frances filled it every morning with fresh flowers and installed canaries, mockingbirds, and a great mastiff. Cleveland himself began to change. "His friends observed that he was happier, brighter, and more companionable," wrote historian Allan Nevins in his biography of the President. "After his marriage he seemed to have been rejuvenated; he worked better, went out oftener, and spent more time in amusements congenial to them both." He may have worked better, but Frances saw to it that he worked shorter hours; breakfast time was set an hour later, and the President was allowed to read only the most urgent telegrams and letters before he ate.

The Clevelands shared two terms of office together. "I'll be back," were Frances's cheerful parting words to the head usher as they left the White House in March 1889, and she was right—they returned in 1893, bringing a 17-month-old daughter with them.

Grover Cleveland died on June 24, 1908, eleven years after leaving office, at the age of 71. He and Frank had three daughters (the second was born in the White House) and two sons. In 1913, Frances was married for a second time, to Thomas J. Preston, Jr., Professor of Archaeology at her alma mater, Wells College, who later joined the faculty of Princeton. She died unexpectedly at the home of her son, Richard F. Cleveland, a Baltimore lawyer, on October 29, 1947. She was 83 years old, and Preston was one year older. She had come to Baltimore from her home in Princeton to help her son celebrate his fiftieth birthday. After a quiet family party, she went contentedly, and apparently in good health, to her room, where she died in her sleep.

CHAPTER XIV

# *THE PRINCESS*

N February 6, 1906, authorities at the railroad station in Cincinnati, Ohio, took into custody a young woman who had no money but had apparently traveled all the way from New Orleans on a total of 10 cents. The girl, who reported her name as Lottie Strickland, said that she was no mere vagrant. A group of her co-workers at one of the biggest stores in New Orleans, where she was employed in the dressmaking department, had dared her to "beat" her way to Washington, D.C. Once there, she was to try, by every ingenious method she could think of, to attend the marriage of Alice Roosevelt, daughter of President Theodore Roosevelt, to Nicholas Longworth, Congressman from Ohio.

Miss Strickland had traveled as far as she did by enlisting the aid and sympathy of fellow passengers, who supplied her with food and let her hide in their sleeping compartments. "We thought that a working girl ought to be at the wedding," said Lottie pleadingly to the authorities, "and I am sure if I get to see President Roosevelt and tell him what I want, he will allow me to attend."

Sympathetic though the authorities were, the girl was denied her wish. All of Washington, not to mention the other capitals of the world, was clamoring for an invitation to the biggest, most brilliant, and most exciting wedding in the history of the White House.

Alice Lee Roosevelt was born at 6 West 57th Street, in New York City, on February 12, 1884. Her mother died three days after her birth, and she was placed in the care of her aunt. When she was three years old, her father married again, and later five more Roosevelt children arrived. Young Alice first came to know Washington when, as a child of five, she moved there with her father, who had been appointed Civil Service Commissioner, and her new stepmother, the former Edith Kermit Carew.

It was early evident that Alice was different from most of the other children in the capital. Although for a while she attended the same private school as the sons and daughters of other government officials, she was described as "a perfect Tartar" as a child.

Women guests screamed and the servants dropped the lemonade glasses at a big reception given by Alice's aunt, when young Alice began firing a toy pistol with dynamite caps that someone had given to her. At the toy tea table, she demanded always a high place for herself or for her doll. Her willful character may have been strengthened because of the fact (little mentioned today) that for some time Alice was unable to join in the other children's energetic games: she had to wear orthopedic braces on both legs, from ankle to knee.

Her early life was a succession of uprootings. The family moved back to New York for two years, and then again to Washington when Roosevelt became Assistant Secretary of the Navy. By this time, she was 14 and a rather serious student, despite her capacity for pranks and other lively mischief. Her father taught her to love reading, to understand public affairs, and to develop into a brilliant conversationalist. She was proud when her father was elected Governor of New York and the family moved to Albany. A governess was hired to help her with the formal education that her father demanded, but the woman was reported to have been "indulgent" and willing to give Alice a little rein.

The third return to Washington was occasioned by Roosevelt's election to the office of Vice President in 1901. Then, on September 6th, fate decreed a completely unexpected move. Gentle President McKinley was shot by an anarchist at the Buffalo exposition, and the White House became the Roosevelts' home. There was a slight delay while the aging mansion underwent extensive restoration, and then the liveliest, noisiest family the old house had ever seen moved in.

Washington could hardly believe its eyes. The three youngest children, Archie, Kermit, and Ethel, borrowed trays from the pantry and slid down the staircase. They roller-skated along the upstairs corridor, drenched the furniture in water fights, hunted ghosts in the attic, and found the high-ceilinged rooms perfect for walking on stilts. Startled visitors sometimes saw a small head pop out of one of the huge vases by the East Room, and one day a group of foreign dignitaries came across a trail of small wet footprints and puddles, leading to a barefoot youngster who had taken a dip in the White House fountain. The President himself staged a Chinese wrestling match between an American wrestler and a Japanese jujitsu expert in the staid old East Room. The White House was full of unusual animals—a black bear, a parrot, a kangaroo rat that lived in Archie's pocket, and a pony named Algonquin, who was once smuggled upstairs in the elevator when Archie had measles and needed comforting. Alice herself, aloof as she may have been from all this childishness, kept a pet green snake called Emily Spinach.

On January 3, 1902, just two days after the remodeled White House was officially opened to the public, Alice made her debut. The occasion was marked by a ball in her honor. Not quite 18, Alice was the center of attention of some seven hundred guests. She considered herself adult enough for champagne to be served, and was disgusted when only nonalcoholic punch was produced during a fairly sedate evening. The function was "non-official," strictly a family affair. Invitations were sent out under the name of Mrs. Roosevelt, and did not bear the seal of the United States. The reception took place in the Blue Room, and the dancing in the East Room, to the music of a Marine Band. *Leslie's Weekly* had only admiration for Alice:

> She has all the honors and pleasures of royalty, without being in the least hampered by its restrictions. Her world-wide popularity was never equalled by any other maiden.... The girl in blue is Miss Roosevelt, it may be added, for that is her favorite color, and blue in all shades predominates her gowns.

Despite this bit of editorial flamboyance, Alice is said to have worn a simple white chiffon dress and a small, conservative diamond necklace.

Alice opened the ball with Lieutenant John C. Gilmore, United States Army, one of the military aides at the White House, and then danced with many of the other young men who were attracted by her personality and her handsome looks.

It was about this time that the press began referring to her as "Princess Alice."

She was growing prettier every day, her attractiveness increased by her lively nature, her social brilliance, and her affinity for high fashion. She also had begun to develop an international reputation, having made a visit to Cuba, during the autumn preceding her debut, where she was the guest of the Governor General of the Island and Mrs. Leonard Wood. Although the visit was only "semi-official," she enjoyed the hospitality of the Palace in Havana, where she met and was entertained by many of the island's notables, all of whom remembered her father's Rough Riders with gratitude.

At home, she flung herself into so many social activities—

the New Orleans Mardi Gras, the St. Louis World's Fair, the Chicago Horse Show, and a party every night for two years (according to the White House chief usher)—that a French publication solemnly predicted a breakdown of her health unless she slowed down.

She was described in *The Ladies' Home Journal* in 1902 as "a typical American girl in the best sense of the term; modest, self-reliant, democratic. Although she has reached an age when many young ladies consider themselves justified in assuming a serious and weary view of the world, she retains with all its charming freshness, her youthful enthusiasm and her girlish love of life and pleasure."

Alice, who had been a little on the scrawny side, was now filling out so that she was described as "gracefully slender." She was not very tall, and had full, wavy light-brown hair, alert blue eyes, and a superb complexion. She spoke several languages well, and enjoyed playing the Sohmer piano in the White House. She could do every dance step from the waltz to the cakewalk. Although she did not share her father's wild enthusiasm for strenuous athletics, she was an excellent horse-woman, swam well, and possessed exuberant good health and energy. She enjoyed driving an automobile as fast as the "machine" would speed, and there was a lot of publicity when she boldly motored all the way from Newport with another girl—and no chaperone.

During these years, her husband-to-be, Nicholas Longworth, was building a more sober reputation for himself in Ohio. Born in Cincinnati on November 5, 1869, of a wealthy and prominent family (his father's estate was said to be worth $20 million), he was educated as a lawyer. At Harvard, he rowed on his class crew, belonged to the popular clubs and the most prominent fraternities, and was later described as "an all-around good fellow." "Everybody likes Nick Longworth," reported *Leslie's Weekly*, and all accounts of him stress his popularity.

In 1899, he won a seat in the State Senate, and in 1903 he was elected Congressman for the first Ohio District. Except for 1914, he was to remain in Congress until his death in 1931 and to serve as Speaker of the House in the Sixty-Ninth, Seventieth, and Seventy-First Congresses.

Longworth was already engaged to a Cincinnati girl, Miriam Bloomer, when he arrived in Washington in 1903, aged 34. Shortly afterwards, Miriam broke off the engagement (but they remained friends, and Miss Bloomer was one of the guests at the spectacular Roosevelt/Longworth wedding three years later). Longworth applied himself assiduously to his duties, served on his first committee, and became noted for his efficiency, fairness, tact as a mediator, and—again—for his position as one of the most popular young men in the House. At balls, dinners, and receptions everywhere, he was a welcome guest. Very soon, of course, he met Alice through some friends and immediately found her beautiful and appealing.

In addition to his personal charm, Nick Longworth had many things to recommend him. He was a good athlete and a strong swimmer, and he excelled at tennis, golf, and fencing. He was a racing enthusiast and had Kentucky thoroughbreds in his own stables. He played the violin much better than average, owned a rare Stradivarius, and even made violins of his own. Most important of all, from Alice's viewpoint, was probably the fact that he was a bright conversationalist who enjoyed the witty badinage at which she excelled.

But 35-year-old Nick certainly did not look like a serious contender for the hand of a girl as attractive and young as Princess Alice. "The first impression one gets of Mr. Longworth is that he looks older than he is," wrote *Leslie's Weekly* in an otherwise enthusiastic article. "With his hat off, his apparent age increases, for his high forehead has become a shiny dome. His figure is stocky, but he is of medium height." The sober-looking official photographs emphasized his heavy eyebrows and black, drooping mustache. Only in informal shots can one catch the mischievous glint in his eye.

There were many better-looking and younger suitors constantly surrounding Alice, and they had time on their hands to press a courtship. Furthermore, Alice did not seem at all of a mind to settle on anyone. She was having too much fun. At the time of the 1905 Inauguration, she and a friend, Bertie Goelet, made up a series of humorous placards that they placed around town, satirizing some of the official Inauguration Committee plaques that had been placed for visitors on buildings of historical interest and on prominent homes. Though Bertie tired of his part in the comedy, Alice continued the sport alone. She placed one of these placards beneath a window and tricked Longworth into peering out through the glass as a sightseeing stage was passing by. The unsuspecting Congressman could not understand why the passengers waved and giggled, until Alice rapturously showed him the sign, "I LIVE HERE, NICHOLAS LONGWORTH."

Despite the seeming odds against him, Nick continued to press his suit. In the summer, he gave a grand costume ball in Hamilton, Massachusetts, with Miss Roosevelt as guest of honor. Races, sporting events, horseback rides, and automobile trips followed quickly. His big opportunity came in the summer of 1905.

Alice had been invited to the coronation of King Edward VII in 1901, but after some negotiation, her father had vetoed the trip. He did, however, promise her a visit to the Orient at some future date. The chance came when it was decided that the Secretary of War, William Howard Taft, would proceed to the Philippines to make an inspection tour. President Roosevelt announced that his daughter could accompany the official party, with her expenses coming out of his own pocket. It was said that one of T.R.'s reasons for wanting his daughter to go on an extended voyage was to give her a breathing spell—away from the throngs of young men who daily besieged the Executive Mansion.

He was not counting on the ingenuity of Nick Longworth. As a Congressman, a member of the Foreign Affairs Committee, and a leading legislator in matters pertaining to foreign trade and tariffs, it was quite natural that he should request, and receive, permission to accompany the Secretary of War.

The official party left Washington at the end of June, from the old Baltimore and Ohio Railroad Station. Alice traveled in a private car, the *Colonial*, along with Mr. Taft, Colonel Edwards, Major Thompson, Mabel Beardman, and a friend, Amy McMillan. The train slowly crossed the continent, with the travelers greeted by crowds, photographers, and reporters at every stop. They finally arrived in San Francisco on the Fourth of July. Four days later, the group embarked on the steamer *Manchuria*, now joined by Longworth, the Herbert Parsons, and Senator and Mrs. Newlands of Nevada, the latter assigned as Alice's personal chaperone. Numerous other Congressmen and Senators were also on board, accompanied by their wives—as was the custom in those days, when a "Congressional junket" was really something to talk about. "Adventure seemed just around every corner and I was ready for it," wrote Alice in her memoirs. "I do not think that I ever slept."

Longworth did not seem to figure very strongly in the picture at first, despite his persistence. Although he sat at the same table as Alice, he had almost as many rivals for her attention as he had had in Washington. Alice was devoted to Mr. Taft, whom she described as one of the most amiable men she had ever known, and with whom she conversed freely and often. In fact, she eagerly joined any discussion where the subject was controversial and she could encourage a heated debate. She was constantly having her picture snapped by the official photographer, Burr MacIntosh, who felt it his responsibility to record every minute of the trip from morning to evening. And she delighted in pranks and activities that might shock the other voyagers.

"I felt it to be my pleasurable duty," she wrote later of her companions, "to stir them up from time to time."

She made it a point to smoke in public—something that just was not done by a woman at that time—flourishing a fat, old-fashioned gold vanity in which she kept cigarettes instead of the hairpins for which the case was intended. In Japan, she smoked little pipes of Japanese tobacco, "about three whiffs to a pipe." On one occasion, she anticipated by more than sixty years the High Society fad of several years ago, by leaping fully clothed into a canvas swimming pool rigged on the ship's deck. Later an over-romantic reporter stated that Nick had jumped in, too.

Alas, this was not the case. She dared Nick to do so, but the person who actually followed, fully clothed, was Bourke Cockran, an old friend and a Congressman noted for his Irish brogue and flowery, booming oratory.

When the ship docked in Hawaii and the party was taken on a tour and entertained by native hula dances, Alice brashly asked the guide if she could slip away from the expurgated tourist version of the dance and see the real thing. She and several others were promptly led to a less "official" locale, where they delightedly witnessed an earthier version of the hula.

The Hawaiians, pleased at her interest, composed a song in her honor, the words of which went:

> Alice Roosevelt, she came to Honolulu
> And she saw the Hula Hula Hula Hai.
> And I think before she reached the Filipinos
> She could dance the Hula Hula Hula Hai.

She enjoyed the Hawaiian stopover so much that she missed the boat when it sailed and had to be rushed out to it in a motor launch.

Where was Nick during the voyage? He was one of the few friends who missed the boat with Alice, because of all the fun on the beach at Waikiki (where Alice put on her full-length bathing suit and went "skid-riding," as it was then called, on the surf). A reader cannot really believe Alice's own account in her book, *Crowded Hours*, which implies that he was not very much in her mind.

But although she devotes more than forty pages to the description of the trip, the greater part of the account is spent on Mr. Taft, the Imperial Household in Tokyo, the sights of Japan, dancing in Manila, Moro natives and the Sultan of Sulu, a rickshaw race in Hong Kong, and the street sights of Korea—not on Nick.

She describes how, in Peking's summer palace on the evening before her audience with the Empress Dowager of China, she became intoxicated on the surprisingly strong rose wine. Only five years earlier, the crafty old Empress had not lifted a finger to crush the Boxers, who had shot or beheaded over two hundred Europeans and Americans in a bloody two-month siege of Peking's legation district. At Alice's audience, the Empress forced the interpreter, who turned gray with fear, to prostrate himself with his forehead touching the ground. "On the lowest step of the throne sat the Emperor, limp and huddled. We were not presented to him. No attention was paid to him. He just sat there, looking vacantly about." Alice's account of the meeting, during which she had to curtsy three times as she advanced toward the throne, gives a hint that the autocratic old Empress may have spotted another woman of extraordinary mettle in the young American. Certainly, she sent unusually extravagant wedding presents to Alice the following year.

Alice also describes how she overcame the boredom of official banquets and speeches, held on every island of the Philippines with monotonous regularity. One imaginative subterfuge was to look around for a scout ant, exploring for food for his fellows. She would then fabricate a trail, scattering crumbles of cake or other sweet food from the ant to the table leg. In a matter of minutes, the banquet site would be crawling with invaders.

Yet somehow, despite the diversions, the romance blossomed as the party crossed the Pacific and the seas of China and Japan. One member of the party, Congressman Grosvenor, is reported to have said, "When we started on the Philippines trip, we noticed Mr. Longworth's friendship for Miss Roosevelt. We also noticed that she apparently liked him, but it was not until we reached Japan that I saw there was something more than mere friendship between them.... The charming scenery of Japan is conducive to love-making and I guess none of it was wasted."

Romantic progress was such that, by the time the party had reached Manila, the kindly Mr. Taft was prompted to ask, "Alice, I think I ought to know if you are engaged to Nick."

To which inquiry, Alice replied, "More or less, Mr. Secretary, more or less."

In December 1905, about a month and a half after their return from the Orient, Nicholas Longworth and Alice Lee Roosevelt announced their plans. On one of the few occasions in her life when she felt any shyness, she told the news to her stepmother while Mrs. Roosevelt was brushing her teeth, so that she would not be able to make an immediate reply. "Nick and I decided ... that we might as well announce our engagement," Alice later wrote, "as the papers were daily doing it for us." During the frustrating period of rumors and no news, the Chicago *Tribune* sent its Washington bureau an ultimatum by wire: "Is Alice Roosevelt engaged or is she not?" The chief cabled back: "She went out driving with Nick Longworth this afternoon without a chaperone. If they are not engaged, they ought to be." The *Tribune* printed news of the engagement in the morning paper; the White House announced it that afternoon.

The official announcement set off a chain reaction across the nation and around the world. People with social, political, or commercial ambitions began devising ways in which they could attend the wedding or the reception or otherwise get into the act. Others, with no illusions of participating, enjoyed the vicarious thrill of reading about the romance and the preparations for the biggest of all White House weddings.

It was to be the first "White House" wedding, in a literal sense, because President Roosevelt had just decreed that this was to be the mansion's official name. It was a great patriotic occasion. The eyes of the world were on the White House. *Leslie's Weekly* published a poem expressing its pride and pleasure that *this* White House bride had not been won by any effete foreigner:

> Oh! Never yet a sweeter maid
>   Has worn a wedding gown;
> The nation's deepest love is hers—
>   A matchless bridal crown!
> And ancient kingdoms, far away
>   Beyond the rolling sea,
> Have honored with their costly gifts
>   The daughter of the free.
>
> No alien on her slender hand
>   Has placed the ring of gold.
> He rode to woo her from the West,
>   Like Lochinvar of old.
> And so among the bridal flowers
>   The flag today is shedding
> The glory of its silver stars
>   Upon the White House wedding.
>                     (MINNA IRVING)

With the wedding date set as February 17, 1906, there were only two months in which to make plans. Many of the details were masterfully planned by Alice herself, the least perturbed of all those involved. For some of the 1,000 guests, the invitations created a certain amount of consternation. Army and Navy officers and members of the diplomatic corps wondered whether they should wear full regalia or appear in morning dress. The answer depended on whether or not the wedding was to be a "state function." The President had made it known that the ceremony would be "private," rather than "public," and that those invited should appear as personal guests rather than as representatives of their governments or services. In the end, most officers and diplomats decided to forgo the gold and lace trappings, preferring to appear conservative rather than overdressed. Afterwards one newspaper ran a headline saying, "UNIFORMS ARE NOT MISSED" —probably a good indication that many observers really were sorry not to see the gold and lace.

Before the wedding, snide remarks about various gifts were whispered around and even printed bluntly in the press. When Mr. and Mrs. George B. Cox of Cincinnati—friends of the groom—proudly revealed that they were sending a "large and beautiful silver ice pitcher," local politicians gleefully pointed out that this was a most appropriate gift—in view of the *chilly* relationship between Teddy Roosevelt and the Cincinnati Republican boss (who declined to attend).

In Columbus, Ohio, a minor crisis occurred when members of the Woman's Christian Temperance Union heard that the Ohio delegation was planning to present the couple with a *punchbowl*. One Congressman Webber took a stand against the "vile object" and received the written appreciation of the W.C.T.U. for his intervention on their behalf. Not having full faith in the abilities of Mr. Webber to swing his colleagues around, however, the members also held a meeting "to pray that the delegation shall not make the Congressional gift a punchbowl."

Their prayers were rewarded. The gift finally selected was a *loving cup*.

Many Washingtonians who had hoped to send flowers were sorely disappointed. As early as three days before the wedding, the leading florists of the city were hopelessly buried in orders; the demand for orchids alone had entirely cleaned out the local market, long considered one of the best in the United States.

The House of Representatives faced a difficult dilemma. On the one hand, the occasion involved one of its own members and would go down as one of the great events in Washington history. On the other hand, it could not declare a holiday, because the wedding was to be private. The House neatly solved the problem by announcing that it would not sit on February 17, but that no official reason would be given for the adjournment. Only the Congressmen from Ohio and New York, the couple's home states, attended the wedding.

Throwing precedent to the winds, the Ohio House of Representatives decided that this was a once-in-history occasion and adopted a joint resolution formally congratulating Miss Alice Roosevelt and its former member on the approaching marriage.

Trying vainly to stop the anticipated flow of valuable gifts from all over the world, Teddy Roosevelt personally asked all governments, as well as private and public organizations, to refrain from sending presents. Most heads of state replied that they really were not going to do so, but would forward small, inexpensive gifts, to express their personal goodwill. One such trifle from the President of France was a rare Gobelin tapestry, six feet by eight feet, woven especially for the bride, and valued at $25,000 or "priceless." Another was an enormous Florentine mosaic table, shipped in a massive crate, from the King of Italy, and later described by Alice as so large and heavy that she could never use it in any of the houses she lived in.

In January Miss Roosevelt and her stepmother made several trips to New York to shop. These forays turned out to be anything but orderly and relaxing, since the two were trailed by reporters and ogled by curious crowds wherever they went. Although the publicity impeded the shopping, Alice gave no indication that she disliked the attention. On the contrary, she likened it to "the sort of thing royalty or a movie star endures, or enjoys."

Back at home, the confusion, equally great, was spiced with a good deal of social controversy. White House assistants tried to keep track of the invitations, while the family pondered over the long guest list. When President and Mrs. Roosevelt gave out a statement to the morning papers, asking the "kind consideration of many friends for not inviting them to Miss Roosevelt's wedding on account of the capacity of the White House," Washington society reacted with "great surprise." Mrs. Roosevelt, it was pointed out, had contracted with a local caterer for a breakfast for 700 people—a small number in comparison with some 2,500 ordinarily accommodated at a state reception. One thousand guests were to attend the ceremony itself.

"Just who is to overtax the White House on February 17th is a matter of much speculation in society circles today," wrote one commentator, "where the non-invited very greatly outnumber the invited friends and acquaintances of the bride and bridegroom as well as of the former's parents." One unlikely guest, whose presence no doubt shook society, was Bill Sewell, the postmaster of Portland, Maine, and the "Czar of Aroostook County," the President's favorite hunting guide. For the first time in his life, he abandoned forest costume for a frock coat, high starched collar, and silk top hat.

It required two full-time secretaries to politely fend off all the requests—sometimes almost commands—from men high in official circles all over the country who wanted personal invitations. It was obvious that no matter how fervently or frequently the Roosevelts described the wedding as "modest" or "private," a great many feelings would be hurt.

On the commercial front, manufacturers were busying

themselves with the production of souvenir trinkets, photographs, and other remembrances. One highly popular item was a souvenir postcard with oval-shaped portraits of the bride and groom. These vignettes were draped with ribbons, roses, leaves, and a dove. Stores that normally did a slight business in such sentimental knickknacks as porcelain cupids, papier-mâché flowers, and bleeding hearts, lured customers by the thousands, simply by calling them "wedding souvenirs."

Business was helped by the fact that Valentine's Day was just three days before the ceremony.

On Monday, February 12th, the week of the wedding began with a dinner and musicale in honor of Alice's twenty-second birthday. The dinner was attended by fewer than forty people, after which several hundred additional guests arrived for chamber music in the East Room. Congressman Longworth is said to have attended, although he was just recovering from grippe and tonsilitis, contracted as a result of having "gone about in the draughty corridors of the Capitol...."

By this time, the presents from all over the world had begun to arrive in great number. The playroom on the top floor of the Executive Mansion had already been filled with the larger gifts. Elsewhere, the White House looked like a jewelry store, laden with elegant clocks, fine watches, valuable necklaces, gold chains, bracelets, rings and other jewelry, leather traveling bags, silver plate, flat table silver, tea services, gold plates, vases, candlesticks, jeweled fans, pendants, and of course, an endless array of china and glass. The Mikado of Japan sent silver vases and a valuable piece of embroidered silk. An enameled snuffbox arived from King Edward of England. The Kaiser sent a heavy antique bracelet of gold, studded with diamonds. Antique jewelry came from King Alfonso of Spain, and a mosaic of the Vatican from Pope Pius X. There was even a gold riding crop and a diamond-studded lorgnette chain.

For his bride, Nick Longworth had ordered from Cincinnati a necklace of perfectly matched diamonds, each weighing about three-fourths of a carat, mounted in unique settings. She wore it at the wedding, together with a diamond brooch from her father.

In contrast, there were what Alice described as "hundreds of freak presents, ranging from mouse-traps to bales of hay." An assortment of live pets included two turtledoves called Nick and Alice, and a box of snakes from a collector. A hogshead of popcorn arrived from a manufacturer, as well as feather dusters, brooms, and a packet of pins from an old lady.

One of the more unusual gifts was a bottle of wine that had been bottled in 1857 for the Golden Wedding Anniversary of "Old Nick" Longworth, great-grandfather of the groom. It was sent by Dr. E. Parmly Brown of New York, who had bought several bottles at auction to save for his own anniversary. The label depicted Longworth's vineyard in Cincinnati, with the identification "N. Longworth" and the caption, in gold, "1857. Golden Wedding." Another bottle of it arrived from Cincinnati from the widow of Fire Captain Leonard, to whom "Old Nick" had sent three bottles of the anniversary wine at the time of the celebration, along with a case of other wine for the men in the enginehouse.

There is no report as to what this liquid treasure tasted like after almost half a century in the bottle.

Among Alice's favorite gifts were those sent to her by the Empress Dowager of China, whom she had met on her trip to the Orient. A marvelous carved teak dowry chest arrived, with many compartments, each of which contained some rare or beautiful gift. These included eight rolls of colored brocade, silks, Chinese paintings, two rings, a pair of earrings, white jade carvings, and two coats, one of fox and one of ermine. "The Chinese," she commented, "had a very proper idea of gifts!"

The bridegroom was not entirely forgotten in the deluge of gifts. On Thursday, February 15th, ten Ponca Indians arrived in Washington, having traveled all the way from their reservation in Oklahoma, to make a presentation, not to Alice, but to Nick. Dressed in beaded buckskin, their faces streaked with ceremonial paint, they plodded solemnly down Pennsylvania Avenue to the Capitol, looking for Congressman Longworth, to present him with a vest made of buffalo skin. The leader of the tribe, Horse Chief, is said to have told the startled doorman that he and his braves "were saddened by the news that came from the home of the Great White Father. In all the talks that reached us about the many presents for the young wife, there was no word of even a blanket for the young sachem. Can a man be boss of his own wigwam if it is so that all the ponies, the beads, the buffalo hides, belong to his wife?"

It was a pertinent question, but Longworth chose to duck the issue and was reported to have been so eager to escape his would-be benefactors that he escaped to the *Democratic* side of the House and hid in a cloakroom. After a council of war, Horse Chief marched down the steps and back along Pennsylvania Avenue to present the vest to whoever would accept it on Mr. Longworth's behalf at the White House. He was trailed by Big John Bull, Mike Roy, George Primaux, White Tail, Yellow Horse, and four others.

To avoid chaos on the wedding day, procedures had to be explained to the guests. On Tuesday, February 13th, a White House statement was issued:

*No one* will be admitted without presentation of the proper credentials.

Carriages will approach from the North to the East entrance of the White House, opposite the Treasury.

Pedestrians will follow the same route.

After discharging passengers, carriages will be parked around the ellipse in the White House lot.

The gates will not be open until 11:15 a.m.

Two carriages will drive under the porte-cochere at the same time. Coachmen will then be presented with numbered checks, necessary for gaining readmittance to the grounds.

Guests will be provided with checks, the same numbers as those of the carriages—necessary for calling the carriages later.

Guests will leave cloaks and hats in the downstairs cloakroom and will then fall into line and pass up the main staircase.

On the afternoon of Friday, February 16th, the wedding rehearsal took place in the East Room, with only the immediate wedding party present. That evening, a celebration was held at the Alibi, a popular supper club. Major Charlie McCawley, a White House aide, was the host. There are some discrepancies in accounts of this party. One report describes it as "most informal," held in a room called the Dutch Kitchen, and attended by Nick and Alice and an assortment of friends, who all left at 10 P.M. to go to a reception at the home of Senator Keen. Other reports, including Alice's, record this as a bachelor party for the ushers, confusing it, apparently, with the stag dinner given the previous evening by Nick. The President is supposed to have gone to the bachelor party, but to have discreetly left before the affair became too boisterous. At least one of the boys seems to have drunk too freely, waking up the next morning "dreaming of icebergs" and finding himself submerged in the chilly water of someone's bathtub.

Saturday, the 17th of February, was sunny and unusually warm for that time of year. By this time, everyone who had had anything to do with preparations was in a state of exhaustion. Everyone, that is, except Alice. She had enjoyed the excitement and stimulation, and was not the slightest bit on edge. When asked recently whether she had been "nervous," she commented sharply, "Heavens, no! I enjoyed my own wedding, and I cannot recall anything—any thought or mishap—that irritated me or marred the wedding."

She recalled looking out of the window ("My bedroom was what is now the dining room on the second floor") at about eleven that morning as she was dressing and watching with some amusement the crowds jostling about outside the grounds.

Alice Roosevelt had served five times as a bridesmaid: in Boston at the marriage of Mr. and Mrs. George C. Lee, Jr.; in Albany, for Mr. and Mrs. David Goodrich; in New York at the marriages of Mr. and Mrs. Theodore Douglas Robinson and Mr. and Mrs. Franklin Delano Roosevelt, and in Philadelphia at the marriage of the Robert Goelets. Yet at her own wedding, she was to have no bridesmaids. It was reported that her half-sister, Ethel (now Mrs. Richard Derby of Oyster Bay), held her flowers during the ceremony, but she does not recall this as a fact.

In an attempt to achieve some kind of journalistic scoop, an unknown photographer took a picture of three little girls and sent them to a newspaper, where they were publicized as being "three little flower girls." This was a total fabrication, according to Alice, done as some kind of publicity stunt. "It was purely imaginary," she says. "There were no children there. Someone later asked me who they were, and I told them they were my *aunts.*"

By 11:15 A.M., the crowd outside the White House grounds had swelled to tremendous proportions. The onlookers were curious and restless, but well-mannered and quiet. The many police on hand had little to do, and there were no incidents. Carriages—some three hundred in all—and a few cars stretched along the avenue for two or three blocks, slowly moving up to the entrance opposite the Treasury Building to discharge their fortunate passengers. Nicholas Longworth had arrived considerably earlier, at about 10:30, followed by some of the other members of the wedding party and several of the Cabinet members and other special guests, all with red or blue cards, which entitled them to enter the Southwest Gate, across from the State, War and Navy Department Building. The regular guests, with white cards, began lining up at the east entrance, which was not opened until 11:15.

The first carriage to arrive at the Southwest Gate was reported to contain Mr. and Mrs. Franklin Delano Roosevelt. However, Mrs. Longworth says that Eleanor Roosevelt was pregnant and would not attend. Nor would one of Nick's sisters, who was in the same condition. "You just didn't do that sort of thing then," she said. In fact, she gave this as one reason why she did not have any bridesmaids. All of her close friends were married and "no one thought of having married people." Besides, she added, briskly disposing of the subject, "I think they're *peculiar*—bridesmaid's processions."

There was some confusion as the carriages maneuvered for place in the separate lines. Apparently, the Department of Streets had decided to fill in some holes along one of the roads, and had left half a dozen asphalt barrels and boards in unfortunate locations. Skirting these, some of the coachmen arrived at the gate for red or blue tickets when they had white, and vice versa. When turning to get into the proper line, they either had to lose their places or else had to risk nasty looks and mutterings by trying to squeeze in where they thought they rightfully belonged.

The only real catastrophe occurred when a large automobile, painted dark blue and brown, headed for the gate at "a smashing speed," pausing just long enough for the footman to hold up a red card. Those close by saw the German coat of arms on the door, and some recognized the German Ambassador and Baroness Speck von Sternburg inside. After this display of mechanical ferocity, the machine suddenly died, 20 yards from the gate. The chauffeur leaped out, his face distorted with anger, and nearly yanked off his arm trying to crank the motor into life, much to the amusement of the onlookers. When it was apparent that no amount of energy was going to get results, Baron von Sternburg stepped out, gave his hand to the Baroness, and escorted her up the road to the White House entrance, leaving the chauffeur in a state of utter fury.

The eyes of the crowd now turned to the roof of the State Department Building, where a group of men were stationed with a large time ball. Precisely at noon the ball dropped. The wedding was ready to begin.

At a few minutes before noon, the bride met her father in the upstairs hall. Together they went down in the new elevator to the State Dining Room. At 12 o'clock, on the arm of the President, she proceeded through the great crowd of guests in the East Room along an aisle formed by white satin ribbons to a broad dais with an improvised altar set up in front of the east window.

The East Room, which had been completely done over some three years earlier, retained its old proportions, but was much lighter than in the day of Nellie Grant's wedding. It was bright with flowers: long-stemmed American Beauty roses, white and pink rhododendron, white roses, and garlands of smilax, all set against a background of gold and white. Behind the altar, the east window had been draped with shining cloth of gold, with Easter lilies arranged to form a sunburst. The dais was covered with a richly colored Oriental rug. The kneeling stand for the couple was decorated with clusters of bride's roses, tied with white ribbons. The entire lower floor of the White House was also blanketed with flowers of all kinds, along with palm trees, asparagus ferns, and other greens.

The beauty and anticipation so overcame one female guest, Mrs. MacVeagh, that at this point she fainted and had to be carried out in the arms of a military aide, missing the whole ceremony.

Alice passed down an aisle lined by 12 military aides (among them was Lieutenant U. S. Grant, III, Fred and Ida's 24-year-old son) and by the eight ushers: Buckner Wallingford, Longworth's brother-in-law; Larz Anderson, a Longworth cousin, of Washington; Guy Norman, Quincy Adams Shaw, Jr., and Francis R. Bangs, all of Boston; Frederick Winthrop of New York; another Longworth brother-in-law, Viscount Charles de Chambrun, formerly with the French Embassy, and Theodore Roosevelt, Jr., brother of the bride.

As the bride entered, the Marine Band, under the direction of Lieutenant William Santelman, struck up the *Lohengrin* music. Unattended except by her father, "Princess" Alice moved gracefully down the ribboned aisle, so regal and so startlingly beautiful that many of the thousand guests gasped and not a few of the ladies found themselves crying openly at the sheer delight of it all! She was dressed in a gown of heavy white satin, in princess style, trimmed with diamonds on the yoke, and with a train of silver brocaded material that trailed behind her on the green velvet carpet. The train's actual length is uncertain, having been described as "six feet" (too little) in one account and as much as "six yards" (too long) in another. The train was topped by the long, voluminous tulle veil, pinned to the only part of the ensemble that gave the bride any trouble in dressing—her high pompadour, which had to be firm enough to hold both the veil and a wreath of orange blossoms.

The gown was trimmed with cream rose-point lace that had come from her mother's and grandmother's wedding dresses. Mrs. Longworth says that she had forgotten the origins of the lace, but on reflecting remarked, "It was point lace, that's rather *elderly*, so that's right."

Completing her ensemble were long white kid gloves, the diamond necklace given her by her fiancé, the diamond brooch from her parents, and two bracelets presented by the German Kaiser. For her bridal bouquet, she carried a shower of white orchids.

At the end of the aisle, the bride was met by the best man, Thomas Nelson Parkins, of Boston, and by Mr. Longworth, dressed in the traditional Prince Albert frock coat (with a moonstone in his pearl-gray tie for luck). In "floods of sunlight," she was then led to the altar, where the Episcopalian Bishop of Washington, the Right Reverend Henry Yates Satterlee, waited. Alice and her father, Nick and the Bishop mounted the dais. The brief ceremony took place in the exact spot where the last wedding of a White House daughter, Nellie Grant Sartoris, had been performed. Nellie herself, now a widow of nearly 50, was one of the guests—wearing a champagne-colored velvet costume trimmed with Russian sable and the diamond-and-pearl necklace she had received as a wedding present thirty-two years before.

At exactly 12:15, a functionary sedately walked out on the knoll in the White House grounds, with megaphone in hand. The ceremony was over, he announced. He began barking numbers toward the line of carriages parked along the street. Some of the guests, not invited for the wedding breakfast, began to depart. As the first one, Justice White of the Supreme Court, came out, the onlookers strained forward to catch a glimpse of notables whom they might recognize. The jovial mood of the moment was caught by an article in *The New York Times* on the following day, describing the Speaker of the House.

When "Uncle Joe" Cannon was seen coming down the walk, twenty cameras closed in about the gate where he must come come out. He saw what was in store for him and laughed. Then he stopped and bowed to the platoon of snapshooters. They all snapped together. Then he turned in another position, took the inevitable cigar from his mouth and sang out:

"Now all together, ready, fire!" They fired. Then he swung his hat off and called out again: "Come on, boys. Get ready, three times up. Now!"

The crowd cheered and hundreds swung their hats in the air. . . .

With the ceremony over, the newly married couple retired to the private dining room to share an intimate breakfast with the rest of the bridal party. Among the delicacies served were rare fruits from the noted conservatories of H. C. Frick, including grapes, strawberries, mushrooms, and a new type of pear, of which there were only a couple of hundred in existence—the "Princess Alice." Other items on the menu were salads, pâtés, assorted sandwiches, ice-cream hearts, petits fours, champagne, claret punch, and lemonade.

There were several wedding cakes, the most unusual being one in four tiers, two and a half feet high and decorated with silver balls, raised fleurs-de-lis, delicate lacy patterns, and a statue of Cupid at the top, ringing a silver wedding bell. It is not known exactly which cake the bride cut, but legend has it that Alice, impatient because the knife supplied was not sharp enough, seized the sword of a White House aide and impetuously slashed out the first slice. Alice, however, on hearing this story, said disdainfully, "Any news accounts of the day which say I *seized* a sword and brandished it aloft before slicing the cake are certainly not correct. That makes me sound like a rude hoyden. I certainly did not leap on Charlie McCawley and take his sword. He was standing beside me and politely offered it, and so I used it to cut the cake."

Asked if she thought that the somewhat misinformed press coverage of the event would have been more accurate if reporters had been present at the ceremony, she replied, "It would have made very little difference. It doesn't seem to be much better today, does it?"

So much went on that the bride barely had time to eat any breakfast, though when an aide toasted her, she is said to have tilted back her head and downed a full glass of champagne without drawing a breath. At one point, she was presented with a little Manchurian poodle, with a huge orange bow on his collar. "Oh, you darling!" she cried, in one report, and she "thrust her plate in one direction and her glass in another and seized the puppy and, regardless of the wedding finery, clasped him in her arms till he was glad to get away."

Next, Nick Longworth arrived with a fistful of congratulatory telegrams and cable messages from abroad. Among them was one which amused Alice particularly. It was date-lined Union City, Pennsylvania. "OUR BABY BORN AT 12 O'CLOCK. HAVE NAMED HER ALICE." Her favorite read: "I ALWAYS KNEW OLD NICK WOULD GET YOU."

While the bridal party was enjoying breakfast, followed by impromptu singing and dancing in the small dining room, the President and Mrs. Roosevelt were in the Blue Room receiving some seven hundred guests, who were then ushered into the State Dining Room for what was described as "a very elaborate and delicious breakfast."

The newlyweds finally left the White House at about four that afternoon. That they got away almost totally unobserved attests to the ingenuity of a special squad assigned to plan their departure. Outside the White House, the crowd (now a little cold and hungry) began to surge back and forth as rumors spread that the young couple would come out one gate, then out another. Finally, an automobile belonging to John R. McLean appeared at the West Gate on Executive Avenue. This must surely be it, thought the watchers, con-verging on the partially guarded point. Then, to their conster-nation, another automobile, belonging to Mr. Longworth, appeared at the Southwest Gate. The crowd split in half. While debates were going on as to which vehicle would be used, a *third* automobile drove up and parked directly in front of the White House, headed north. This, too, belonged to Mr. Longworth. The farce was carried still further when a *fourth* automobile appeared at the East Gate.

Then, all at once, the McLean automobile started off to the south. Although no one but the uniformed chauffeur was in it, the crowd, sensing action at last, started in pursuit, think-ing that it would stop at one of the gates and pick up the couple. Not so. It disappeared behind the State Department Building, where it deliberately gave away its presence by an occasional fit of honking, which was answered in turn by Longworth automobile number one. The exchange of honks kept the crowd on its toes.

Just about the time the crowd was getting discouraged and rumors began that Alice and Nick intended to stay at the party until late in the evening, out popped the newlyweds, followed by a few young laughing guests. They simply went to the Red Room, raised a window and stepped through to the back steps of the White House, from the South Portico, on the garden side. At that precise moment, the McLean machine darted up to receive the young couple. Nick dexterously fielded a bag of rice hurled by an enthusiastic friend—and they were off. Not more than fifteen or twenty of the patient watchers outside even caught a glimpse of the bride (in a plumed hat and brown dress that she remembers as "dingy") as the car careened up the road and turned into 15th Street.

One movie photographer, told by his boss to come back with news footage, at any cost, is said to have been so frightened at the consequences of missing the bridal party that he took his employer's words in the broadest sense and hired an automobile and another couple to reenact the scene. Moviegoers of the day, looking at the jumpy, out-of-focus action, were probably just as impressed with the results as if the photographer had filmed the real thing.

The McLean automobile had been carefully selected for its assignment. It was described as "a twelve horsepower machine, made in Paris in 1901 for George Heath, the winner of the first Vanderbilt Cup Race in 1904. He used it for racing until Mr. McLean bought it . . . ," after which a limousine body was added.

Another reason Alice and Nick chose McLean's car was that they were headed for his country place, "Friendship," on the Tenallytown Road, where they planned to stay for a few days before traveling south on their honeymoon trip. Their ultimate destination, Cuba, was kept such a good secret that they were able to arrive on the island with relatively little publicity or annoyance from sightseers.

The honeymoon in Cuba turned out to be delightful. Alice had been there a few years earlier and, as Teddy Roosevelt's daughter, had enjoyed the finest in hospitality. The Cubans had sent her the most magnificent wedding gift of all—a necklace of 63 enormous matching pearls with a diamond clasp, valued in 1906 at $25,000. Now, with her new husband, she was equally well received, and everyone went out of the way to show the couple the sights of the island, whether along the coast by boat or over the Rough Rider trail to San Juan Hill. One of Alice's recollections of the trip was the return from Santiago and a heated debate with Nick under the Peace Tree. "I have not the faintest recollection what it was all about," wrote Alice in her memoirs, adding, "I remember the feeling that I held my own and was successfully obnoxious."

After two weeks, they returned to Washington and established themselves in a gracious mansion at 18th and I Streets.

It soon became a featured point on the regular sightseeing tour of Washington, where the open buses paused long enough for the guide with the megaphone to tell the story about the marriage of Princess Alice and the Congressman from Ohio.

Today, a grandmother of 83 and a widow (Nick died in 1931), Alice is still such an institution in the capital that she was referred to in a recent profile as "the other Washington Monument." When asked about that day in 1906, she referred to the affair as "just a wedding of family and friends and acquaintances" and capsules the day in this fashion: "Got up. Ate breakfast. Got dressed. Walked down with Father. Had ceremony. Greeted people. Cut cake with Charlie McCawley's sword. Put on dingy dress. Said goodbye to all the aides, Douglas MacArthur among them. Drove to 'Friendship,' had our wedding trip."

CHAPTER XV

# A MEMORABLE GARDEN PARTY

URING the third week in June 1911, the whole world was focusing attention on a great historic event, the coronation of George V, King of Great Britain and Emperor of India, with all of the pomp and circumstance attendant thereto. It seemed rather petty that *The Independent*, a weekly magazine, should have picked this particular time to run an editorial downgrading the British monarch as "nothing remarkable or unusual" and "the puppet of his Ministers," a man who "must obey the will of the untitled Herbert Henry Asquith." The editors pointed out how absurd it was that "millions are spent on the pageantry," that all of Britain had gone out of its mind, and that the very reason for the splendor and the attendance by the highest-ranking nobility had long since been "lost to our democratic memory."

Why this ungracious censure?

The fact of the matter is that the editors of *The Independent* were miffed. While the rest of the American press lauded this magnificent British spectacle, it was unjustly all but ignoring the significance of an event at home, just because it offered "no processions, no ceremonial, no show." That was the Silver Wedding Anniversary celebration of President and Mrs. William Howard Taft, on Monday, June 19th, one of the largest receptions in Washington's history, to which more than 5,000 guests had been invited. "There is nothing to describe," said *The Independent* proudly, "for it was very simple; only the great heart of the people went out to their President to felicitate him and her on their happy domestic occasion. It had no political significance, for Mr. Taft had been inaugurated before —but so, in fact, had King George."

The Tafts had been married just 17 days after the White House wedding of Grover Cleveland and Frances Folsom in 1886, at a time when Taft was a lowly assistant county solicitor in Ohio. Although they had been born and brought up in the same town and their fathers were warm friends and lawyers practicing at the same bar, they did not meet until Taft was 21 and graduated from Yale, and his wife, then Helen ("Nellie") Herron of Cincinnati, was 18. They had become engaged in May of 1885, six years after their first meeting, and shortly after their marriage they had moved into a new home, overlooking the Ohio River, built on a plot of land given to the bride by her father. A year later, Taft was appointed a judge of the Superior Court of Ohio, and after that he moved up the ladder fast.

A huge, amiable man, Taft was the perfect host for a White House party that was "the most brilliant social affair" of the time (despite the assertion of *The Independent* that there was "nothing to describe"). Everyone liked him. Alice Roosevelt adored him, and said that he never became irritable or even looked cross; during the most exasperating days of their trip to the East, he looked pleasant and cool after shaking hands for hours in the hot sun. His enormous size may have had something to do with his genial disposition. In 1911 he weighed 332 pounds. He liked all food—and lots of it—except eggs, and Mrs. Jaffray, the White House housekeeper, reported that for breakfast he would eat a 12-ounce steak, two oranges, several pieces of toast and butter, and a "vast quantity" of coffee with cream and sugar. Shortly after the Silver Anniversary, the doctor sentenced him to eat only a six-ounce steak for breakfast: "Things are in a sad state of affairs when a man can't even call his gizzard his own," grumbled Taft, amiably. Mrs. Jaffray said he was the best-natured of the four Presidents she served under for seventeen years.

Mrs. Taft, too, was universally liked. She was described by *Good Housekeeping* in that year (1911) as "an ideal home-maker," and "the type of woman we would all like to be." She filled the White House with flowers and with music, and, during the holidays, with happy young people attracted by the three Taft children—22-year-old Robert (the future Senator), studious 20-year-old Helen, and Charles, 14.

The Tafts wanted to enjoy their anniversary and to have everyone share their happiness. But they were temperamentally poles apart from the sticky sentimentality that pervaded the Rutherford B. Hayes anniversary, thirty-four years earlier. Helen Taft's parents, the Herrons, were lifelong friends of the Hayes family and had been present on that occasion, when Helen's youngest sister was sentimentally christened Lucy Hayes Herron. Helen herself, then a 16-year-old girl, seems to have accompanied her parents. Possibly she remembered the event, all these years later, and determined to do something different.

Taking a gamble, the Tafts planned an enormous garden party, to be held in the evening on the South Lawn. There were many worried moments that morning under an overcast sky, especially after Professor Willis Moore, Chief of the Weather Bureau, made a personal visit to the White House to report gloomily, "Conditions are most unfavorable. There will probably be showers this afternoon and tonight. It is raining almost everywhere, even in the British Isles and Scandinavia." The refreshment tables were set up indoors, with appropriate caution.

The rains fortunately never materialized, or as one wag put it, "the only thing wet was Mr. Moore."

By that evening, the yard was bright with strings of colored electric light bulbs and lanterns and alive with people in dresses, suits, uniforms, and costumes of every conceivable hue.

There were 5,000 guests (one account says as many as 8,000; and three years later Helen Taft herself could not remember how many invitations had been issued, but guessed there were "four or five thousand people present"). Outside the fences, the newspapers reported the next morning, another 15,000 spectators took in the lights, the laughter, the crowds, and the music. One White House historian said that it looked "as gay as any musical-comedy scene."

In an article three years later in *The Delineator*, Nellie Taft recalled:

It was a night garden-party with such illuminations as are quite beyond description. Every tree and bush was ablaze with myriads of tiny colored lights; the whole stately mansion was outlined in a bright white glow; there were strings of bobbing, fantastic lanterns wherever a string would go; the great fountain was playing at its topmost height in every color of the rainbow; while on the gleaming point of the Monument and on the flag stretched in the breeze from the staff on the top of the White House shone the steady gleam of two searchlights.

On the hour of eight, the Presidential procession marched out into the grounds on a carpet, led by military officers, to the accompaniment of the scarlet-uniformed Marine Band and the acclaim of the guests. The marchers proceeded in a large circle, arriving at an illuminated arch by a large tree, halfway between the house and the fountain, where the Tafts and others in the receiving line were to stand. Mrs. Taft was wearing a white satin gown, heavily embroidered with silver roses and carnations, and a long embroidered train. On her head perched the expensive diamond tiara that the President had given her as her anniversary gift.

The receiving of guests followed strict protocol, with members of the diplomatic corps at the head of the line, followed by lesser notables, all of whom were officially introduced. It was reported that the Tafts shook hands with everybody, and this must have taken close to three hours.

At about eleven, dancing began in the East Room, and a buffet dinner was served from heavily laden tables in the State Dining Room. Champagne and Rhine wine punch flowed freely. Tables had been set up on the West Terrace for those who preferred to eat out of doors and watch the fountain. The prize display was a huge cake, described in one newspaper as being:

> .... circled with twenty-five crystal hearts imbedded in scrolls at regular intervals. Out of the top were seen dainty cherubs whom the froth of a frosted sea seems to have cast up against a great cornucopia filled with reproductions of a rare exotic of the gardener's art, with clinging angels clamoring for them. Around the great circle of confectionery, and alternating with the hearts, were twenty-five miniature silken reproductions of Stars and Stripes and the President's flag. At the base were roses, cut from their stems and flung against the towering sides. Fluttering on the edge of the cake were turtle doves in their customary attitude as the poet sees them.

It was not until two the next morning that the music stopped, the final guest departed, the lights were dimmed, and the delighted, but exhausted, Tafts had retired upstairs to bed. Mrs. Taft called it "the greatest event of our four years in the White House."

The crowds, the champagne, the late hour and, above all, the gaiety of this garden party had been as different as anyone could have wished from the sedate East Room reception given by President and Mrs. Hayes—who served nothing more intoxicating than coffee and who ended their celebration promptly at midnight, even though it was New Year's Eve.

It was highly appropriate that the Tafts' Silver Anniversary should have taken place in the White House. During the quarter-century of their marriage, all but a single year had been spent in the public service.

CHAPTER XVI

## "HALF ANGEL, HALF GRECIAN STATUE"

OME two weeks after his election to the Presidency in the fall of 1912, Woodrow Wilson was vacationing in Bermuda with his wife and three daughters. He had planned the trip specifically as "an escape from the confusion and publicity." Hence, he had asked the press to respect the privacy of his family and not to include the ladies when they took his photograph. The reporters obeyed his wishes, with the exception of one brash young man who aimed his camera at daughter Jessie, no doubt expecting some kind of journalistic scoop.

Wilson is said to have blanched noticeably, then reddened. With fists clenched, he approached the intruder, then, gaining control of himself, he roared, "You're no gentleman! I want to give you the worst thrashing you've ever had in your life—and what's more, I'm perfectly able to do it!"

Whether this description of the incident is accurate or not, it does convey the protective environment in which the Wilson girls were brought up and the extent to which—during the course of their father's career as college president, Governor, and Chief Executive—they were shielded from publicity. At the time of their holiday in Bermuda, two of the girls, Jessie and Eleanor, were successfully hiding secret engagements from the prying press. Wilson insisted that all the women in the household, including his wife, Ellen, should remain unspoiled and be allowed to develop outside the public eye. He refused to let them engage in any work, social or personal, which had, or might seem to have, political overtones. His daughters were Margaret, Jessie, and Eleanor ("Nellie"), respectively 26, 25, and 23 years old when Wilson became President in the spring of 1913.

No two young ladies could have been more unlike in personality and temperament than Jessie Woodrow Wilson and the bride who had preceded her in the White House, Alice Roosevelt Longworth. Jessie was quiet, religious, studious, and extremely close to her father. She had a frail prettiness, with a shy, appealing manner and a natural sweetness of temperament. Although referred to as a "sensible young woman," she was by no means dull and adapted herself well to the social demands made on her when the family moved to Washington.

Woodrow Wilson had what was almost a fixation about family unity and solidarity. For a man in his position, he devoted a remarkable amount of time to his wife and daughters. Yet it was never enough. He could not face the time when the family might be broken up, either by marriage or by death. His possessiveness was openly apparent whenever some young man began to show something more than friendship for one of his girls. Eleanor later recalled that, although her father strove to remain polite to these suitors, he would invariably exclaim, "What on earth does she see in that fool?"

Mrs. Wilson, who faced her daughters' future more realistically, would then reply, "Is he a fool because he is interested in your daughter?"

Jessie herself tried to avoid any serious attachment and was constantly trying to discourage her suitors from proposing. When they did, she would turn them down with tears. Though she was not sentimental, she could not help being extremely sensitive about the feelings of other people. "When she did succeed in expressing her love," wrote Eleanor in her memoirs, "we were deeply touched and her rare moments of anger always surprised us. It was usually on the heights of the soul that she lived, however, and we all recognized this and adored her as one a little apart from the rest of us, not quite on this earth."

Jessie was a scholar and had earned her Phi Beta Kappa at Goucher College, Baltimore, where she majored in political science. She also possessed considerable talent for writing and art. Her most serious interest was in social work, and when the Board of Missionaries turned down her request to become a missionary because she was not physically strong enough for assignment to the field, she took up settlement welfare work. While the Wilson home was in Princeton, she lived during the week at the Lighthouse in Philadelphia and also worked for the YWCA, on whose behalf she made numerous speeches.

Also interested in settlement work during those years was a good-looking young man named Francis Bowes Sayre. He was born in 1885 in South Bethlehem, Pennsylvania. He spent two years at the Hill School in Pottstown and two years at Lawrenceville, from which he graduated in 1904. He entered Williams College, where he was Phi Beta Kappa, manager of the football team, and founder and president of the Good Government Club. In the fall of 1909, he entered Harvard Law School, from which he graduated in 1912. During undergraduate summers he spent his time as a missionary assistant in Labrador with the noted Dr. Wilfred Grenfell, giving medical aid to Eskimos, Indians, and fishermen; right after graduation from law school he worked for several months in the summer of 1912 in Alaska and northern Siberia. Later that year, he entered the office of the District Attorney of New York, Charles S. Whitman, and moved into an apartment with his mother near Columbia University.

Despite their mutual interests, Mr. Sayre and Miss Wilson

might never have met if it had not been for a delightfully colorful character, "Auntie Blanche."

Miss Blanche Nevin, an eccentric sculptor, poet, painter, and world traveler, had met the Wilsons on holiday in Bermuda in 1910. She modeled a head of Governor Wilson, while she listened to him speak proudly of his children, Jessie in particular. Auntie Blanche turned an eye on Jessie as a likely wife for her favorite nephew Francis, or Frank. In the spring of 1912, with calculated shrewdness, she invited Jessie and Eleanor to visit her for a weekend at her charming old country place, "Windsor Forges," near Churchtown, Pennsylvania. Frank was on holiday during the law school's spring recess, and she also invited him, determined she would engineer a match.

Although such arrangements usually end up with the couple cordially disliking each other, Eleanor later recalled: "They were instantly attracted to each other, and for the first time in our lives Jessie seemed to have forgotten my existence."

Only Auntie Blanche could have pulled off such an unblushingly calculated plot. She was herself an unforgettable personality. She was in the habit of adorning her ample person with an uncountable number of bracelets, necklaces, earrings, rings, and other jewelry. Her pet accessory was described as "a silver snake belt," so constructed that its various parts tinkled like wind chimes and clacked like castanets whenever she moved. The girls could hear her coming from anywhere in the house.

When interviewed for this book in the spring of 1966, Frank Sayre had the fondest memories of his aunt, her home, and his first meeting with Jessie.

"My aunt's house, 'Windsor Forges,' was a rare and beautiful place," he said. "I used to go there often to visit for a day or so. It was an old-fashioned house. I think James Buchanan either lived there or near there. My Aunt Blanche wrote verse, painted, was a sculptress, and traveled a great deal. She was a distinctive, charming person, and one of the most colorful I have ever known."

Asked if he knew his aunt was matchmaking for him, he grinned and said, "I imagine she did wonder if it might not be possible for me to win Woodrow Wilson's daughter. I don't remember if she told me that Jessie and Nell were coming to visit, but we were all invited for the same few days."

About the visit he said, "On the day Jessie and Nell were due, I went to meet them at the nearest railway station. We had no cars then, just horses. It was a little country station. There was no office. I drove them back, and for the next several days I took them driving around.

"I quite fell in love with Jessie. She was so wonderful, everyone loved her.

"One day during their visit, I drove them to where we could take the electric trolley, and I took them to a Wild West show in Lancaster. It was a very happy afternoon in spite of the rain. They departed the next day."

During the course of that first weekend, Auntie Blanche kept pulling Eleanor aside and urging her to let Jessie and Frank have time to themselves so that true love could take its course. Then with tactics drawn straight from comic opera, she would attempt to tiptoe to a position where she could eavesdrop on the young couple and determine how her plans were going. Naturally, she could be heard as easily as a cat with a bell around its neck. It is a wonder that the romance flourished at all. Yet perhaps Frank and Jessie were drawn together in part by their amusement over the antics of Auntie Blanche.

On the way home, Eleanor could not refrain from teasing her sister about her new beau and tried to determine just how serious Jessie was about Frank. She was curious, and to some extent she was also concerned. What if Jessie finally had found the man she wanted? It would suddenly break up their wonderful family. So Eleanor began to talk about welfare work and its importance and how fine it was that Jessie was devoting her life to helping the settlement program and the YWCA.

All at once Jessie turned to her, with a far, faraway look on her face and a deep blush in her cheeks, and said in a musical and dreamy voice, *"Oh, Nell, he has asked me if he might call!"*

Mr. Sayre explained in his interview that he was not able to call often. Jessie was working at a settlement house in Philadelphia, while he, after finishing law school, went out West to work in Montana for the summer, then on to Alaska. They did correspond, however. That September (1912), Frank got his position in the New York District Attorney's office.

"When I returned to New York in the fall," said Francis Sayre, "I wrote to Jessie and arranged to take her for a drive from Princeton. I was to meet her at two o'clock at her home. Her father, Woodrow Wilson, then Governor of New Jersey, opened the door. When I asked if Jessie was in, he told me that she was out, teaching her Sunday School class. Just then Jessie came down the stairs, and we all laughed together." They drove out into the peaceful countryside behind what Sayre has called "a very understanding horse." "That afternoon, October 27th, I asked her to marry me," he said. Taken by surprise, apparently, Jessie asked him for a little time.

In his memoirs, *Glad Adventure*, Francis Sayre described the outcome in words he would perhaps not choose in a face-to-face interview: "On the following Tuesday evening I was back in Princeton and called at the Wilson house. Jessie met me at the door, threw her gray cloak about her, and led the way out into the foggy, deserted street and down a dark pathway. Then, almost without a word she raised her face to mine and put herself into my arms. Our hearts beat close together, and Heaven that night touched the earth. Under the misty moon we plighted our troth. The evening of October 29th will always be a holy time for me."

Woodrow Wilson was at this time in the final hectic week of his campaign for the Presidency. Jessie and Frank agreed not to tell him about their engagement until the election was over. The following incident, recalled by Eleanor, shows that the great strain of keeping her secret from the close-knit family was almost too much for Jessie.

Two days after Jessie had accepted Frank, on Thursday, October 31st, Mrs. Wilson took her three daughters to New York to attend a big Democratic political rally, where Woodrow Wilson was to make his last campaign speech in New York before thousands of people in Madison Square Garden. While they were dressing that evening, Mrs. Wilson noticed that Jessie looked rather pale.

"Are you ill, dear?" she asked.

Jessie glanced down sheepishly and did not say anything, whereupon her mother scurried off to order some medicine. Alone with her sister, Jessie began to giggle uncontrollably, almost hysterically. "Nellie," she said, "Mother wants me to take medicine—can one take medicine for love?" It was at that moment that Eleanor and Margaret knew for sure that Jessie was overwhelmingly in love with Frank. They threw their arms around their sister and all three began weeping and laughing.

When their mother returned, Jessie took the medicine without even knowing what she was doing. Then they all set out for Madison Square Garden, with Jessie hardly aware that her father stood on the threshold of becoming President of the United States.

Exactly a week later, on November 5th, Woodrow Wilson won the election. Late that night, as the bell of Nassau Hall rang in triumph, Princeton students marched by torchlight to the nearby Wilson house and gave the President-elect a rousing ovation. It may have been that night, or early the next day, that Frank and Jessie also received the congratulations due to them.

Even though the young couple had kept their secret for a

week, the Wilson family may have suspected what was coming. Woodrow Wilson had been too heavily involved in political life to pay much attention to the comings and goings of the young men who called on his daughters. One afternoon, however, as he walked up the front steps, the Governor met a young man he did not remember, coming out of the door. He smiled at him politely in passing, Eleanor recalls in her memoirs, and the young man in turn tipped his hat. That evening Wilson asked his wife who "that nice-looking sandy-haired boy" was.

Mrs. Wilson looked at him with a twinkle in her eye. "You'd better stop and make his acquaintance the next time," she said. "That's Frank Sayre, and I think you're going to be his father-in-law!"

That was enough to change Wilson's opinion. For the next hour or so, Mrs. Wilson tried her best to assure her husband that Jessie knew what she was doing and that this young man was really worthy of her. In the end, Wilson grew so fond of Sayre that he grudgingly admitted in a letter a month and a half after the engagement was officially announced that summer, ". . . we love our prospective son-in-law more and more. He is almost good enough for Jessie."

It did not hurt matters a bit that Sayre had frequently been likened to the President in appearance. He had "the strong Wilson jaw," the "Wilson smile," and the alert "Wilson eye."

Francis Sayre's resemblance to Woodrow Wilson also helped to get him past the sharp-eyed reporters, who were often watching the Princeton house of the President-elect when the young man came out by train from New York for an evening's visit. Mr. Sayre, when interviewed, said he and Jessie did not want the public to know of their engagement until very shortly before the wedding (for this reason, he did not attend the Inauguration in March 1913). "Jessie and I were always doing our best to escape newsmen," he recalled. "We had to make special arrangements to meet outside the White House, although people said I looked like the President, so that when I went to the White House I passed for a cousin."

Asked whether his courtship was plagued by the presence of Secret Service men and whether Jessie, like more recent Presidents' daughters, had to be accompanied everywhere by them, he replied, "No, Jessie could go about at her own pleasure."

July 2, 1913, was the date set for the announcement from the White House. The engagement party was held on the 4th at "Harlakenden," in Cornish, New Hampshire, the recently-rented family summer home. Wilson was not on hand, having a Fourth of July speaking engagement at Gettysburg, but he joined them the next day. Sayre spent a great deal of the summer in New Hampshire, he recalled in his interview. "Woodrow Wilson came up whenever he could, and we had a very, very happy summer."

One revealing report in the papers, the day after the White House announcement, stated that Sayre's business associates had no idea that he was even acquainted with the President's daughter! The news eclipsed accounts of a $100,000 jewel robbery. The District Attorney called his young associate into his office to express personal felicitations. "Mr. Sayre is a man of a great deal of ability," he said later, "and I have grown very fond of him in the year he has been working with me."

The public immediately wanted to know more about this young man. What kind of a future did he have? "My ambitions are all along the lines of social service," said Sayre in an interview. "I have been interested in settlement work ever since I entered Williams College in 1905. While in Harvard Law School I did work for the Boston Social Settlement. I concluded that in a position such as the one which I now occupy there would be a better opportunity for gaining a knowledge of human nature, which is the underlying basis of all social work."

What about his politics? "Why, I'm a Republican," he admitted, "although I am not a strict party man. I voted for

Governor Wilson because I thought he was the best man, in spite of my admiration for Colonel Roosevelt."

The wedding plans? Sayre replied that he preferred to have them disclosed by his fiancée's family.

At the time of the engagement announcement, it was indicated that the wedding would take place in the White House, in late November. Sayre recalled that they arranged to have their wedding in November because he was so attached to Sir Wilfred Grenfell. "You know, Grenfell discovered how little help the Eskimos in Labrador and Newfoundland had. If they broke a leg or became sick, there was no help for them. So he built hospitals and also cruised about in a hospital ship. I spent one summer on the hospital ship and another in a hospital with him. I loved him so much, and I asked him to be best man at my wedding."

Late November was a time that was convenient for Grenfell to be in Washington. The 25th was picked as the day because it was a Tuesday, the day of Frank and Jessie's engagement.

Sayre could not recall much of a discussion about the location of the wedding and whether it should be in the White House or in a church. "Everybody agreed it was to be a White House wedding. As a family, we were all deeply devoted to Christian activities, but we wanted our wedding to be where Jessie was living. It meant so much more than to have everyone going to an outside church, especially since the Wilsons' home church was in Princeton."

An unknown reporter spread the unsettling rumor that the Wilson/Sayre wedding would be the *thirteenth* to be held in the White House! Was the bride-to-be superstitious? She was widely quoted as saying that she was not at all concerned about bad luck. Accounts varied, anyway, and some writers counted this wedding as only the eleventh, or less. Just to flout the pessimists, Jessie and Frank deliberately arranged their bridal party to include 13 people—bride, groom, bride's father, best man, maid of honor, four bridesmaids, and four ushers.

The day of the engagement announcement was a time of triumph for Miss Blanche Nevin. Auntie Blanche, noted as a sculptor and artist, also seems to have had some ambitions as a writer. To record the great event, she composed a "Song of Welcome" for the bride, which she obligingly distributed to the press around mid-July:

> Fling the door open, swing the gate wide,
> Welcome the entering feet of the bride;
> Eager the groom on the threshold stands,
> Holding his arms and his outstretched hands:
> Blessed are you who true love win;
> Jessie, come in, come in.
>
> In heat of Summer, in Winter's cold,
> This roof shall shelter young or old;
> Come weal, come woe, whate'er betide;
> Palm to palm and side to side,
> Into the house of your true love's kin,
> Jessie, come in, come in.
>
> Sweet pink clover bloom over the grass,
> Welcome the lover here with his lass;
> Pride of the golden hair and eyes,
> Blue with the luminous hue of the skies,
> Blessed are you to true love win;
> Jessie, come in, come in.

It was widely circulated and reprinted.

On September 6th, Mrs. Wilson announced through her personal secretary, Miss Isabella L. ("Belle") Hagner, that the wedding would indeed be in the White House and would take place on Tuesday afternoon, November 25th. Although she gave out no details, it was "understood" that the wedding would be "as brilliant as any that had taken place in the President's official residence."

All through August, while the Wilsons quietly enjoyed country life at "The Summer White House" in Cornish, New Hampshire, workmen were noisily and messily remodeling the interior of the Executive Mansion in Washington. Reconstruction included a slight raising of the roof, to add five bedrooms and two baths to the third floor without destroying the classic lines of the old two-story building. The rooms would be used for the first time to accommodate wedding guests in November.

Jessie and Frank themselves had little interest in the details of the ceremony. Frank had decided that he would accept a job offered by his alma mater, Williams, and that they would move to Williamstown, Massachusetts, to live after the honeymoon. They had already picked a spacious, ten-room house near the campus as their future home.

In the matter of her trousseau, Jessie revealed the appealing blend of the practical and the romantic in her personality. On the one hand, she observed "a conspicuous amount of common sense" by choosing all her dresses, except the bridal gown, from ready-to-wear stock. On the other hand, she had all her lingerie hand-made in a style of old-fashioned elegance. Jessie was *feminine* in all the most attractive meanings of the word.

On October 17th, Mrs. Wilson returned from her extended summer in New Hampshire to confer with Miss Helen Woodrow Bones, cousin of the President, about preparations. Reporters who expected her return to be an occasion for a public announcement of the wedding plans were disappointed. The ceremony, said Mrs. Wilson, would be a private affair, details of which would not be available for comment in the daily press. Following a pattern now familiar in connection with earlier weddings, the President let it be known that he and his family were discouraging presents from everyone except the close friends of the bride and groom. This proclamation moved one editor to report that Alice Roosevelt Longworth had received so many valuable gifts—despite her father's protests—that "thousands of dollars' worth of silver, cut glass, rare hangings, pictures and some jewels have never been out of storage since that date." Whether it was true or not, Wilson did not intend to have such extravagance reflect on a daughter who was moderate in her tastes and completely unspoiled.

At the same time the President was pleading for moderation, the House of Representatives, at the suggestion of James R. Mann, of Illinois, was deliberating over the purchase of an official gift. The House had not bought a joint present for Alice Roosevelt (who received presents only from the Ohio and New York delegations). The new idea was received "enthusiastically," and a committee was formed, headed by Speaker of the House Champ Clark.

"How much shall we chip in?" asked Mr. Mann. "Will five dollars a member be too high?"

"No, no!" the House is said to have replied in chorus.

The acclaim was not unanimous. Five days later, Congressman Finley H. Gray of Indiana rose to his feet on the floor of the House in heated protest. It was not the matter of losing $5 out of pocket, he assured his colleagues, since he had already given the money to the committee. However, he had made it quite clear that the $5 was to go toward Christmas presents for poor children. "I don't believe," he shouted, "that this is a fitting and proper manner for members of the House to show their respect for the President . . . or that it is the proper way for us to express our wishes to Miss Wilson. . . .

"I regard the practice of people making gifts to high officials and members of their families as a lingering shadow coming down to us from the ancient days, from the days of feudalism."

He wound up charging that the gift was "in bad taste," was "indiscreet" and an "intrusion." He then had the Clerk read the text of a letter he had sent to the committee collecting funds, specifying that his check was "for the benefit of the children who are observed every Christmas standing in the cold before the show windows looking wistfully at the simplest presents, but whose parents are without means to purchase them."

When Mr. Gray had finished his maudlin comments, Congressman Mann rose in rebuttal.

"After hearing the gentleman from Indiana," he said, "I think it will be hopeless to put into his soul the expression which finds itself in the heart of every other member of this House. The other members do not need to be told why."

An outburst of applause greeted his remarks. The House went on to establish a gift-giving precedent, which took the form of a diamond necklace and a pendant in the form of a large canary diamond, pear-shaped and 6¼ carats in weight, surrounded by 85 small diamonds. It was considered a personal, not an official gift. With it went a handsome jewel box, with an engraved inscription:

> Presented to Miss Jessie Woodrow Wilson by the members of the United States House of Representatives, as a token of their affectionate interest and regard, on her marriage, November 25, 1913.

According to Eleanor's recollection, when Jessie opened the case and saw the magnificence of the present, she suddenly collapsed in a chair and moaned in consternation, "What can a poor professor's wife do with such things?"

By the first week in November, the members of the wedding party had been decided on and announced. Dr. Wilfred Grenfell, the medical missionary from Labrador, was to serve as the best man for his old friend and helper. Margaret Wilson, eldest of the three daughters, was to be maid of honor, while the four bridesmaids were to be Eleanor Wilson; Mary White of Baltimore, a college friend of Jessie's; Adeline Mitchell Scott; and Marjorie Brown, daughter of Mrs. Wilson's cousin, Colonel E. T. Brown of Atlanta, Georgia.

The four ushers were to be Benjamin Brown Burton, of New York, who had graduated several years after Sayre from Williams and worked with him in Alaska; Dr. Scoville Clark, of Salem, Massachusetts, whom Sayre had known in Labrador; Dr. Gilbert Horrax of Montclair, New Jersey, who was a classmate of Sayre's at Williams; and Charles Evans Hughes, Jr., son of the Supreme Court Justice and a friend of Sayre's at Harvard Law School.

The minister selected to officiate was the Reverend Sylvester W. Beach, pastor of the Presbyterian church which the Wilsons had attended while living in Princeton, and at which Jessie had taught a Bible class.

The Reverend John Nevin Sayre, Frank's brother, an Episcopalian missionary formerly serving in China, would arrive from Europe in time to assist the minister at the ceremony. The place selected was the East Room.

Reports stated that invitations had been sent out to fewer than seven hundred guests and that the only ones invited on an official, rather than personal, basis would be the diplomatic corps, Supreme Court Justices, "with their respective womenfolk," the Vice President and Mrs. Marshall, and Cabinet members and their wives. Few Senators or Congressmen were invited, and then only if they were close to the family. Almost no members of Washington society were asked to attend. Since the Wilsons had been in residence such a short time, and since the Sayres were from out of town, they had between them only a sprinkling of old friends in the capital.

As in the case of the Roosevelt/Longworth wedding, there was considerable hullabaloo about the matter of uniform. Should diplomats appear in gold lace and military officers in full dress? The resultant debate was unresolved until almost the last minute. Then, to the complete satisfaction of the guests and outside onlookers, these officials appeared in all their finery. In addition, the White House had a corps of young and handsome Army, Navy, and Marine officers to act as aides. Resplendent in full-dress uniform, they were to draw the admiring eyes of many a bridesmaid and female guest.

A topic of great discussion—and for reasons different from those stimulated by previous weddings—was the bridal gown. Although Jessie had "succumbed to the prevailing French modes" and had included several Continental imports in her trousseau, she had decided that the wedding gown should be "all-American." The soft, shimmering satin fabric was specially ordered from a textile mill in Paterson, New Jersey, in what many lauded as a "patriotic" move, while the gown itself was sewn in New York City. Although concealed from the gaze of all outsiders, it was described as having a three-yard train of lustrous satin that blended beautifully with Jessie's blonde hair and fair complexion. The foundation skirt was in the prevailing silhouette—close at the ankles, with a slight crinkled effect at the hips. The skirt was to be slashed at the wide back seams, to make for easier movement, but with the slashes completely concealed by the train. The top of the gown was a surplice draped in satin, "of a purer white tone than is usually employed by the Paris couturiers." The wedding veil was of conventional tulle, held in place by orange blossoms.

On November 22, Cincinnati papers carried an announcement from the Home Products Committee of the Chamber of Commerce:

> We congratulate you on your loyalty to your country in ordering your trousseau entirely of American manufacture. Your patriotism is a good omen, and will do much to further the cause of more patronage of home industries by our people. All good wishes for your happiness.

The announcement was not entirely correct, as Jessie had selected among her trousseau gowns one just off the boat from Paris, of ivory-tinted velvet, a long-piled weave of the finest spun silk. She had also purchased a second dress from the French Callot sisters, who were "famous for designing gowns for the youthful and slender." This was of pure white satin, with a round, scant skirt and what was described as a "minaret tunic," somewhat modified to suit American tastes.

It was noted, too, that Jessie's engagement ring was getting a great deal of attention—a pure white stone in a conventional setting of dull gold.

As the presents started coming in, it was evident that President Wilson's protests had not been much more effective than Teddy Roosevelt's. By mid-November, the gifts were overflowing the largest of the second-floor apartments in the White House, where they were on display for intimate friends of the family. An article in *The New York Times*, referring to the presents, said, "... the exaggerated statements concerning their value are most distasteful to her [Jessie]." It then went on to emphasize the lavishness of the display by adding, "Silver plates, compotes and bowls of various sizes have been received by the gross, rather than by the dozen...." One of the rarest gifts was a pure white vicuña rug, presented by the Peruvian Minister and Señora Pezet, which was used at the wedding ceremony itself. The appropriate legend from the Andes mountains was that vicuña fur brought good luck to its owner.

Another imposing gift was the set of silver plates received from Mr. and Mrs. Andrew Carnegie. Auntie Blanche sent an antique "hand-wrought Roman silver lamp of the Flying Mercury design." Jessie also received a cookbook containing "all the good old recipes grandmother used to make." It had been compiled from contributions sent in by some four hundred fifty wives of Cabinet members, government officials, Governors, and other noted people. The Senate, not to be outdone by the House, had passed a resolution and ordered an elegant silver service of 14 pieces, valued at $1,000. The Chargé d'Affaires of Persia and Madame Ali Kull Khan dispatched a toilet mirror, 12 inches high, with frame and back of lacquer, appropriately inlaid with flowers, singing birds, and tiny Cupids. Another gift was a white linen skirt, hand-embroidered, and containing the initials "J.W.S." All of the 500 women employed in a New York City skirt-and-waist factory had had a hand in its preparation. The workers had started the skirt as soon as the engagement had been announced, and a delegation of three came to Washington to present it in recognition of Jessie's participation in social welfare work. Thirteen other young women at a local cooking school sent a 35-pound cake with pink-and-white icing.

One of the presents most cherished by the bride was a small beaded bag, made by a 4-year-old cousin. Other gifts which, while of little monetary value, were received with considerable pleasure by Jessie and her mother were two washtubs and six boxes of soaps; coal scuttles; sacks of potatoes and Bermuda onions; a rustic rag rug; hand-made quilts from mountain women of the South, and many other articles lovingly and carefully made by various people who knew the Wilsons through their welfare work.

On the day before the wedding, the bridal party assembled at the White House for the wedding rehearsal. The full Marine Band was present, running through the usual bridal chorus from *Lohengrin*. It is interesting to note that President Wilson—in contrast with President Cleveland, who barely had time on his wedding day for his own rehearsal—"laid aside all care this afternoon and entered into the joyous spirit of the occasion as merrily as the youngest member of the company."

Tuesday, November 25th, was the fifth occasion on which a President's daughter was to be married in the White House. The city of Washington can sometimes have superb days in late November, warm, and slightly crisp, and this was just such a day. Around four in the afternoon, a crowd started to gather outside the White House grounds, but it was neither as large nor as active as the one at the Roosevelt/Longworth wedding. Diplomats representing all the nations of Europe and the Orient arrived in full regalia, along with the military officers. They came in a curious mixture of horse-drawn carriages and automobiles. Members of the Cabinet and other high officials went through the gate flashing their much-coveted tickets of admission. Conspicuous by their absence, however, were Vice President and Mrs. Marshall, who had been visiting relatives in Arizona and had not returned.

Legend has it that Frank Sayre, as nervous as any other

Nellie Grant, the President's 18-year-old daughter, married an English diplomat in one of the most lavish of all White House weddings. Her choice upset her father and a patriotic nation, but her American citizenship was restored when she was forced to leave her husband.

These portraits of Nellie and Algernon Sartoris appeared in *Frank Leslie's Illustrated Newspaper* in June 1874.

ABOVE:
Columbia aims a slipper at Nellie and Algernon as they leave the White House in this cartoon from New York's *Daily Graphic*.

BELOW:
Mr. and Mrs. Sartoris began their honeymoon by traveling to New York in a luxurious Pullman "palace car."

*Culver Pictures*

*New York Public Library*

RIGHT:

Beautiful Ida Honoré, whose society-queen sister arranged for her to marry Nellie's brother in Chicago instead of in the White House, was painted, like her husband, by G. P. A. Healy.

BELOW:

Fred Grant was painted in Europe two years before his marriage by Healy, who made portraits of Europe's royalty and America's social and business leaders.

*Chicago Historical Society*

*Frick Art Reference Library,*
*courtesy of Ulysses S. Grant, III*

*Rutherford B. Hayes Library, Fremont, Ohio*

President and Mrs. Rutherford Hayes greet guests in the East Room at their Silver Anniversary reception, after a private "sentimental orgy" the day before.

*Rutherford B. Hayes Library, Fremont, Ohio*

The President's niece, Emily Platt, surprised many friends
when she married an aging General. Drawn here for the New
York *Daily Graphic* (June 25, 1878), the ceremony took
place in the Blue Room, with many children among the guests.

President Cleveland issued firm instructions that no floral bells or
horseshoes were to decorate the Blue Room when he married his
young ward there. But this well-meaning cartoon in *Puck* gave
him a bell, a horseshoe, and a long poem of congratulation.

Frances Folsom was so much younger than the
President that Cleveland was rumored to be courting
her mother. Mrs. Folsom, standing in front of Cleveland, is shown by *Leslie's* artist kissing her daughter
after the wedding.

Nicholas Longworth joined a Congressional junket so that
he could be with Alice Roosevelt aboard the *Manchuria*,
far away from other suitors. This snapshot, taken on the
journey to the Philippines, was published in *Harper's
Weekly* (Feb. 17, 1906).

The 1906 East Room wedding of "Princess Alice" to the enterprising Congressman outshone all other White House ceremonies in splendor and expense.

The Tafts gave a huge garden party to celebrate their Silver Anniversary in 1911. Young Robert Taft stands at left in back row, with aunts and uncles.

*Culver Pictures*

The Wilson women are caught in a carefree moment at their summer home in Cornish, N.H. Left to right are Jessie, the social worker; Margaret, a singer who thought up madcap pranks when they lived in the White House; the first Mrs. Wilson, who died a few weeks after the White House wedding of her youngest daughter, Nellie.

**LEFT:**

Jessie Wilson took up social work when frail health prevented her being a missionary. Her sister Nellie wrote: ". . . we all adored her as one a little apart, . . . not quite on this earth."

**BELOW:**

Frank Sayre pretended, for the sake of newsmen, to be a Wilson cousin while he courted her. His co-workers were unaware that he even knew the Wilsons.

Jessie with Margaret on her right, Nellie at her left. In back row: The Wilsons, Frank, and Grenfell.

*Culver Pictures*

During their courtship, President Wilson took Mrs. Edith Galt to a World Series game in Philadelphia where (on October 9, 1915) they saw the Red Sox beat the Phillies. Mayor Blankenburg is beside Edith Galt; her mother is partly seen at center.

*Culver Pictures*

Eleanor Wilson, shopping for her trousseau, and her fiancé in New York about five weeks before their White House wedding.

Nellie's wedding dress was of ivory satin, trimmed in old lace; inside it she pinned a blue ribbon with a brooch borrowed from her ailing mother.

Seconds before a "perfect tornado" whisked up Alice Wilson's veil and tore awnings from their frames, she posed on the South Portico for her favorite wedding photo. The thunderstorm ended the hottest day in 40 years.

*Courtesy of Mrs. Isaac Stuart McElroy*

*Wide World*

Harry Hopkins took Louise Macy to Washington
to visit the Roosevelts on July 4, 1942, the day
after their engagement was announced. At the
end of the month, they were quietly married
in F.D.R.'s study.

bridegroom, had arrived in plenty of time at one White House gate, but was unable to find his ticket. The over-zealous guard refused to let him in. As Sayre now remembers the incident, the accounts were true:

> I had been staying at Justice Hughes's house a few days before the wedding. I had known his son, Charlie Hughes, in college, at Williams, and Charlie was to be one of my ushers. I spent the morning of the day of my wedding walking on the Virginia shore with Grenfell. We both enjoyed walking and being out-of-doors. But in the afternoon I went to the White House alone. When the guard asked me who I was, I told him I was the bridegroom. He said anyone could claim to be the groom. I suggested he call the Captain, because if I did not get inside there would be no wedding.

In his memoirs, Sayre records that the Captain marched out of his sentry box, listened sternly to his explanation, gave a slight wink, and let him in.

At precisely 4:30, the full Marine Band, in scarlet coats and gold trappings, began the opening measure of the bridal chorus. Bandmaster Santelman, who had conducted at Alice Roosevelt's wedding, this time had Margaret Wilson to contend with. She was the musician of the family, a trained singer of professional standards. At her firm suggestion, the program included music by a composer few had heard of—Ethelbert Nevin, Mrs. Sayre's cousin.

Sayre and his best man entered the East Room and took up positions directly in front of the low dais with its white satin-covered prie-dieu, which was backed by a wall of green foliage set off by roses and lilies. As in the Grant/Sartoris and the Roosevelt/Longworth weddings, the ceremony took place in front of the large east window. Under the prie-dieu was spread the pure white vicuña rug from the Minister of Peru. Tall white candelabra stood on each side.

The bridesmaids, escorted by the ushers, formed a study in pink. Their gowns, said to have set a fashion trend across the nation, had been designed in four different shades of satin, ranging from the palest pink to a deep rose. They bore Elizabethan ruffs of silvery lace. The skirts were draped so that they almost touched the floor in back. In front, they were considered quite "daring" for the day, revealing four inches of silk stocking through silver petticoats.

Eleanor had rashly designed headdresses, which she described as "little rose velvet caps with silver lace, wired and standing up in the Russian manner." Although at the time she created them she thought them "triumphs of simple chic," and "a stroke of artistic genius," she was horrified when, on the day before the wedding, they were tried on and found to be so bizarre and ungainly as to be "hideous failures." Sitting up most of the night, she and Margaret and the ladies' maids cut, sewed, and reworked them so that they "weren't too awful." As a result of her exertions, Eleanor woke up the next morning completely hoarse and unable to speak above a whisper.

When the bride walked down the aisle on her father's arm, she looked, said Eleanor, "half angel, half Grecian statue, and she had that lovely shining look that always brought a lump into my throat." She wore no jewelry except for the diamond pendant and chain that had been given to her by Frank.

On reaching the foot of the dais, the bridesmaids and ushers formed a semicircle with a space directly in the center. Through this the bride and groom stepped to stand before the minister. The service was a combination of the Episcopalian and the Presbyterian. At the bride's request, the word "obey," not normally a part of the Presbyterian vow, was included.

It was a double ring ceremony, at which everyone present spoke the Lord's Prayer "in fervent monotone."

The Reverend Dr. Beach wore his dark collegiate gown with a Master's hood of white silk. John Sayre, wearing a contrasting white surplice of the Episcopal church, gave the benediction as the couple knelt on the little prie-dieu.

At a hushed moment, just before the blessing, guests near the bridal party were startled to hear the most unusual sounds emanating from the front row. It was dear Auntie Blanche. Overcome by emotion and by the overwhelming realization that *she* was responsible for all this, she was shaking like a leaf, her breath coming in gasps of joy. And, of course, with every breath, her necklaces and bracelets and that fabulous snake belt all set up a metallic cacophony.

Then the Marine Band began the triumphant recessional march, and Jessie and Frank went back down the aisle.

For nearly an hour, the guests filed through the Blue Room, offering warm congratulations. Refreshments were served in the State Dining Room for the guests, and, after the reception, the wedding party had an old-fashioned Southern supper in the breakfast room. Then an informal and unplanned dance took place. The Marine Band moved into the East Room, the carpets were rolled back, and "the tango and other late dance steps were gracefully danced by the young folk." Before eight o'clock, Frank and Jessie (dressed in a green skirt and coat) managed to slip away.

"After the wedding," said Sayre, "we had a tricky time getting away. I believe something like a thousand dollars had been offered to the newsman who could find out where we were, but we had everything arranged. We drove away from the White House in a little car that belonged to Secretary Tumulty, rather than in a White House car. The Secret Service man [on a motorcycle] managed to tie up all the other cars until we could make a getaway. We drove across Chain Bridge, where another car was waiting on the other side of the river. It was parked so that it faced Washington. We got into it and drove right back to Washington. Anyone who might have found the first car would have found it empty. We drove right past the White House again and saw all of the crowd. It was just a simple car we were in, so no one would suspect. Then we went on to Baltimore, where we spent our first night at the home of friends. No one found us, but later the maid of our friends in Baltimore said that someone had called to ask if we were there, and she said, 'I very frankly denied you were here.'"

After a brief return to Washington on Thursday the 27th for Thanksgiving dinner, they went to Hoboken, to sail aboard the North German Lloyd steamer *George Washington*, for a two-month honeymoon in Europe. President Wilson was on hand to wish them bon voyage that Saturday morning. The German band played "The Star-Spangled Banner," an ironic gesture in view of the tragic relationship that Wilson was soon to have with the German people.

Characteristically, Jessie and Frank avoided the first-class gangway and slipped aboard ship unnoticed, just 20 minutes before sailing time, when everyone except the President was worried that they might not make it. How did they manage to do it?

"It was just this way," said Sayre. "We came over in the Hudson tube with a lot of other passengers and took one of those ancient hacks from the Hoboken Terminal to the pier. The driver took us to the entrance of Pier 1 and we came up in an elevator filled with people." Then they chose the third-class gangway.

For Woodrow Wilson, the marriage of his daughter was not all happiness. In a letter on February 1, 1914, he wrote:

Jessie and Frank came back from across the water last week; today they started for their home in Williamstown. The pang of it is still deep in my heart. When they went off on their wedding journey the thing somehow did not seem final: they would be back after their honeymoon! But now! This going to make a permanent home for themselves comes on me like a new realization, or—rather—a first realization of what has happened, and I feel bereaved. They are very happy—delightfully happy—it is a joy to see; but that does not fill the gap here.

Jessie and Frank shared much happiness together for twenty years, until her death on January 15, 1933. When she died, they had two sons and one daughter, all in their teens.

Francis Bowes Sayre is one of the most distinguished of all the White House bridegrooms. He later served as a Harvard professor of law, was Assistant Secretary of State in the Franklin D. Roosevelt administration, and was United States High Commissioner to the Philippines when the Japanese attacked Pearl Harbor. In 1942 he dramatically escaped from Corregidor, rescued by submarine a few weeks before the last-ditch fortress was overwhelmed by the enemy forces. After the war, he served as a diplomatic adviser to the United Nations Relief and Rehabilitation Administration, heading missions to Egypt, India, South Africa, Iraq, and other countries. He has high honors from a dozen or more nations, has been a delegate to the United Nations, and has written many books and articles. At the height of his career, it required a column 11 inches long to record his accomplishments in Who's Who.

Today he lives quietly with his second wife, Elizabeth Graves Sayre, in a lovely home on a cul-de-sac near the Potomac River, in the Spring Valley section of Washington, D.C. He is a delightful, charming old gentleman of 82, but the "old" should be qualified, for he stands proudly erect and alert. He would have been vastly amused to know that we had called the office of his oldest son (born in the White House in January 1915), who is now Dean of the Washington Cathedral, to ask if the former bridegroom were "still living." He has a lively twinkle in his eyes and gives the appearance of spending a great deal of the time outdoors. When called upon for an interview, he appeared at the door with a devoted cocker spaniel.

In the entrance hall stands a very beautiful bust of Jessie, and from the way Dr. Sayre speaks of her it is evident that he had nothing but wonderful memories of his White House bride of more than half a century ago.

CHAPTER XVII

# A SIMPLE EVENT

RESIDENT WILSON's deep feeling of loss was not touched off entirely by the departure of his beloved Jessie. He knew only too well that his youngest daughter, Eleanor or "Nellie," would soon follow.

On the evening of November 25th, after Frank Sayre and his bride had departed, it was Nellie who sparked the party and kept things lively. It was she who induced the dignified Marine Band to abandon the conventional numbers and play the turkey trot and other popular dances. Whenever it seemed that the music might stop, Nellie would wave appealingly at the leader, Lieutenant Santelman, and what could he do but keep playing?

During the course of the evening, Eleanor was sought out again and again by William Gibbs McAdoo, Wilson's Secretary of the Treasury, a widower who had come to the wedding with his daughter. McAdoo, although nearly 50 (with six children, and already a grandfather), was handsome, tall, youthful in appearance, and considered by Washington hostesses as a fine catch for some lucky lady. Eleanor led him into the Blue Room, where she gave him lessons in the one-step and the fox trot, all the time straining her hoarse voice to speak in something above a whisper.

Eleanor had met McAdoo, whom she called "Mac," for the first time at Sea Girt, New Jersey, Woodrow Wilson's summer home when he was Governor of New Jersey. It was in the summer of 1912, for McAdoo, as Vice Chairman of the Democratic National Committee, was in the habit of visiting Wilson that year for party conferences. At the time the two met, Mac had his arm in a sling, which 23-year-old Eleanor thought "most becoming to his tall, youthful figure." He was popularly referred to as "The Tunnel Man" because he had been an advocate of the Hudson Tunnel, and apparently had experienced several "adventures" under the river. Wilson was greatly impressed by McAdoo, whom he referred to as "attractive and dynamic."

On one occasion, Eleanor, hearing that he was coming to Princeton to spend the night, broke a date. But at the time Mac was interested only in the Governor and his wife and paid little attention to any of the daughters. Eleanor's big opportunity came when, at the end of the evening, Mac announced that he had to leave on an early train in the morning, and he insisted that Mrs. Wilson should not trouble herself to get up and see him off.

"I will let Nellie be your hostess," replied Mrs. Wilson. "She is taking an early train, too, and will see that you are taken care of." Eleanor commuted daily to an art school in Philadelphia.

The next morning, Eleanor was so nervous that, trying to prepare her guest's coffee, she dropped the sugar tongs and spilled the cream. McAdoo, with characteristic Southern courtesy (he was born in Georgia and became a lawyer in Tennessee), "put me at my ease, talking to me as though I were a wise woman of the world."

After the election and the move into the White House, Eleanor quickly adapted herself to the new life and soon had the personable young White House aides charmed by her manner. On one occasion one of the aides, Charles Rockwell, admitted that before the arrival of the Wilsons he and his colleagues had been certain that the three girls would all have thick glasses, straight hair, and high-button shoes. When he asked her whether she could dance, Eleanor replied, "Goodness, we were raised in a college town. I'm a very frivolous person!"

After the move to Washington, Eleanor, as well as her sisters, soon discovered that their social life was public property. If they even looked at a man twice, some newspaperman would appear to ask if there was a romantic attachment. And whenever Eleanor let herself be carried away by the fun of singling out an especially good dancer for her partner at parties, there were sure to be hints of an "engagement" in one paper or another.

Eleanor also discovered something else: she possessed a power that was both fascinating and dangerous. According to protocol, at dances and dinners where a Wilson daughter was guest of honor—and there were a good many—no one could leave until the President's daughter was ready to go. On several occasions, she far overstayed the intended time, thus earning a scolding from the alert Belle Hagner, who not only functioned as Mrs. Wilson's personal secretary, but acted as a kind of social conscience for the daughter. Three o'clock in the morning, she commented several times, might be the time Nellie Wilson wanted to call it a day, but it was no time for an official function to end.

"One night I was invited to a big dinner party and a charity performance at the theatre afterwards," wrote Nellie. "After coffee we just sat and sat until at last I got nervous and blurted out, 'I thought we were going to the theatre.' At once everyone sprang up and dashed for their coats and wraps, and I realized that I had slipped again.

"The young army and navy officers were my particular beaux," she recollected in her autobiography. "There were thrilling dances on the *Mayflower*, the President's yacht, and at the War College; dinner-dances at Chevy Chase, Washington's famous country club; small theatre parties and *thé dansants* almost every afternoon at private houses . . . I ruined dozens of pairs of slippers, flirted outrageously, took moonlight walks by the Potomac, and fell off Charlie Rockwell's horses, one after another, in Rock Creek Park."

By her own admission, Eleanor says that neither Margaret nor Jessie succumbed so often to the frivolous pursuits that she indulged in. Margaret was always wrapped up in her singing, while Jessie dedicated herself to social work—and to Frank. Shortly after they moved to the White House, Eleanor discovered a brand-new game. She and Margaret, dressed in old clothes, draped veils over their faces and took a guided tour of the city. "Margaret assumed a high nasal voice and a Midwestern twang," Nellie wrote later in her memoirs, "and kept a running fire of comment. When we reached the White House she cried, 'Oh, mister, can't we go in? I want to see where the Wilson girls sleep. Please take us in. . . . Why can't we go in?' He soothed her condescendingly, explained that she would have to have a pass and promised to get it and take her through himself, but for all her pleas, he said that she couldn't see the bedrooms. Weak with laughter, I dragged her off as soon as I could."

During happy family days in the summer of 1913 at "Harlakenden" in Cornish, New Hampshire, the three girls enjoyed parties, picnics, tennis, and other sports and recreations. That September, Nell and Margaret and three young men, including the noted poet, Witter Bynner, staged a "Bird Masque" to help naturalist Harold Baynes promote interest in a bird sanctuary. Nellie was dressed as the "bird spirit" in a headdress of white wings. The others all had on outlandish costumes, including a blue hooded gown, a leopard-skin mantle, and bird feathers. On the way back from the performance, they passed through a village where some of the country people were holding a dance. They went inside, "swooped three times around the hall," and then disappeared into the night.

"I have never known," wrote Eleanor, "whether they thought us a dream, or a visitation from an insane asylum."

Nellie saw McAdoo occasionally when he visited her father in New Hampshire, but she was surprised whenever he paid much attention to her. On one occasion, he asked her if she would play tennis with him the next day. Whereupon she slipped out of the house, dashed downtown, and bought herself "a tricky tennis costume." The game, described by her as amateurish and interrupted by chit-chat, was followed by tea in the garden. Woodrow Wilson was amused enough by the incident to tease his youngest daughter about it that night at dinner—indicating by his amusement, of course, that he was not the slightest bit concerned that the relationship would ever become serious.

When Jessie and Frank returned from their honeymoon trip in Europe at the end of January 1914, they stayed for a few days at the White House. For a while it seemed like old times, with the family together again and all the girls "in residence." But the newlyweds were anxious to move into their new home in Williamstown, and so they soon departed, leaving Eleanor "desperately homesick for the old days, most of all for the long nightly conferences with Jessie, as we lay in bed in the dark."

It was perhaps this sense of loneliness that led Eleanor to start thinking more seriously about her future. Ever since she had traveled on holiday to Mexico, some time before her father became President, she had been "secretly engaged" to a mysterious friend she had met on the trip. Her memoirs do not tell us anything about him, except that she exchanged letters with him regularly.

But during the early weeks of 1914, McAdoo saw her more and more. They started taking informal walks together, and he showed signs of being rather possessive. For one thing, he was almost rude about permitting other men to cut in on them when they were dancing. Finally one night he proposed. Eleanor had to refuse. But she cried endlessly at night and finally had to confide in her mother. Mrs. Wilson advised her by all means to break off the previous "engagement," but not to take any steps regarding McAdoo for the moment—at least until she had time to compose herself and think things out.

It had been growing obvious to the President that William Gibbs McAdoo was interested in their youngest daughter. One evening when the family was together in the Oval Room, one of the servants, Brown, appeared in the doorway and announced the arrival of the Secretary of the Treasury. The President started to get up, but then Brown added in his booming voice "—for Miss Eleanor!"

Brown began to realize over a period of days that perhaps this was something he should not be shouting up and down the halls. On the next visit, he discreetly advanced farther into the room and lowered his voice when making the announcement. And so it continued. The climax came when, after having advanced farther and farther each time, announcing the Secretary in a lower and lower voice, he finally walked right over to Nellie, bowed from the waist, grinned, and rolled his eyes in the direction of the door without ever uttering a word.

Then Mac was called away from Washington on an extended trip for the Treasury. Eleanor was so lonely during this period that when Mac returned and proposed again, she kissed him and said "Yes" without hesitation. For a few weeks, they managed to keep the engagement a secret. Then, by mistake, while she was on a visit to New York, a letter to her from McAdoo was opened as official mail and the secret was out. On March 13th, the couple announced their engagement.

"Official Washington" was reported as taking it for granted that there would be a White House wedding in June. Papers also made special note of the fact that McAdoo was 50 and his intended bride 24, and that he had just recently become a grandfather when his daughter—one of six children, and exactly Miss Wilson's age—gave birth to a son in Arizona.

Some hint of the publicity to come can be found in a news item, datelined Washington and headed: "CAMERA MEN GET McADOO." The account described how the Secretary of the Treasury had been constantly waylaid since the engagement by "an army of photographers and moving picture men." He was reported to be most unhappy about the situation, but in a quandary as to what to do about it.

Now, too, the rumor spread that after the wedding McAdoo was going to resign his post as Secretary, to avoid any suggestion of nepotism. It is apparently true that McAdoo did bring up the matter with the President, wondering whether the relationship might not prove embarrassing to him. Wilson immediately settled the issue by saying that at the time of the appointment there had been no hint of marriage and that McAdoo had been appointed simply because he was the most able man for the job.

Reactions to the engagement were mixed. Eleanor was very close to her uncle, John Wilson, and his wife, Aunt Ida, partly because she resembled a daughter of theirs who had been killed in an automobile accident. When she told Uncle John that she was engaged, his first reaction was one of indignation, until she reassured him by saying, "But it's Mac, Uncle John."

He thereupon hugged her and replied, "Thank God—I was afraid it was one of those young whippersnappers!"

Woodrow Wilson was beset by inner conflicts. "I shall be poor without her," he wrote. "She and I have been such ideal chums. It's hard, very hard, not to be selfish and rebel,—or repine!" On many occasions, as college president, Governor, and President, he had displayed his deep affection for all of his daughters by forgoing interests of his own—even official duties—in order to be with them on special occasions.

Now, too, there was another factor that made the President's depression more pronounced than ever. His wife, Ellen

Louise Wilson, was seriously ill. She had suffered from a kidney ailment for many months, all the time showing devotion and courage as she tried to ignore the pain and distress and continue with her work. Not only did she serve with distinction as First Lady, but she had plunged into slum clearance projects with dedication, often walking through the most squalid tenement sections of the capital, dragging with her many a member of Congress reluctant to face the dismal realities of the problem.

At the end of February 1914, before the engagement had been revealed openly, Ellen Wilson fell on the floor of her bedroom. The fall  caused such extreme pain and shock that she was confined to bed under care of the White House physician, Dr. Cary Grayson, for more than two weeks. It was at the end of this period of misery and worry that the news of the engagement leaked out. The President was furious, not only because Nellie's mail had been opened, but because there were other rumors being fabricated by the press that Margaret was engaged.

"I am a public character," he said bluntly and angrily one day to an assembled group of journalists, "but the ladies of my household are not servants of the government and they are not public characters. I deeply resent the treatment they are receiving at the hands of the newspapers at this time." He referred to his oldest daughter, who was "constantly represented as being engaged to this, that or the other man in different parts of the country; in some instances, to men she has never even met in her life." He threatened to deal with reporters, not as President, but "man to man."

All things taken into consideration, it was quite remarkable that the Wilson girls managed to live their lives normally in the White House. Nellie found much truth in her father's statement on one occasion that "Washington is, I should judge, the worst place in America to keep normal. One's perspective goes wrong along with one's nerves, and there are a lot of people here who get on your nerves." If Washington in general was difficult, the White House was impossible!

Because of Mrs. Wilson's illness, Nellie and Mac decided to have a small, private wedding in the White House, inviting no one except close relatives, intimate friends, and the Cabinet members and their wives. Mrs. Wilson objected, saying that Nellie should have a large, gay wedding to suit her temperament and to include all of the many, many friends she had made in Washington during the preceding year or so. Of course, Mrs. Wilson was right. If ever there should have been a historic White House wedding, with all the splendor and joyfulness possible, it should have been at the marriage of Eleanor Randolph Wilson!

But, alas, there is no place for "the things that could have been" in the pages of history.

Almost in a matter of weeks, Nellie had changed from a gay sprite to a rather serious young lady, absorbed in plans, not so much for the wedding as for life as Mrs. McAdoo. Her mother was a little concerned that, while Nellie had been well instructed in the social graces, perhaps she had not received enough of a practical education in matters of housekeeping—especially since she would be a Cabinet member's official hostess as well as a wife.

By the end of March, it had been tentatively announced that the wedding would take place on the 29th or 30th of April. Eleanor had already decided on the oval-shaped Blue Room as the setting for the ceremony. She had always been impressed by the "palatial grandeur" of the East Room, with its broad expanse of polished floor, its three huge crystal chandeliers, and the two great marble fireplaces. But the Blue Room was her favorite, paneled in soft blue brocade and with an atmosphere of security and dignity. She particularly liked the curving bay windows, tall and stately, from which one could look straight ahead to the Washington Monument.

The President still did not consider the event to have

reached the planning stage. "As for the wedding, there are no plans," he had written to his brother as late as April 1st. "Practically everything depends upon the rapidity with which Ellen regains her strength, because Eleanor and Mr. McAdoo do not wish her to be troubled about the plans until she is fully fit to consider them and take part in them."

As the days went on, it became more and more apparent that Mrs. Wilson was little likely to improve. The date was set for Thursday, May 7th, for six o'clock in the evening, and it was decided to limit the guests to fewer than a hundred people. Once again, as in the case of Jessie's wedding, both the House and the Senate appointed committees and set about purchasing appropriate gifts. Curiously enough, they reversed the selection—this time the House sending a costly silver service and the Senate personal jewelry. Of the latter, Nellie said, "I have always been sure that some clever woman chose the Senate's gift—an exquisite pearl and diamond bracelet."

The small bridal party was selected: Jessie as matron of honor; Margaret as maid of honor; Dr. Cary Grayson, U.S.N., the President's medical aide, as best man; and Sally McAdoo, 10-year-old daughter of the bridegroom, and 12-year-old Nancy Lane, daughter of the Secretary of the Interior, as flower girls. The colors selected by the bride were pink and blue. The Blue Room was decorated with apple and cherry blossoms and with branches of flowering dogwood (although one newspaper reported it decorated "entirely in white lilies").

The total guest list was set at eighty, since the situation had been further complicated by recent international developments, not the least of which was an increasingly strained relationship with Mexico. Vice President Marshall and his wife, who had not returned to Washington in time for Jessie's wedding, managed to make it this time.

On the afternoon of the wedding, Nellie went to her mother's bedroom to help her with her dress—of creamy lace, with violets on the shoulder—before putting on her bridal gown.

She recalled later that her mother was wearing a set of amethysts that the President had given her and that, despite the miseries of illness, she looked "radiantly pretty." Somehow, Ellen Wilson had managed to rally during the few days before the event, and friends remarked at the time that she seemed her old self again. Reassured, Nellie returned to her own bedroom to put on her bridal gown of heavy, ivory-colored satin, trimmed with valuable lace and designed in "an almost mediaeval style." The old point lace was believed to have once belonged to the Empress Eugénie. Nellie's bouquet consisted of white orchids, gardenias, and lilies of the valley. To be "on the safe side," she pinned a piece of blue ribbon inside her dress with a brooch borrowed from her mother. She also put on the necklace Mac had given her.

Margaret and Jessie wore diaphanous organdy gowns, styled alike, but of blue and rose, respectively, and carried old-fashioned shepherd's crooks festooned with lilies of the valley and roses.

At 6 P.M. that Thursday, as the sun set at the end of a perfect spring day, less than six months after Jessie's large wedding, Nellie and her attendants assembled at the head of the main stairway, where they were joined by the President. The Marine Band, unaccountably delayed for a short time, finally struck up the wedding march, and they proceeded slowly down the stairs toward the Blue Room. All at once Nellie realized that her train had flopped over, revealing the lining. She whispered quickly to Irwin Hoover, of the White House staff, who as in the past was right at hand for any emergency, and he lifted it back in place. The President gave a little laugh, and they started down the corridor.

The bride and groom kneeled on a small satin-covered priedieu that rested on the same white Peruvian vicuña rug that had been used at Jessie's wedding. Once again, the Reverend Dr. Sylvester Beach, who had married Jessie, officiated, using the Presbyterian service. This time it was a single ring ceremony.

The wedding was followed by a small supper, with guests seated around 20 small tables in the State Dining Room. Cary Grayson's sword was used again to cut the cake (a present from the junior members of the National School of Domestic Arts and Sciences). Dancing followed in the Blue Room, where Nellie had taught Mac the fox trot only six months earlier.

There was one tearful moment, when Nellie went upstairs with Jessie and Margaret to change and was suddenly overwhelmed by the thought that she was leaving them. But they simply laughed at her sad face and helped her into a blue suit with a long, slit skirt and a sailor hat with a single large rose in the front. Then she was hurried down the stairs. As might have been expected, the bride's bouquet was aimed at Margaret, but the "luck" was not there. Margaret deliberately remained single for the rest of her life.

McAdoo, aching to get even with the press for the way photographers had mobbed him after the engagement announcement seven weeks earlier, devised a clever scheme to frustrate them. He had ordered three of the White House automobiles and one of his own to be placed in conspicuous locations, two at the front and two at the South Entrance—all with drawn shades. When he and Nellie were ready to leave, Frank and Jessie scooted into one of the cars; Margaret, with Cary Grayson, took a second; and friends dashed for the other two. Then all four whirled through the gates. As expected, reporters and photographers set off in quick pursuit. Mac and Nellie quietly slipped into a fifth automobile, hidden behind some bushes, and drove off in complete anonymity.

Having also "leaked out" fictitious information that he planned to honeymoon in Europe, Mac then whisked Nellie off to "Harlakenden," where they enjoyed a couple of days of privacy before any outsiders knew they were there. After that, as was to be expected, the press ferreted them out, and they were back in the public eye. Two weeks later, they were back in Washington and right in the thick of social and official activities.

Even though Nellie was living in Washington and was much closer to the White House than Jessie, the President missed her deeply. "How desperately my heart aches that she is gone," he wrote to his friend Mary Hulbert not long after the wedding. "She has married a noble man, who I feel sure will make her happy and proud, too. But just now I can realize in my selfishness, only that I have lost her for good and all."

Nellie and Mac were to gladden Wilson's heart in the future by presenting him with two granddaughters, Ellen Wilson, born in 1915, and Mary Faith in 1920. But Nellie's mother did not live to share this happiness. After the wedding, her health began to grow much worse. By late May, it was evident to Dr. Grayson and other doctors that she had Bright's disease and that her case was hopeless. From that time on she declined rapidly, although there were occasions when she seemed to rally and recapture some of her former spirit. On August 6, 1914, she died.

In just nine months, the strong, exuberant solidarity of the Wilson family had been broken apart three times.

Nellie's own family was broken by divorce in 1934. She lived in Santa Barbara, California, until her death in 1967, twenty-six years after her former husband's.

CHAPTER XVIII

# A PRESIDENT'S EMOTIONAL CRISIS

o anyone intimate with the President, it was not surprising that Woodrow Wilson formed a very close attachment with another woman less than a year after his wife's death and that shortly thereafter he announced he would marry again. Wilson was very dependent upon women, so much so that the fall of 1914 found him in a state of depression and despair that had members of his Cabinet alarmed over the political consequences. He had sat beside the body of his dead wife, almost uncomprehending, for two entire nights, and for weeks after the funeral would wander through the White House mute with grief. With Ellen in her grave and his only unmarried daughter, Margaret, wrapped up in her music and concert tours, he felt completely alone. He kept thinking back to the period just after the Inauguration—such a short time ago—when they had all been together and he was a happy father and husband.

Bess Furman, in her book *White House Profile*, explained Wilson's nature this way: "One Princeton friend compared Wilson to Disraeli in that he was dependent on women in an extraordinary degree. Their companionship, admiration, attentiveness, adoration brought out his original thought and scintillating conversation."

On her deathbed, Ellen Wilson is said to have whispered to her physician and great family friend, Dr. Cary Grayson, the often quoted plea, "Promise me that when I go you will take care of Woodrow." Another version has it that she told her husband herself that he should find someone to take her place and help him bear the great responsibilities of his office. Whatever actually took place, it is certain that Ellen realized how desperately this man was going to need strong female companionship and love.

The President's cousin, Helen Woodrow Bones, had been living at the White House, to assist the retiring Margaret as hostess. Helen herself became rather lonely there. Consequently Dr. Cary Grayson thought it would be a good idea to introduce her to the guardian of Alice Gordon, the girl with whom he was in love and whom he was later to marry. The woman in question was Edith Bolling Galt, a handsome, personable, and lively widow in her early forties. During the winter of 1915, the friendship between Helen and Edith flourished. They enjoyed walks in Rock Creek Park and tea afterwards at Edith Galt's house on 20th Street.

Then one day at the end of the third week in March, when they were finishing a brisk walk, Helen suggested that for a change they return to the White House for tea. Edith protested that her boots were muddy and that she was not properly dressed for such an occasion. But Helen pressed the invitation, saying that Grayson had insisted the President join him on the golf course. No one would be there.

"I promise you that you will not see a soul," she said.

It was with considerable surprise, therefore, that the two friends stepped out of the elevator on the second floor and were confronted by Grayson and the President, who had returned earlier than expected. "I think you might invite *us* for tea, too," Grayson is said to have remarked to Helen, turning to introduce Edith to the President. Edith Bolling Galt did not have an eye-catching type of beauty, but she possessed a special charm that immediately appealed to people. And her dark eyes expressed all the warmth and sympathy that Wilson so desperately needed.

The informal little tea that had been suggested on the spur of the moment was suddenly transformed into an event that was to have historic consequences. The four retired to the Oval Room, where they enjoyed the tea and conversation for more than an hour. It was evident to Grayson that a remarkable change had come over the President. He could not recall how long it had been since he had seen Wilson laugh and carry on a discussion with anything like his old animation. It was no surprise, therefore, when several days later the surgeon was invited to join the President and Helen Bones for dinner at the White House, along with Mrs. Galt and Colonel E. T. Brown (the late Mrs. Wilson's cousin from Atlanta), who was staying there at the time. The date was March 23rd.

If the President had seemed animated at the impromptu tea, he was now even more responsive, absorbed and fascinated by Edith Galt. After dinner, the group adjourned once again to the Oval Room, and at his cousin's request the President read three English poems with great feeling. Edith Galt (who had recalled seeing Wilson when he was Governor, a "thin man on a horse—he was wearing a frock coat and high hat") found her host most appealing. "He is *perfectly* charming," she wrote in a letter almost the minute she reached home that night, "and one of the easiest and most delightful hosts I have ever known . . . full of interesting stories and a fund of information . . . and as a reader he is unequalled."

From that moment on, the courtship proceeded in whirlwind fashion. More White House dinners were interspersed with teas and drives through the park and visits to other points of interest around Washington. The President began sending Edith flowers from the White House gardens and copies of books that he particularly enjoyed, among them Wordsworth's poems and the writings of Lord Bryce and Edmund Burke.

When they were together, he often read aloud. It was a natural thing for him to shift from conversations about great literature to discussions on world affairs—and then, in a personal way, to his immediate political problems. Once again, he looked alert and able to cope with the burdens that rested on his shoulders. He was no longer the grief-stricken President described by his brother-in-law, Stockton Axson, who wrote:

> I can see the lonely figure of the President now, walking down the long hallway, the hair so much whitened in the few months.

Carrying on a courtship in the White House has always been a complicated business, and Wilson found it almost impossible to be alone with the woman he had fallen in love with. For one thing, there was the matter of security. At a time when the lives of public figures were threatened repeatedly, he was kept constantly in view by Secret Service men. They followed him whenever he went for a drive; they stood outside his doors at night and day; they checked on the food he ate and the people who visited, whether socially or on business. For another thing, it was not considered entirely proper for a man so recently widowed to be receiving an unattached lady alone.

One evening, however, on either the third or fourth of May, Wilson managed to have Edith for a time to himself. He had invited her to dinner with the others in their intimate little group. She arrived looking more attractive than ever, dressed in a white satin and lace dress, cut with a deep square neck trimmed in green velvet. After dinner, he quietly maneuvered her out onto the South Portico in the mild spring air. His friends, by now fully aware of Wilson's deep feelings for Edith, did not follow. There, barely six weeks from the day that he had first met her, Woodrow Wilson revealed his love and proposed marriage. Edith was almost too overcome to speak, but she finally replied that he could not be sure he loved her, that he did not really know her, and that it had been only nine months since his wife had died. Wilson did not press for an answer, and they agreed to continue seeing each other while Edith came to a decision. She did not want to be overwhelmed by the prospect of becoming First Lady or be swayed by sympathy over his admitted loneliness.

Although the President had agreed to be patient, he could not contain his emotions. He told his daughters and his cousin that he was in love and wanted to marry Edith. And when he could not be with her for one reason or another, he would sit down and write long, ardent letters, some as long as fifteen or twenty pages. He continued to send her flowers in great profusion and books that he felt would interest her. The more intimate members of his staff began to grow concerned, for the man was acting, they felt, more like a lover in his early twenties than like the Chief Executive of the United States. It must be remembered that these were extremely critical times. The Germans were conducting submarine warfare, and on May 7th the *Lusitania* had been torpedoed with a loss of 1,195 people, including 124 Americans.

Ten days after this disaster, Wilson invited Edith to accompany him on the Presidential yacht, *Mayflower*, to New York harbor to review the Atlantic Fleet. It gave him an excellent opportunity to be near her and to share some precious hours in comparative privacy on the darkened deck each evening. A little more than a month later, at the end of June, Edith joined Helen Bones for a trip to "Harlakenden," which the President had again rented for himself and his family. For over a month, he was almost constantly with her. He shared his official duties with her and consulted her about decisions of state. Whenever there was relief from the problems that his staff and Cabinet relayed to "The Summer White House," the two would spend time reading aloud to each other.

By the end of the first week together, Edith knew that she

was in love and confessed it to him, but she declared that she would marry him only if he were defeated for re-election.

On August 2nd, Edith left to visit friends. The rest of the month was intolerable for the President, since he did not see her again until she returned to Washington on September 1st. It was a memorable occasion. After dinner and a drive through Rock Creek Park, Edith said that she would marry him whether or not he served a second term. The President had won a victory more dear to him than any political conquest.

During the course of the next few weeks, Wilson told the immediate members of his family and the official household of the White House that he was engaged. His daughters were delighted, for they knew their father had feared losing Edith, and they realized that such a disappointment might be more than he could bear. Cousin Helen was frankly triumphant. She had long urged Edith to accept and could now consider herself one of the noted matchmakers of American history.

The President's happiness shines through the pages of his letters. Writing on September 26th to Mary W. Hoyt, the late Ellen's cousin, he said, "A great happiness and blessing has come to me in the midst of my loneliness," asking her to keep the matter secret until they had decided on a date for an official announcement.

On October 4th, he wrote a similar note, this one to a woman whom he had met during a family trip to Bermuda and to whom, over a period of seven years, he had written some two hundred letters: Mrs. Mary Hulbert. "Before the announcement is made, I want you to be one of the first to know of the good fortune that has come to me ... a blessing greater than I can measure in words has come to me. . . ."

There is an ironic twist connected with this excited communication to his old friend. It was written right after Wilson's innocent relationship with Mrs. Hulbert became part of a political plot to prevent his marriage. For several months,

Dr. Cary Grayson had been concerned over the political consequences of a possible engagement. He was aware that there would be considerable opposition in the Democratic Party to Wilson's remarriage. The President's political popularity was at a low point that fall. There are numerous discrepancies in the accounts of what happened, but developments seemed to have followed this general course.

Some time in late June or early July, Grayson revealed Wilson's "infatuation" for Edith to Colonel Edward House, the President's adviser, who had for some time been abroad and who, Grayson supposed, was not aware of White House matters. Grayson, according to the Colonel's diary, told House that he feared the President was "wholly absorbed in this love affair" and "is neglecting practically everything else."

Actually, Wilson had already told his adviser about his love for Edith and asked for his advice. House had replied that remarriage might be good for the President's well-being, but had recommended that any engagement be held off until the following spring. He was certain, as was the President's secretary, Joseph P. Tumulty, that an earlier marriage would result in criticism and even political suicide. Sometime in early September, members of the Cabinet, along with other Democratic leaders, are said to have met to determine who should tell the President bluntly that remarriage before the election of 1916 would most certainly bring defeat. Secretary of the Navy Josephus Daniels was nominated first, but he quickly declined what he referred to in *The Wilson Era* as the "exalted position of Minister Plenipotentiary and Envoy Extraordinary to the Court of Cupid on a mission in which neither my heart nor my head was enlisted and in the performance of which my official head might suffer decapitation."

Then Wilson's son-in-law, Secretary of the Treasury McAdoo, became involved. From time to time, political enemies had tried to start whispering campaigns about the President's "affairs" with other women. One such target was Mrs. Mary

Hulbert. With the Galt problem foremost in mind, Grayson reminded McAdoo of the effects of this kind of whispering campaign and added that at one time Wilson had sent Mary a check for $15,000. (The amount was actually $7,500, and it had been sent by Wilson to purchase some mortgages so that Mary's son could start a business.)

As the story has it, McAdoo decided on a calculated ruse to save Wilson's career. On September 17th, he told the President he had seen an anonymous letter from California saying that if an engagement were announced, Mary Hulbert would show the press all of the letters she had received from Wilson. This startling news about a friend to whom he had entrusted many personal (though not romantic) thoughts had a traumatic effect upon Wilson. He not only was deeply upset and shocked, but he became physically ill. His immediate desire was to communicate with Edith Galt. Yet he could not compose himself enough to talk to her on the private telephone line that ran to her home from the White House. He sat down to write her a note, but his hand trembled so violently that he could not hold the pen. In desperation he called Grayson and urged him to go to Edith Galt immediately and tell her what had happened. He had nothing to hide, he said, but he could not involve her in a scandal, frabricated though it might be. His only alternative was to release Edith from her promise of marriage.

For the next two days and nights the President is said to have remained in his room with the shades drawn.

Edith Galt, for her part, spent that night in her home trying to think things through. Finally, early the next morning, she wrote a letter that began:

Dearest—
The dawn has come—and the hideous dark of the hour before the dawn has been lost in the gracious gift of light.
I have been in the big chair by the window, where I have

fought out so many problems, and all the hurt, selfish feeling has gone with the darkness—and now I see straight—straight into the heart of things and am ready to follow the road "where love leads."

She continued that she was "not afraid of any gossip or threat, with your love as my shield. . . . This is my pledge, Dearest One, I will stand by you—not for duty, not for pity, not for honour—but for love—trusting, protecting, comprehending love. And no matter whether the wine be bitter or sweet we will share it together and find happiness."

Although the letter actually reached the President the next day, he put it into his pocket unopened, terrified that Edith had written the expected words of rejection. A day later, worried about not having heard from the White House, Edith came to see him. She found him still in darkness, her letter unread, and quickly repeated what she had written. There was now no doubt that they would proceed with marriage plans. On October 1st, Colonel House wrote the President, "I do not believe that there is anything to gain by delaying the announcement of your engagement."

Wilson never believed that Mary Hulbert was party to the supposed blackmail, although he did fear that political enemies might have somehow located his letters to her. On October 4th, to reassure her of his continuing regard, he wrote her the note announcing his engagement. He never mentioned the "blackmail" threat to her.

What actually did happen, and who was to blame? Much later, Colonel House admitted to Edith Wilson that he and McAdoo together had devised the hoax out of deep concern for the President, hoping to spare him from the political attack that they felt would surely follow an announcement of his engagement.

In his diary, House attributed the idea to McAdoo, referring to it as "cruel." Yet, says Mrs. McAdoo in her memoirs,

"When I asked McAdoo about it, he said that it was entirely 'the Colonel's idea.' "

The scheme failed, anyway, and plans for the wedding went ahead. The President sat down and personally typed out a statement on his own machine:

> The engagement was announced to-day of Mrs. Norman Galt and President Woodrow Wilson.

> Mrs. Norman Galt is the widow of a well known business man of Washington who died some eight years ago. She has lived in Washington since her marriage in 1896. She was Miss Edith Bolling and was born in Wytheville, Virginia, where her girlhood was spent and where her father, the Hon. William H. Bolling, a man of remarkable character and charm, won distinction as one of the ablest, most interesting and most individual lawyers of a State famous for its lawyers. In the circle of cultivated and interesting people who have had the privilege of knowing her Mrs. Galt has enjoyed an enviable distinction, not only because of her unusual beauty and natural charm, but also because of her very unusual character and gifts. She has always been sought out as a delightful friend, and her thoughtfulness and quick capacity for anything she chose to undertake have made her friendship invaluable to those who were fortunate enough to win it.

> It was Miss Margaret Wilson and her cousin Miss Bones who drew Mrs. Galt into the White House circle. They met her first in the early part of the present year, and were so much attracted by her that they sought her out more and more frequently and the friendship among them quickly ripened into an affectionate intimacy. It was through this association with his daughter and cousin that the President had the opportunity to meet Mrs. Galt, who spent a month at Cornish this summer as Miss Wilson's guest. It is, indeed, the most interesting circumstance connected with the engagement just announced that the President's daughters should have picked Mrs. Galt out for their special admiration and friendship before their father did.

On Thursday, October 7th, newspapers across the nation carried the announcement. In some, the headlines were slightly incongruous. Characteristic was the one in *The New York Times* which read:

PRESIDENT TO WED MRS. NORMAN GALT,
INTIMATE FRIEND OF HIS DAUGHTERS:
ALSO COMES OUT FOR WOMAN SUFFRAGE

What had happened was that, after Wilson had given the typed pages to Joseph Tumulty to release, the Secretary had tacked on another announcement—that the President would vote for the upcoming New Jersey amendment in support of woman suffrage. The news would, said Tumulty hopefully, neutralize any unfavorable reaction that female readers might have about a wedding so soon after a funeral.

This strategy may have had some effect, yet it was not really necessary. Except for isolated expressions of "shock," public reaction was quite warm. Although the press went a little bit overboard in depicting the bride-to-be as a "descendant of Pocahontas," the accounts of Edith Bolling Galt were highly flattering. She was described as "very beautiful," a "social favorite," and "greatly accomplished." The dreaded public protests failed to materialize.

With the wedding date set for Saturday, December 18th, the couple announced that the marriage would be simple and would take place in Mrs. Galt's own home, 1308 20th Street, N.W. The nation was so disappointed that many a public protest was made. It had been assumed, of course, that the President would be married in the White House. As Edith wrote later in her autobiography, "So many of my friends told me, 'Oh you should be married in the White House; it would be so historic.' But I told them that we preferred simplicity to historic background, and that nothing would induce me to be married there."

The President also insisted on a simple ceremony and was greatly relieved to be able to have it in the Galt home. He had another reason for not wanting it in the White House: weddings there had for him become symbolic of sadness rather than of joy, of loss rather than of gain. He wanted his own wedding to represent something positive and happy.

The period of the engagement was not all smooth sailing. Although the general public approved it, by November 1915 it was clear that Wilson's political enemies really were attempting to turn the betrothal against him. The next Presidential election was only a year away. In late November, newspaper editors across the country began receiving phone calls with "tips" that Wilson was involved in legal action. There were rumors that Mary Hulbert had sued for breach of promise. It was also whispered around that not only had Wilson had immoral relations with Mary Hulbert, but that his relations with Mrs. Galt had not been exactly platonic. It was easy for his enemies to depict the President as something of an aging playboy (although he was then only 58) who was spending more time carrying on affairs than attending to duties of state.

Though Wilson was furious, he weathered the slanderous campaign, largely through Edith Galt's calming reassurance that love would surely win out over evil. They were married at 8:30 in the evening of December 18th as planned, in a simple ceremony witnessed only by relatives and a few friends. The day was clear and cold. Two ministers officiated, the Reverend Herbert Smith, rector of St. Margaret's Episcopal Church, which Mrs. Galt attended, and the Reverend James H. Taylor, of the First Presbyterian Church, to which Wilson went.

There is an interesting story that Edith later revealed. She had originally asked a Bishop of the Episcopal Church to perform the ceremony, carefully explaining to him that she could not invite his wife, because of the extremely limited guest list. She was therefore surprised and hurt to receive a letter on the morning of the 16th from the Bishop saying that he had arrived in Washington, that he had brought his wife with him, since they were sailing for Europe, and that she would be chagrined to have to tell "titled friends" abroad that she had not been invited to the President's marriage, at which her own husband had officiated.

Edith immediately dispatched a curt note to the man. She thanked him for letting her know of the embarrassing situation his wife found herself in, reminded him why she could not add another person to the guest list, and let it be known that she was herewith excusing him from his promise to officiate.

There were no bridesmaids and no best man. When the moment came for the bride to be given away, her mother stepped forward and put Edith's hand in that of the President. The bride wore a plain gown of black velvet, orchids, and a velvet hat with a crest of feathers. The President wore his cutaway and striped trousers.

Desperately wishing for privacy, Wilson had planned the "getaway" with great care. He and Edith slipped into a limousine with drawn shades and headed for the tiny railroad station in Alexandria, Virginia, rather than the Washington depot. There they boarded a private parlor car that took them to Hot Springs, where they spent Christmas and New Year's. They had expected to honeymoon for three weeks, but on January 3rd, the worsening international situation required the President's immediate attention.

Woodrow Wilson returned to shoulder once again the burdens of state. He won the election of 1916. And he had beside him now in the White House a woman who, during her husband's illness, was to share his work and help shape the destiny of the nation as no other First Lady had done.

CHAPTER XIX

# ROMANCE IN RETROSPECT

*T*HE former Alice Wilson, niece of the 28th President and daughter of his younger brother, Joseph R. Wilson, today lives in Richmond, Virginia, with her husband, the Reverend Isaac Stuart McElroy, Jr., a retired Presbyterian missionary. They were married in the White House just before the end of the First World War, on August 7, 1918. Both are now in their early seventies.

They live in the Richmond suburbs in a modest but charming one-floor white frame house, situated on a corner lot among a great many old trees. Mr. McElroy is tall, slender, erect, and energetic, a fine-looking man with piercing blue eyes. His glasses give him a somewhat detached and studious air. He wears a hearing aid, yet he is a good listener and seemingly prefers not to talk very much. Perhaps, too, this is because his wife is a congenial and excellent conversationalist.

Alice Wilson McElroy was a dark-haired girl of 23 when she became a White House bride. She still has the same warm, round face with large brown eyes and a broad mouth. In stature, she is in direct contrast to her husband—short and with a full figure. The McElroys have five children and sixteen grandchildren. One daughter, Jessie McElroy Junkin, also married a missionary, and she and her husband were interned during World War II in a Japanese concentration camp, where a son, William, was born.

At the time of our visit, in late January of 1966, the McElroys had just finished adding a room to their home, and Mrs. McElroy kept apologizing that she had not put things "quite straight yet," although the place seemed immaculate and rather cozy. A fire was burning in the fireplace, and several hobbies were in evidence: a partly completed jigsaw puzzle, a crocheted bedspread still unfinished, and picture frames in the process of being gilded, all in comfortable disarray. Mrs. McElroy was gaily dressed in a mandarin jacket and seemed delighted to open a large metal chest which she had brought out, containing a collection of old letters, yellowed newspaper clippings, snapshots, and other memorabilia. Except for the contents of the chest, there was no other evidence in the room that she was the niece of Woodrow Wilson—no Wilson family portraits on the walls, no pictures of the President, although there were two "Wilson pieces" of furniture. Prints and other decorations reflected the couple's interest in the Orient where they had served as missionaries.

Perhaps the most startling indication of any Presidential connection was Mrs. McElroy's announcement that she had felt it necessary to have the F.B.I. make a security check before the interview.

"You know, when my family lived in Baltimore, we had no protection, and it was very difficult. We had to be very careful." During World War I, a demented crank had apparently told Mrs. McElroy's parents that, unless President Wilson permitted her son to be protected by a special helmet, "the world will blow up."

Alice's father, Joseph R. Wilson, was born in July 1867, eleven years after Woodrow, who was his only brother.

"Uncle Woodrow was worried about nepotism," said Mrs. McElroy. "He didn't like it. My father was a newspaper editor in Nashville, a political commentator, and you know, as a newspaperman, he could have been accused of nepotism. So he went with U.S. Fidelity and Realty, and later with Maryland Casualty in Baltimore."

The young Alice Wilson did not attend the other two weddings at the White House while her uncle was President. "I was much too busy in school," she said, pointing out that at the time she was attending Belmont College. "When Jessie was married, Mrs. Wilson made duplicate cakes and candies and sent them to me at school. Later, when Nell was married, I was busy getting ready to graduate, so I did not go to her wedding."

Nell did not attend Alice's wedding. Neither did Jessie. "Jessie wanted to be there, but she had undergone surgery on her neck. At that time, she said that she envied my bridegroom and me so much, because she, too, had always wanted to be a missionary. Margaret Wilson was at our wedding. We asked her to sing, but she didn't because she was not feeling very well just then."

The McElroys first began seeing each other seriously when he was a student at Union Theological Seminary in Richmond. "Father said that he thought that a young man who was planning to be a missionary should be a chaplain. But Uncle Woodrow said, no, that there were plenty of chaplains, and that there would never have been a war at all if there had been more missionaries!"

The McElroys announced their engagement on Thanksgiving Day, 1917. "I remember," said Mrs. McElroy, "that Mother asked Father if he had asked Stuart [she calls him Stuart rather than Isaac] *all* the questions he should ask. We were all dressed in evening clothes to go to the theater, and father asked Stuart if he would like to lead us in prayer. Stuart read the last part of the Seventh Chapter of Romans. It was the part that says, 'what I hate, that I do.' And he went on reading until he came to 'O wretched man that I am! Who shall deliver me from the body of this death?' "

Mrs. McElroy laughed heartily at this recollection, but her husband interrupted and said, "Now I think that bears a little explanation." He went on to say that he had been studying this part of the Bible at the time and the passages were fresh in mind. He had not chosen it because he felt "wretched."

President Wilson first met Isaac Stuart McElroy at about the time of the engagement, and again on December 7, 1917, when the young couple went to Washington to hear the President read the Declaration of War on Austria-Hungary. By the spring of 1918, Alice and her fiancé were starting to make plans for the wedding. Their original intentions were changed by a number of factors. "I had expected a church wedding in Baltimore," said Mrs. McElroy. "We lived in an apartment, though, and we could never have given a big reception in it. And we didn't belong to any country clubs. It was Uncle Woodrow who suggested the White House wedding. The White House was in mourning because of the War, so we couldn't have a large number of wedding guests. Furthermore, I knew that some people wanted to come because they were curious to see the White House. One friend from Tennessee wanted desperately to go to the wedding after she heard the plans. 'Oh, Mr. President,' she pleaded, 'I'm a third-termer for you.' We had to be very careful, so we only invited sixteen guests. When I told Edith we were having so few people, she said naturally since the White House was in mourning, we couldn't have a large number—but we didn't have to limit our guest list to that extent!'"

In her memoirs, Edith Wilson says, "Alice's parents lived in an apartment in Baltimore, and a wedding would have been such an undertaking for them that I suggested it be held in the White House. The President's daughters, thinking only of their father's comfort, opposed this, but Woodrow wanted the girl to have a nice wedding. Only relatives of the bride and groom were asked, but these were sufficient to fill the White House. Nearly all of them were there by the evening of the 6th, which was dreadfully hot. They seemed ill at ease, and so in view of the event of the morrow, I proposed early bed for everyone and got them all off to their rooms at 9:30."

Having thus neatly disposed of the in-laws, she added, "Then I ordered a car sent around to the Treasury entrance and my husband and I stole out through a basement door and had a lovely ride."

The situation was difficult on both sides. As Mrs. McElroy said, "Our family was not a 'publicity family.' It was hard on us. Uncle Woodrow used to say, 'My Wilson nature likes people, but my Woodrow nature does not like publicity.'"

The wedding was held a little sooner than had once been planned. Isaac Stuart McElroy, Jr., had assumed the duties of pastor of the Presbyterian Church in White Sulphur Springs, West Virginia, on June 9th, a few weeks after his ordination. In keeping with his duties, he therefore had to have a parsonage. "We were to have been married in October," said Mrs. McElroy, "but Stuart had rented a house in White Sulphur Springs and he seemed mighty lonely there, so we were married earlier, in August."

The wedding day turned out to be one of the hottest in the city's history. As Edith Wilson describes it in her memoirs, "Next day was worse than ever. Heat shimmered on the surface of the streets and buildings ... I shall never forget one relative of the groom. She arrived in a tailored suit, skirt and coat, with a starched high-collared waist, and not a hair turned from the heat. While we were all suffocating in the thinnest of white dresses with open necks, this lady really seemed comfortable as she sat bolt upright on the edge of a chair and said she preferred hot tea to iced lemonade!"

That woman, says Mrs. McElroy, was her future mother-in-law!

Woodrow Wilson emerged from his study to face all the house guests at lunch. In the afternoon he had to meet with the "War Cabinet" in the basement, because the upper part of the White House was by this time completely taken over by the wedding preparations.

When evening brought no relief from the heat, Edith Wilson wrote, she and the President suggested that, since only family guests were on hand, the gentlemen might wear their white clothes, instead of formal dress, "for it did not seem humanly possible to put on stiff shirt and black, long-tailed coats." The suggestion was not approved.

"No, indeed!" wrote Edith indignantly. "Full dress was essential, decreed the mother of the bride. My poor, long-suffering husband and all the other men yielded, but I should hate to speculate on what their thoughts must have been!"

Mrs. McElroy's version is somewhat different. "Uncle Woodrow asked what the men were to wear. I told him it was just too hot for white tie and tails. Then he asked me, 'What are the ladies wearing?' When I said they would be in formal dress, he said, 'Well, then we will, too!' "

Alice herself was hardly prepared for the hot weather and the switch in dates. "My going-away clothes were all for fall and winter, because I was getting ready to be married in October." She could not recall whether she had followed the tradition of wearing something old, something new, something borrowed, and something blue, except that she had borrowed a bit of lace from Edith.

It would not have been natural if the bridegroom had not forgotten something. "One of the funniest things that happened," said Mrs. McElroy, "was that Stuart forgot his suspenders. Since dress trousers aren't made for belts, Brooks, the President's valet, helped Stuart make eyelets around the top of the trousers to hold one of Woodrow Wilson's belts—with safety pins! Who would have thought that a man who had to be held together with safety pins would become the father of five children!"

About the wedding itself, Mrs. McElroy did not remember a great deal. "I didn't notice the decorations. I was too excited.

And I didn't know what the dinner tasted like. It was very elegant, and there was a big wedding cake." The thing she recalled most vividly about the wedding cake was that, when she went to cut it, she knocked over one of the tall-stemmed glasses. (She still has two pieces of the cake, ensconced in tiny white boxes, monogrammed and tied with white ribbon, as well as two place cards, autographed by the President.)

The floral arrangements were quite simple. The Blue Room, where the ceremony was to take place, was decorated with leaves and white blossoms. The long windows leading to the South Portico were lined with palms, fronted by gladioluses and white hydrangeas. In strategic locations, electric fans were positioned, particularly in the dining room, to provide some relief from the heat.

By the time of the wedding dinner, however, the fans were not so badly needed. Just before the ceremony, the bride was asked to step out on the South Portico in her wedding gown for an official portrait. There was some delay in setting up equipment and arranging the folds of the gown properly. In the midst of all of this arrived what Edith Wilson later described as "a perfect tornado." Without advance warning, the wind hit. It not only twisted Alice's veil around and sent attendants leaping to the rescue, but it was strong enough to rip some of the green awnings from their iron frames. The thunderstorm that followed brought a downpour of rain—and quick relief from the heat, which was described as "the worst in 40 years."

The wedding was one of the smallest ever held in the White House. The bridegroom had as his best man Professor M. R. Turnbull of the Union Theological Seminary. Several newspapers reported that Mrs. Martin Crook, sister of the bridegroom and matron of honor, was "the bride's only attendant." This was not so, explained Mrs. McElroy. For what she thought might have been the first time in history, the President and the First Lady were in the bride's party. However, it was a spur-of-the-moment act. "Before starting down the stairs to begin the wedding," said Mrs. McElroy, "I asked Uncle Woodrow if he and Edith would be attendants, and he said 'Of course.'"

The wedding may have set a record as the *shortest*, even though it was a double ring ceremony. It was all over in about five minutes. The bride, on the arm of her father, entered the Blue Room from the main corridor, while the bridegroom and his best man entered from the Red Room. She wore a gown of white georgette crepe, embroidered with beads and silk thread, floating on satin. Her tulle veil, which formed a train, was held in place with a coronet of orange blossoms and rare old lace (the piece borrowed from Edith Wilson). Cradled in her arm, she carried "a shower of bride roses and lilies of the valley."

As for music, "The Marine Band played for our wedding," she said, "and the music was lovely. No one was having German music played at that time, but we did—*Lohengrin*."

With the couple kneeling on a small satin-covered prie-dieu, without an improvised altar, they were married by Stuart's father in front of the long windows of the Blue Room. Everything went off smoothly, although there had been a slight crisis that morning. Irwin H. Hoover, of the White House staff, who had made application for the marriage license, suddenly realized that the Reverend Mr. McElroy was from Georgia and could not legally perform a marriage in the District of Columbia.

It might have been quite embarrassing to the nation to have a marriage performed in the White House and then find out that it was not valid! Fortunately, the License Officer, Colonel William A. Kroll, recognized Hoover, and expedited the authorization for the Reverend Mr. McElroy to officiate.

On the official papers, the groom's age was given as 25, the bride's as 23.

After dinner in the State Dining Room, the couple departed

in a White House automobile, but quietly and without any high jinks. Alice did not throw her bouquet to the guests, because of possible embarrassment—Margaret Wilson and one of Alice's college friends, Elizabeth Perkins from Muncie, Indiana, were the only two single women present. Alice had told the guests they could see her off to the station "if they wanted to and if they promised not to throw any rice." She was somewhat in a daze, anyway. She recalled that they boarded the train and that somewhere they were supposed to change trains down the line. But they were so excited and so engrossed in each other that they paid little attention to where they were. They did notice at one station, however, the train seemed to be lingering an unusually long time. Finally, there was a knock on their stateroom door. A porter stood there politely, cap in hand.

"Are you the White House couple, sir?" he asked.

"Yes, we are," replied Stuart.

"Well, sir, we don't want to be impolite, but we're just waiting for you to get off."

One of the things that struck Mrs. McElroy as particularly amusing about the wedding was a confused newspaper headline. The story of the ceremony had been placed next to an account of an epidemic abroad. The typesetter had neatly switched words around so that the headline read:

NIECE OF PRESIDENT IN GRIP OF PLAGUE
ALL SWITZERLAND TO MARRY IN WHITE HOUSE

CHAPTER XX

# A WEDDING IN WARTIME

Mrs. Louise Gill ("Louie") Macy was a good-looking girl who radiated high spirits, was always in bright humor, and had boundless energies. In the spring of 1939 she was the Paris editor of *Harper's Bazaar*, a position for which she dressed with suitable elegance. Having lived in France for some time and having attended any number of dances, dinners, and other social functions, she began to accrue a formidable list of people to whom she owed some form of party in return. The situation was complicated by two problems. The first was that she could never invite such hosts as the Duke and Duchess of Windsor and numerous princes and princesses to her Left Bank apartment (rented from a retired French general who had decorated it principally with guns). The second was that she had saved up only about $500. How could she entertain a couple of hundred people on this kind of budget?

With characteristic imagination, she conceived a magnificent and totally preposterous plan. She had seen a deserted mansion in the old 17th-century section of Paris, an aging pile called the *Hôtel Salé*, whose windows had been shuttered for decades. She went to the agent and said that she wanted to have the place opened for a party for a single night. The agent suggested a high fee, but Louie was prepared. Ridiculous, she replied, and indicated that she was doing him a favor by giving him publicity and that she did not expect to pay any fee at all. The agent, startled but a true Frenchman, bowed and graciously handed over the key.

It took about a week for Louie and a small army of friends to remove the dust and cobwebs and give the sweeping interiors a thorough airing. Through a stroke of luck, she located an old candlemaker who had purchased the original chandeliers from the *Hôtel*, and who agreed to lend them back to her for nothing. She did have to use part of her $500 for some candles. She had to install rudimentary plumbing. For tables, she ordered makeshift affairs on trestles, arranging to borrow other necessary furniture and furnishings from friends. But the banquet—that was the real coup. Armed with only a letter of introduction, she went to the noted restaurant, Tour d'Argent, one of the most elegant in Paris, and spoke with the proprietor, André Terrail. She had, she explained, only $400 left, with which to furnish food and liquor for two hundred people. Monsieur Terrail was intrigued with the whole idea of reopening what he considered "the most beautiful house in Paris." He agreed to supply the food and wine at cost, and to donate all of the table settings, along with waiters, who would be dressed in 17th-century livery.

With the grand occasion all arranged for, Louie Macy then sent out her invitations, specifying that the ladies were to wear "white ball gowns and tiaras" and the gentlemen "white tie and decorations." On what was described as a perfect Paris evening in June, wearing a white Schiaparelli gown of stiff, heavy lace and a jeweled tiara borrowed from Cartier, she presided over the incredible banquet in a setting of Old World magnificence. Monsieur Terrail had even furnished two tall footmen, who received the guests and directed them to tables designated by different kinds of flowers. After the dinner, the guests danced until dawn.

The next morning, the phone in Louie's Left Bank apartment rang. It was the famed hostess, Elsa Maxwell. "My dear," she began, "I'm supposed to know how to give parties, but I want to tell you that yours topped anything I've ever seen in my life."

On the other side of the Atlantic, a man named Harry Hopkins was wrestling with some very different problems. As Secretary of Commerce under Franklin Delano Roosevelt, he had little time for parties. He had also been troubled by serious illness that gave him, at 49, a sallow complexion and worry-lined features. He was described several years later in a *New Yorker* profile as looking "like an animated piece of Shredded Wheat." He was, on the one hand, introverted, hard-working, and intent, and on the other, talkative, sociable, and often witty and whimsical.

Hopkins had been born in Sioux City, Iowa, where he had grown up (the son of a harness maker) and plunged into social work—a career that took him from the cornfields to New York, New Jersey, and then Washington, where in the mid-Thirties he served first as head of the Federal Emergency Relief Administration and then as administrator of the Works Progress Administration (WPA). It was remarkable that Hopkins had been able to develop a rather dull welfare career into such a high position in Washington. Along the way, he had married two social workers, Ethel Gross, whom he later divorced, and Barbara Duncan, who died in the fall of 1937.

It was highly unlikely that this ailing, often unkempt man with straggly hair, who had a habit of slumping like a limp pillow in chairs, would ever become part of the life of the urbane Louise Macy.

They met for the first time in March of 1942, when he was 51 and she was 36.

Hopkins had received a letter from Mrs. Lawrence Lowman, a former *Harper's Bazaar* editor, asking for his help in placing a friend of hers, Louise Macy, in a Washington job. Louie had been in Paris when The Netherlands and Belgium had fallen and had immediately volunteered to help the war refugees who began arriving in Paris. (For her outstanding work, she was named "Godmother" by a regiment of Americans who had volunteered to fight for France.) She had become interested in war work and had returned to New York to become a member of a nurses' aide class in New York—one of the first in the city—held at Memorial Hospital. Now, wanting to contribute more toward the war effort, she felt that Washington was the place for her.

Hopkins immediately agreed, suggesting that Mrs. Macy meet him at the St. Regis in New York. They had a chat of about half an hour, during which time it was quite apparent to Hopkins, always attracted by poised and handsome women, that his assignment was not the chore he had feared it might be. They parted, with Hopkins saying that he would see what he could do. There would be a short delay, though, because he was about to leave for England on a special mission.

By this time, Harry L. Hopkins had achieved a unique position in the Administration. He had resigned his post as Secretary of Commerce in 1940, because of his health, but had been enticed back again by F.D.R. in 1941 to serve as Lend-Lease Administrator and then in 1942 as a member of the War Production Board. Despite various titles, his real position was that of adviser to Roosevelt, an assignment which he took on so capably that he was soon referred to as "the Assistant President."

He was also referred to as "The Shadow," because F.D.R. insisted on having him by his side at all times. The story went that he had been invited to dinner by the President in May 1940, on the day Belgium and Holland fell. He stayed overnight in borrowed pajamas, and F.D.R. then urged him to stay on at the White House. He did just that. His little daughter Diana (then aged about five) had moved into the White House, at Mrs. Roosevelt's insistence, when her mother died in 1937, just before Hopkins himself had a serious operation. Later she lived with her father in Georgetown; in 1940 she went back with him to the White House and was mothered by Eleanor Roosevelt, who worried about whether the little girl's solitary life in the White House was too lonely.

After returning from England in April, Harry L. Hopkins immediately phoned Louise Macy and invited her to dinner in New York. They discussed possible jobs, including one that he said he could offer her in the Office of Price Administration, which she did not feel was suitable. Mostly, though, they just talked, exploring subjects of mutual interest—of which there were far more than might have been imagined.

Although Hopkins later said, of Louise's set, "Three-fourths of her friends, I think, are fine," many of them loathed the New Deal policies represented by Hopkins, who in three years as head of WPA distributed over $10 billion for public works and relief of unemployment. *Time* said (July 1942): "Many a wealthy New-Deal-hater has been doubly horrified, after a week's grind in the factory, making money for Hopkins to boondoggle with, to find him in the house for the weekend."

During April and May, they saw each other on an average of at least once a week. Louie spent one weekend at the White House, where she became friendly with Mrs. Roosevelt, who then invited the couple on two weekends to visit her at Hyde Park. In New York they were seen together at the theater, at Manhattan night spots, and at a party given by close friends of Hopkins, the W. Averell Harrimans.

It was quite apparent that they were both interested in something more than finding Louise an appropriate job in the war effort.

Louise, like Harry Hopkins, had been married before. In 1932, she had become the wife of Clyde Brown, a New York attorney, but the marriage had ended in Reno within a year. Having no children, she had resumed her maiden name, although she retained the "Mrs."

On June 22, 1942, Mrs. Macy and Hopkins went together to a Russian War Relief rally at Madison Square Garden, where Hopkins had been asked to speak, topping this off with a much more interesting visit to El Morocco. Hopkins was an engaging conversationalist, with a knack for telling jokes and anecdotes. He was somewhat more serious this particular evening and was dismayed to see how fast the time went by before he had to make a dash to catch the last train back to Washington. As he recalled it later, he was up in the clouds. "I had never dreamed of marrying again. I got to my room the next morning and thought: You're in love with her. You talked like a sixteen-year-old last night."

He picked up the telephone and called her, asking her to come right down to Washington that day. To make it more difficult to refuse, he said that Churchill was in town and he had already promised him he was going to share the dinner table with "the nicest girl he'd ever seen."

Louie said she was on her way. Hopkins met her at the train and took her to the Mayflower Hotel, so that she could go up to the Harrimans' suite and change for dinner. For a few minutes they were alone. It was a perfect opportunity. He proposed to her, and she, having known all along what was going to happen, accepted him on the spot.

The only disappointment, said Hopkins, was that "Marie Harriman came in just as I was going to kiss her."

A little later, they drove to the British Embassy for dinner, accompanied by the Prime Minister. Churchill was the first person besides the Harrimans to learn of their engagement. That night, Hopkins walked into the President's study, saying "Hang onto your chair," and explained that he was going to be married. The President laughed, knowing at once who the bride was.

At the time the engagement was publicly announced, on July 3rd, Louie said that she had no idea where, or exactly when, the wedding would take place. When a reporter said that he had heard rumors that the event might be in the White House, Louie replied, "You know Mr. Hopkins is a very busy man and we haven't had an opportunity to discuss wedding plans fully. We definitely will be married in about a month, however, and as I expect to see Mr. Hopkins this weekend (over the Fourth of July) perhaps we can then decide."

On July 4th the announcement was made: the couple would be married on July 30th in a simple ceremony—in the White House. The information was given during a press conference in the office of Presidential Secretary Stephen T. Early. The decision had not yet been made whether the ceremony would take place in the East Room. It was revealed, however, that after a brief honeymoon, the bride and groom would live in the White House. Hopkins would carry on his usual duties as the President's closest adviser, and his wife would transfer her nursing and war activities to a Washington hospital.

Eleanor Roosevelt personally expressed her approval of the arrangement. "I am very glad," she said, officially presenting the couple to the press, "that Mr. Hopkins and Mrs. Macy will be married in the White House. They are being unselfish because they can carry on the work of the war better and will stay with us for a while. I hope they will find it very comfortable and pleasing, for a while, anyway."

Hopkins said of the forthcoming marriage, "I like the whole business. It suits me. That's an unqualified endorsement."

A week later, Mrs. Macy announced that she had made further plans. She said that the ceremony would take place at noon and that in keeping with the hour and the circumstances her gown would be a "simple one." Furthermore, she was ordering it from Hattie Carnegie, because Hattie had given her her first job, as a saleslady, in 1933. She had decided, too, that, out of loyalty to *Harper's Bazaar*, that magazine would be the only one she would permit to picture her in the gown before the wedding.

The Reverend Dr. Everett Russell J. Clinchy, a Congregational minister from Hartford, Connecticut, President of the National Council of Churches, would officiate at the wedding. The application for the marriage license listed the "local residence" of both applicants as "1600 Pennsylvania Avenue, N.W.," which is, of course, the address of the White House.

The wedding was one of the simplest performed in the White House. The day before, Hopkins said, "I get a haircut and I'm ready."

The simplicity was more than a matter of personal choice. The dark days of 1942 were no time for an elaborate ceremony. On the wedding day, advancing German divisions forced the Red Army to retreat to within 80 miles of Stalingrad; Axis planes bombed the British near El Alamein; and at home in the States, nationwide gasoline rationing was being proposed.

Tragic circumstances were to haunt this unlucky couple throughout their lives. Already they had suffered the unhappiness of divorce and illness. After their marriage, they became the target of anti-Administration gossip—there was talk that Lord Beaverbrook had given Louie a $500,000 emerald necklace, as a token of Great Britain's appreciation for Lend-Lease, and a rumor that Baruch had held a "Lucullan" dinner for them during the days of wartime rationing. When the Hopkins couple and young Diana moved into a house of their own in Georgetown, after a year and a half in the White House, a rift with the Roosevelts was hinted at. Hopkins lived for only four years after the wedding. Louie was married again in 1947, to Geoffrey Gates, an architect, but tragedy followed once more. Gates died in 1961. Louie began to suffer periods of despondency, although she tried to keep busy by running an antique shop in the 250-year-old "Mill Pond House" at Oyster Bay, New York. On Saturday, May 11th, she was found dead in her bed, aged 57. A note was found beside her, and the police recorded the death as "an apparent suicide."

Luckily the sadness of the future was hidden from the little party assembled in the President's oval study at noon on July 30, 1942. It was the first time that anyone had been married in this room, and the first White House wedding in almost a quarter of a century. The group that witnessed this informal ceremony included about eight relatives and a very varied assortment of guests, among them General George C. Marshall, Army Chief of Staff; the playwright Robert Sherwood; Justice Samuel Rosenman of the New York Supreme Court; Admiral Ernest J. King, Commander in Chief of the United States Fleet; and 23 members of the White House staff, including the old doorman and Hopkins's favorite maid, Lizzie McDuffie.

President Roosevelt was there, too, of course, in a white linen suit, with Mrs. Eleanor Roosevelt beside him in a blue and white polka-dot chiffon dress. They watched with affection as Louie was led toward the marble fireplace by her brother-in-law, Lieutenant Nicholas Ludington, U.S.N. Louie's costume had a naval touch, too: her tailored blue dress was ornamented by specially designed bracelets, a lapel pin, and earrings—all in the shape of sailors' "victory" knots. Hopkins, with a fresh haircut, wore a plain blue business suit, but his best man, his son David, proudly wore his new Navy lieutenant's uniform. As the Reverend Dr. Clinchy conducted the simple service, Louie handed her bouquet of purple orchids and deep purple-blue delphiniums to Diana Hopkins, Harry's 10-year-old daughter.

The popular Meyer Davis replaced the Marine Band, and his orchestra must have given a very different rendering of the inevitable wedding march from *Lohengrin*. It was followed by "The End of a Perfect Day" and "O Promise Me." Later, at the simple lunch of salmon and chicken, the band swung into the couple's favorite, "Buckle Down, Winsocki" and "I Married an Angel," as well as a specially composed love song that has not survived the years.

Newspaper accounts of the wedding, buried among the headlines of war, must have been read with mixed feelings by the seven men and women who had themselves been married in the White House.

Alice and Stuart McElroy may have scanned the stories, but they were not in a mood to linger over the details of frivolity and happiness. They were too busy worrying about their missionary daughter, Jessie McElroy Junkin, interned with her husband and small son in a Japanese concentration camp. The senior McElroys had themselves served as missionaries in Japan, and their stay there had also come to an unhappy ending; they had to leave the country, and most of their possessions behind them, after the disastrous earthquake of 1923 destroyed half of Tokyo and all Yokohama.

Only a few weeks before the Hopkins wedding, the headlines had told the story of Francis Sayre's dramatic nighttime submarine escape from Corregidor. After saving five and a half tons of gold and millions of dollars' worth of paper securities from the hands of the Japanese, the 57-year-old Commissioner to the Philippines and his second wife got out just in time. The besieged fortress fell to the Japanese on May 6th, just seven weeks before the wedding.

Memories of an earlier wartime wedding may have passed through the mind of Mrs. Edith Bolling Galt Wilson, a 75-year-old lady still living in the capital. The closing days of World War I had broken her husband's health and hastened his death in 1924 only eight years after their marriage.

A younger widow, 53-year-old Mrs. Eleanor McAdoo, had just passed the first anniversary of her divorced husband's death the previous February. She was left with two daughters: 22-year-old Mary Faith, not yet married, and 27-year-old Ellen, divorced from Rafael Lopez de Onate after their three-year marriage produced one son.

The ever lively Alice Roosevelt Longworth may have read the stories of the Hopkins marriage with the keenest eye of all. Widowed since Nick died in 1931, she was still in the foreground of Washington's social and political life. It has been said that she looked upon each of her father's successors as a White House usurper. She bitterly opposed Wilson's plans for the League of Nations, and when he returned from his European trip on the League's behalf, she stood while he passed "with fingers crossed, making the sign of the evil eye, and saying 'a murrain on him.' " Harding was "just a slob" to her, and she thought Coolidge "looked as if he had been weaned on a pickle." Associated with the arch-Republican and reactionary lobbyists, and with isolationist groups such as the America First Committee, she was outspoken and witty in her opposition to the administration of another Roosevelt. To her, distant cousin F.D.R. was "one-third sap and two-thirds Eleanor." She entertained her salon of admirers by doing bitterly funny imitations of Eleanor Roosevelt, and she may have searched the newspaper accounts with relish for new material to work with.

The oldest living White House bride at that time, Mrs. Frances Cleveland Preston, must have turned her thoughts back to a gentler and more gracious time in the past. A 19th-century aura still lingered around her. Now 78 years old, she lived in quiet retirement in Princeton with her second husband, a former professor of art history and archaeology, surrounded by the beauty of art works and the peace of the countryside. She derived the greatest pleasure from the families of her four married sons and daughters (all children of President Cleveland) and from the gracious friendliness of women's-club life. If stories of the Hopkins wedding intruded into her world at all, she must have thought with nostalgia of that June evening in 1886—of the gas light flickering in the flower-filled Blue Room—the stirring music of John Philip Sousa himself—the beautiful dresses with their long skirts—and the leisurely carriage rides through the Maryland mountains. She may have remembered, too, stories she had read of the earlier White House brides: the "merry widow" Washington; young Maria Monroe under the shadow of a nation's mourning for its hero;

the Southern belles of Andrew Jackson's day; Julia Gardiner's secret marriage to the widowed President Tyler, whose children were older than she was; Nellie Grant's spectacular East Room wedding to her young English diplomat.

Administrations come and go. Wars shake the nation. Prosperity follows depression. But love, romance, and weddings go on and on, even in the most important home in the land.

# APPENDIX

LIKE the making of a patchwork quilt, the fragments of this book were pieced together by many hands. Tadd Fisher visited Francis Sayre in Washington and traveled to see Alice Wilson McElroy and her husband in Richmond, Virginia. Carol Montgomery struggled through a Washington snowstorm to spend an hour with Alice Roosevelt Longworth, the oldest living (and liveliest) White House bride. A few months before her recent death, Eleanor Wilson McAdoo was visited in her Santa Barbara home by Robert Austin.

Clues to the earlier weddings were tracked down in libraries by researchers as well as by the two authors. Susan Hartung pieced together the story of President Cleveland's secretive courtship and sudden White House marriage; she typed so long and hard, transcribing newspaper accounts of the day from illegible microfilms, that she was later seen in the New York Public Library with her right hand in a sling, taking research notes with her left. Deirdre Randall Ryan and Mary-Rose Rogers copied the stories of Jessie Wilson and Alice Roosevelt from old newspaper pages of 1906 and 1913. Cornelia Haldane and Vera Scriabine found magazine articles about more recent White House courtships and weddings. Catherine Reinis discovered portraits of brides and bridegrooms in art libraries and hanging on the walls of descendants' homes.

The long search through published material in libraries began with books on the history of the White House itself. The more books were read, the more the different tales about weddings in the mansion began to conflict with one another, and the worse became the muddle about names and dates. Many of the feminine writers of the earlier histories were more interested in romance than in fact. Even those chroniclers who did their best, in the 1800s and early 1900s, to get straight the details of White House weddings, did not have access to today's microfilms of old newspapers and magazines, careful genealogical records, newly published family papers and diaries, or the professional services of large modern libraries. We look back across a longer span of years, but we see the past perhaps more clearly than was possible at the beginning of this century.

Among the many White House histories combed for wedding stories were Bess Furman's *White House Profile* (1951), Ona Jeffries's *In and Out of the White House* (1960), Amy Jensen's *The White House and Its Thirty-Two Families* (1958), Ethel Lewis's *The White House*

(1937), Benjamin Perley Poore's *Perley's Reminiscences of Sixty Years in the National Metropolis* (1886), Esther Singleton's *The Story of the White House* (1907), Mary Whitton's *First First Ladies* (1948), and Gilson Willets's *Inside History of the White House* (1908).

Living White House brides and bridegrooms gave us reminiscences about their courtships and wedding days in interviews. In addition, many of the men and women whose stories are told in this book recorded their memories in autobiographies, letters, and diaries. Their published memoirs include Alice Roosevelt Longworth's *Crowded Hours* (1933), Eleanor Wilson McAdoo's *The Woodrow Wilsons* (1937), Francis Sayre's *Glad Adventure* (1957), Edith Wilson's *My Memoir* (1939), and Woodrow Wilson's *Life and Letters*, edited by Ray Stannard Baker (1931-1939). Helen Taft's recollections of her Silver Anniversary party were printed as part of a serialized autobiography in the November 1914 issue of *The Delineator*. Relevant parts of the unpublished *Genealogy and Autobiography of General Russell Hastings* (manuscript, 1900) were kindly sent by Watt P. Marcham, director of the Rutherford B. Hayes Library in Fremont, Ohio. Some of Julia Gardiner Tyler's ecstatic letters to her mother have survived the years to be much quoted in books and articles, and President Tyler's account of the disastrous explosion on the *Princeton* has been handed down in Lyon Gardiner Tyler's *Letters and Times of the Tylers* (1884).

Other descendants and relatives were courteous in giving us facts and portraits for the book. Mrs. T. P. Yeatman of Mount Pleasant, Tennessee, who married the grandson of Mary Ann Eastin and Lucius Polk and is herself directly descended from the Eastins, still lives in "Hamilton Place," the house built for the newly married couple in 1833 by slaves sent from North Carolina. She took down from the walls the oil painting of Lucius made a year after his marriage, as well as Earl's double portrait of Mary Ann Eastin and Mary Ann Lewis (Mrs. Yeatman, in family tradition, is herself called Mary Ann), so that they could be carried to Columbia and photographed for this book. Lawrence Gouverneur Hoes, great-grandson of Maria Monroe and Samuel Gouverneur, is now in charge of the James Monroe Law Office and Memorial Library in Fredericksburg, Virginia. When he gave us permission to reproduce the Cardelli plaque of Maria, he revealed that the oval painting that has often been published as being that of his great-grandmother is really a fraud: it was seen in a shop window by her son, Samuel Gouverneur, Jr., who bought it because it reminded him of his adored mother, and the painting is still owned by the Gouverneur family.

Among other helpful descendants was Lyon Gardiner Tyler, Attorney General of Virginia, who did his best in the search for an authentic portrait of Elizabeth Tyler and referred us to his distant cousin, Elizabeth Tyler Coleman, author of *Priscilla Cooper Tyler* (1955). One descendant we were just too late to meet was Miss Bessie V. Todd of Shelbyville, Kentucky. Great-granddaughter of Judge Thomas Todd, she died in April 1964. Mysteriously, the original portrait of Judge Todd, owned by her for at least 10 years before her death, has disappeared; her executor wrote us that no one knows what happened to it. Dr. John A. Washington of Washington, D.C., gave permission to reproduce the portrait of the Judge's White House bride, Lucy Washington, painted by Charles Peale Polk. General U. S. Grant, III, Fred and Ida's son, allowed us to use Healy's painting of his father.

Even those relatives and descendants who are no longer living offered a lot of useful information in their published accounts of the romances and weddings they witnessed or later heard about. Accounts turned up in John Quincy Adams's manuscript diary (in the Adams Papers at Columbia University); in Julia Cantacuzene's *My Life Here and There* (1921); in Allen Clark's edition of *Life and Letters of Dolly Madison* (1914); in Lucia B. Cutts's *Memoirs and Letters of Dolly Madison* (1886); in *As I Remember, Recollections of American Society in the Nineteenth Century* (1911), by Marian Gouverneur, daughter-in-law of the White House couple of 1820; in Jesse Grant's *In the Days of My Father, General Grant* (1925); and in Rutherford B. Hayes's diaries and letters, published by the Ohio State Archeological and Historical Society (1924).

Housekeepers of the Executive Mansion, secretaries, military aides, doctors, and doorkeepers were in some cases as close to the weddings as actual members of the First Family. Elizabeth Jaffray, housekeeper for Presidents Taft, Wilson, Harding, and Coolidge, described in detail her version of *Secrets of the White House* (1927). Another housekeeper, Victoria Henrietta Nesbitt, was running the White House when Harry Hopkins married Louise Macy there; she released her *White House Diary* in 1948. Irwin Hoover, the doorkeeper and chief usher who secured the marriage license or quickly stepped forward to right an overturned wedding train in more than one White House ceremony, left his impressions in *Forty-Two Years in the White House* (1934). *Grant in Peace* (1887) is a personal memoir by Adam Badeau, the military secretary and aide who joined the General's staff during the Civil War and later grew close to the whole family. Cary T. Grayson, Woodrow Wilson's friend and doctor, whose Navy sword was used to slice two wedding cakes, published his *Intimate Memoir* in 1960.

Other observers of the Washington scene included journalists, leaders of society, and officials' wives, several of whom commented in print on the White House weddings of their day. Particularly useful were Mrs. Josephus Daniels's *Recollections of a Cabinet Minister's Wife 1913-1921* (1945); Margaret Bayard Smith's *The First Forty Years of Washington Society*, edited by Gaillard Hunt (1906); Francis Williams's *The Bride of the White House* (1886); and Jessie Benton Fremont's *Souvenirs of My Time* (1887).

For each Administration, almost countless histories and biographies have been written. Many of these are scholarly studies to which the authors of this book owe an obviously heavy debt. The authoritative works are the results of years of research—carefully indexed, footnoted, and written with a painstaking attention to accuracy that is missing in most of the general histories of the White House and in many of the rambling personal reminiscences. Among the many dozens of serious volumes on which this lighter account of romance and marriage has leaned heavily are Samuel Flagg Bemis's *John Quincy Adams and the Union* (1956); Irving Brant's *James Madison, the President, 1809-1812* (1961); Pauline Burke's *Emily Donelson of Tennessee* (1941); Oliver Perry Chitwood's *John Tyler, Champion of the Old South* (1939); William Hesseltine's *Ulysses S. Grant, Politician* (1935); J. R. Irelan's *Life, Administration and Times of John Tyler* (1888); Marquis James's *Andrew Jackson, Portrait of a President* (1963); Arthur Link's *Wilson* (1956-1964); Robert McElroy's *Grover Cleveland, the Man and the Statesman, an Authorized Biography* (1923); George Morgan's *The Life of James Monroe* (1921); Allan Nevins's *Grover Cleveland, a Study in Courage* (1934); Arthur M. Schlesinger's *The Age of Jackson* (1945); and Arthur Walworth's *Woodrow Wilson* (1965).

Contemporary newspapers and magazines, often inaccurate about details but always interesting, balanced the judicious perspective of the historians. Because the earliest weddings, in particular, often involved people of no historical importance, the press of those days is almost the only source for accurately dating these first marriages and for finding details about the men and women concerned. The Washington *National Intelligencer*, above all, was useful for verifying the dates of the marriages between 1812 and 1842. Like bits of a jigsaw puzzle, facts about these early events were fitted together from the *Intelligencer* and other old newspapers and periodicals. In the *Western Monthly Magazine* (July 1836), for example, we found a "Sketch of the Life of Judge Thomas Todd," published some ten years after his death and giving the only description of his physical appearance. Todd's earlier obituary in the *National Intelligencer* gave us contemporary opinions about his estimable character. Notices of his death and accounts of official mourning for him were found also in the Frankfort (Kentucky) *Argus of Western America*, in the Lexington (Kentucky) *Gazette* and *Reporter*, and in the Washington *Daily National Journal*. Notices of the death in 1825 of Congressman John G. Jackson, the "forgotten" bridegroom of 1801, turned up in the Charles Town (Virginia) *Farmer's Repository*, as well as in the Washington *Gazette* and *National Intelligencer*. The Washington *Globe* gave us the date on which President Andrew Jackson sent Lewis Randolph, pretty Betty Martin's lover, out to the wild Territory of Arkansas. The New York *American* in 1842 wedged a 4-line notice of Elizabeth Tyler's White House wedding in between advertisements and commercial news.

The breakthrough to modern journalism happened, luckily, just before the first really spectacular White House wedding: that of 1874, when Nellie Grant married Algernon Sartoris. The day of the society writer, and of extended female readership, had just begun. Never again could the marriage of a President's daughter be covered in a mere 4 lines. The New York *Daily Graphic* rushed to press with a 12-page pictorial supplement for Nellie's wedding. Artists were dispatched to sketch every detail of the decorations, dresses, and refreshments. The Washington *Evening Star* gave Nellie and Algernon front-page coverage, as it did every succeeding White House couple—with the curious exception of the three Wilson girls, who were relegated to pages 5, 3, and 8 respectively. *The New York Times* also began its coverage of Presidential weddings in 1874 and, with its useful annual index, it became one of the best sources for reasonably reliable details.

Magazines, too, began to multiply year by year. Both *Harper's Weekly* and *Frank Leslie's Illustrated Newspaper* were on hand to describe Nellie's marriage to the British diplomat in the East Room. *Harper's Bazar*, *Lippincott's*, and *Puck* were among other news magazines at the end of the nineteenth century. We found great detail, a lot of sentiment and almost as much misinformation in magazines such as the *American Monthly Review of Reviews*, *Hearst's International Cosmopolitan*, *Current Opinion*, *The Delineator*, *Independent*, *McClure's Magazine*, *Munsey's Magazine*, and *Pearson's Magazine*. By the time of the 1942 White House wedding of Louise Macy to Harry Hopkins, many of these had passed into oblivion, to be succeeded by *Time*, *The New Yorker*, and others, more factual, more sophisticated, and considerably less sentimental.

Genealogy is a field in which the amateur should tread delicately, and our excursions into this area were largely limited to looking up relatives and children in two basic works: Reginald Henry's *Genealogies of the Families of the Presidents* (1935) and Walter L. Zorn's *Descendants of the Presidents of the U.S.A.* (1955).

A slightly longer excursion was needed to solve the riddle of the "forgotten" first White House wedding of 1801, believed to have taken place years before the generally accepted "first" wedding, that of Lucy Washington to Judge Thomas Todd in 1812. This 1801 marriage is mentioned by very few sources as having happened in the White House, although a letter from the groom implies that Madison gave the bride away. We searched through every available book on the bridegroom's family, the Jacksons, trying to learn where his 1801 marriage to Mary Payne took place. (Marriage license records in the District of Columbia do not go back far enough.) Finally, in a biography about the most famous member of that family, "Stonewall" Jackson, we found it: "He [J. G. Jackson] married Miss Mary Payne, sister of the famed Dolley Madison, and also a sister of Mrs. George Steptoe Washington, whose husband was a nephew of George Washington, and one of the administrators of his estate. This marriage of John G. Jackson and Mary Payne is said to have taken place in the White House, being the first ceremony of the kind solemnized therein." The book is Thomas Jackson Arnold's *Early Life and Letters of General Thomas J. Jackson, by His Nephew* (1916). A footnote gives the source of the information: "On the authority of their eldest daughter, the late Mrs. John J. Allen, wife of Judge Allen, long a member of the Supreme Court of Virginia, who stated that she had often heard it related by her parents."

Yet another forgotten wedding may be buried in White House history. Although most authoritative directories give John G. Jackson only two wives, Mary Payne (1901) and Mary Meigs (1810), a surprising number of books and articles say that he was married for a third time, once again in the White House, in 1811 or 1812. A great deal of very painstaking research would be needed to prove or disprove this story. The bride at this third wedding is said to have been "a Quakeress from Philadelphia," a Miss Anna Todd, a niece or cousin of Dolley Madison's. A typical account of this supposed White House wedding was published in *Harper's Weekly* (February 17, 1906), at the time of Alice Roosevelt's marriage:

> The first to be solemnized was that of Miss Todd, of Philadelphia, to Representative John G. Jackson, of Virginia, the great-uncle of General "Stonewall" Jackson. It was in the winter of 1811, during the Presidency of James Madison. Miss Todd was a cousin of Mrs. Madison. The wedding took place in the East Room and was one of the brilliant functions of the year, as Mrs. Madison was the social leader of her day.

But John Jackson was "Stonewall's" first cousin once removed, not his great-uncle. And the East Room was not furnished until the Monroes moved into the White House. Almost every other account of this mysterious wedding raises dozens of questions, and the details of the story are changed as they pass from book to book. Miss Todd (only once named Anna) is sometimes Dolley's niece and sometimes her cousin. Jackson is here a Congressman, there a Judge, and sometimes a Colonel or even a General. The wedding date jumps from 1811 to 1812 and back again.

Do we have the wrong Representative Jackson here, named as the bridegroom? More than one account says that the husband was "Stonewall's" great-uncle—which would have made him John George Jackson's *father*. The father, George Jackson, who was a famous Indian fighter and a Congressman from Virginia, would have been 54 years old in 1811. He lived to be 74 and to father fourteen children, which could explain a certain amount of confusion about which Jackson married whom and did what. The father had been a colonel in the Continental Army during the Revolution, and some versions of the story do refer to the bridegroom as "Colonel Jackson"; the title applies more logically to old George than to his son, who reached the rank of Brigadier General in the winter of 1811.

Miss Todd's elusive husband may even have been another of old George's many sons, Edward Brake Jackson (who is in fact named in one account of this wedding). Edward was 16 years younger than his brother John George, and would have been barely 18 at the time of the supposed 1811 White House wedding. But he did accomplish a great deal in a short life, practicing medicine in Virginia, serving in Ohio during the War of 1812, and at 27 being elected to the Sixteenth Congress (as yet another Representative Jackson from Virginia). He left four children when he died (but no one reported his bereaved wife's name) and he is buried in Miss Todd's home state, Pennsylvania.

The mysterious 1811 Todd/Jackson wedding may never have happened at all. The whole story may be nothing more than a highly scrambled version of John George Jackson's first marriage in 1801 to Mary Payne. Like the unknown Miss Todd, Mary Payne was a Quaker from Philadelphia. She was closely related to Dolley Madison—her youngest sister, in fact. It might have been an easy mistake for writers to think of Mary Payne as being Mary "Todd," because her sister Dolley had been married to John Todd before she became Mrs. Madison, and she was sometimes mistakenly referred to in print as "the former Miss Todd" rather than as Mrs. Todd or Miss Payne. Only a printer's error was then needed to transform "1801" into "1811" and create a brand new White House wedding.

Such a mistake would have been nothing out of the ordinary. The frequency of printers' slips, as well as muddled reporting, can be traced through White House history. Dates are changed; couples are reported honeymooning in two different places at once; wedding guests materialize out of thin air; names become hopelessly mangled.

John Adams's bride, Mary Hellen, is turned into a "Miss Johnson" and even a "Miss Jackson" by some writers. Famous Nellie Grant becomes "Ella." One bride married in Jackson's Administration, Elizabeth Martin, is given the President's name and changed into "Emily Jackson." Major Lewis's daughter, Mary Ann, is for some unaccountable reason turned into the Major's niece and renamed "Delia." And her unfortunate husband, the first foreigner to be married in the White House, fares worst of all: a French diplomat named Alphonse Pageot, he has been called everything from Depageot, Paqeot, and Paqueol to Paquerel. Even as recently as 1913, *The New York Times* renamed Francis Sayre "Thomas" just three days before he married President Wilson's daughter.

Descriptions of the flowers, the cakes, and the bride's gown were very detailed but often completely wrong in days when reporters had to rely on memory, on other people's secondhand accounts, and on rough sketches hastily drawn by the newspaper's artist. Barred from the 1886 marriage of President Cleveland, journalists from the competing *Harper's Weekly* and *Leslie's Illustrated Newspaper* eagerly pressed the guests for descriptions of Frances Folsom's gorgeous gown, then did the best they could. When the magazines came off the press that week, staff artists had carefully drawn two completely different dresses, as dissimilar to one another as both of them were to the real gown, recorded accurately by a studio photographer a few days later.

Photography has not always been a help to researchers, though. Mistakes were occasionally filmed on purpose, as by the newsreel photographer who hired a couple to stand in for Alice Roosevelt and her husband, or by the editor who was so desperate for more "news" that he published a photograph of Alice's three nonexistent flower girls. Picture captions often gave historians one more chance for error. A recently published book on the White House and its families shows a photograph of the great East Room, "decorated for a wedding," supposedly in 1893, a year in which not one White House wedding took place. The picture of this ghostly wedding scene must have been taken when Alice Roosevelt was married in this room 13 years later.

Writers who lengthened the list of White House weddings to make Jessie Wilson's the unlucky thirteenth may have had similar ghost weddings in their notebooks, or they may have included the elusive Congressman Jackson, or even the fraudulent Elizabeth Sheits Chandler from Lincoln's day. In their eagerness to make the list as long as possible, some writers even moved the 1835 wedding of Elizabeth Martin and Lewis Randolph into the White House. The wedding did take place—but 600 miles away in Tennessee, not where legend put it.

A final word of thanks is due to the librarians and archivists who helped us straighten out the many muddles along our road. They provided accurate information, illustrations, and encouragement. Mrs. Paul M. Rhymer, curator of prints at the Chicago Historical Society, sent us Healy's portrait of Ida Honoré Grant. Stephen S. Lawrence, director of the Ladies' Hermitage Association in Tennessee, sent us pictures of Sarah Yorke and Andrew Jackson, Jr. Miss Marie Ellis, reference librarian at The College of William and Mary, kindly mailed us extracts from Robert Seager's book, *And Tyler Too*. James Milling, of the Sumter Library, South Carolina, verified the date of Angelica's marriage to Abraham Van Buren and found the name of the plantation where the ceremony took place. Miss Kendall Cram of the Tennessee State Library and Archives, Nashville, led us to the two most informative books on the many weddings of the Jackson Administration.

If everyone who gave a helping hand were to be mentioned by name, the list might be endless. So the last acknowledgment goes to those professional helpers who accept with grace their usual anonymity and who cheerfully assist the researcher who wanders through the doors of the New York Public Library, the New York Historical Society, the Museum of the City of New York, the Frick Art Reference Library, the Library of Congress, the White House Historical Association, the National Archives, and the Smithsonian Institution.

# INDEX OF NAMES